Praise for Halloween Delights

A Collection of Halloween Recipes
Cookbook Delights Series

…"**Halloween Delights Cookbook** is a sweet treat for kids of all ages!

From "Booberry Brew" to "Bat Wings" to "Liposuction Lard," these recipes are as original as their titles! This collection is filled with fun food ideas that are sure to add more intrigue to your holiday party. It will keep your guests wondering where you came up with such imaginative ideas!"…

Kimberly Carter
Publicist

…"Halloween, a much-loved autumn tradition with roots in the ancient Celtic festival of Samhain and the Christian holy day of All Saints, has been part of our custom at least as far back as 1846. *Halloween Delights Cookbook,* which contains over 250 ghoulish and haunting recipes, fun-filled facts and tidbits on Halloween and its origin, as well as exciting poetry, promises to tickle your fancy and funny bone. *Halloween Delights* will make a splendid addition to your holiday cookbook collection."…

Mary Scripture-Smith
Graphic Designer

Praise for Halloween Delights
A Collection of Halloween Recipes
Cookbook Delights Series

…"*Halloween Delights* is a great cookbook because it not only includes over 250 recipes, but it also contains information and facts about nutrition, health, and cultivation to support the recipes. Reading the 'Did You Know' facts is fascinating, and the poetry by the author is an added extra feature that you won't find included in other cookbooks. *Halloween Delights* is definitely a great value because it is packed with rich information. It makes an interesting book to read as well as a resourceful cookbook with delicious-tasting recipes arranged for easy use. I highly recommend this book to give as a gift."…

Dr. James G. Hood
Editor

…"It's that time of year again! The weather is turning crisp and cool, leaves are changing to vibrant autumn colors, and the holidays are just around the corner. First up is Halloween, a favorite for the child in each of us, a magical and spooky night filled with delicious goodies, fun costumes, and frights galore. More than just a cookbook, *Halloween Delights* is a treasure trove of creative ideas to make your fright night celebration one to remember! The book is also packed with extras, like information on how to grow your own pumpkins, interesting facts about the history, folklore, and symbolism of Halloween, and a helpful glossary of cooking and baking terms."…

Kim Saunders

Praise for Halloween Delights

A Collection of Halloween Recipes
Cookbook Delights Series

Halloween Delights was featured on "Good Morning Northwest" on September 7, 2008. The live news program is broadcast on KXLY Channel 4, the ABC TV affiliate in Spokane, Washington. Author Karen Jean Matsko Hood presented an array of cookbook recipes which were posted on news4.com. The segment also featured a live cooking demonstration.

Halloween Delights

A Collection of Halloween Recipes
Cookbook Delights Series

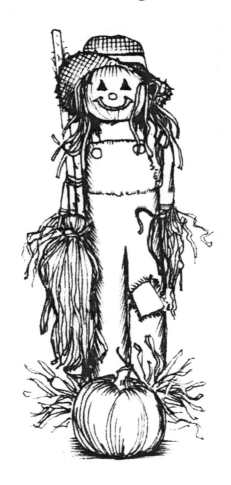

Karen Jean Matsko Hood

v

Current and Future Cookbooks

By Karen Jean Matsko Hood

DELIGHTS SERIES

Almond Delights
Anchovy Delights
Apple Delights
Apricot Delights
Artichoke Delights
Asparagus Delights
Avocado Delights
Banana Delights
Barley Delights
Basil Delights
Bean Delights
Beef Delights
Beer Delights
Beet Delights
Blackberry Delights
Blueberry Delights
Bok Choy Delights
Boysenberry Delights
Brazil Nut Delights
Broccoli Delights
Brussels Sprouts Delights
Buffalo Berry Delights
Butter Delights
Buttermilk Delights
Cabbage Delights
Calamari Delights
Cantaloupe Delights
Caper Delights
Cardamom Delights
Carrot Delights
Cashew Delights
Cauliflower Delights
Celery Delights
Cheese Delights
Cherry Delights
Chestnut Delights
Chicken Delights
Chili Pepper Delights

Chive Delights
Chocolate Delights
Chokecherry Delights
Cilantro Delights
Cinnamon Delights
Clam Delights
Clementine Delights
Coconut Delights
Coffee Delights
Conch Delights
Corn Delights
Cottage Cheese Delights
Crab Delights
Cranberry Delights
Cucumber Delights
Cumin Delights
Curry Delights
Date Delights
Edamame Delights
Egg Delights
Eggplant Delights
Elderberry Delights
Endive Delights
Fennel Delights
Fig Delights
Filbert (Hazelnut) Delights
Fish Delights
Garlic Delights
Ginger Delights
Ginseng Delights
Goji Berry Delights
Grape Delights
Grapefruit Delights
Grapple Delights
Guava Delights
Ham Delights
Hamburger Delights
Herb Delights
Herbal Tea Delights
Honey Delights

Honeyberry Delights
Honeydew Delights
Horseradish Delights
Huckleberry Delights
Jalapeño Delights
Jerusalem Artichoke Delights
Jicama Delights
Kale Delights
Kiwi Delights
Kohlrabi Delights
Lavender Delights
Leek Delights
Lemon Delights
Lentil Delights
Lettuce Delights
Lime Delights
Lingonberry Delights
Lobster Delights
Loganberry Delights
Macadamia Nut Delights
Mango Delights
Marionberry Delights
Milk Delights
Mint Delights
Miso Delights
Mushroom Delights
Mussel Delights
Nectarine Delights
Oatmeal Delights
Olive Delights
Onion Delights
Orange Delights
Oregon Berry Delights
Oyster Delights
Papaya Delights
Parsley Delights
Parsnip Delights
Pea Delights
Peach Delights
Peanut Delights
Pear Delights
Pecan Delights
Pepper Delights
Persimmon Delights

Pine Nut Delights
Pineapple Delights
Pistachio Delights
Plum Delights
Pomegranate Delights
Pomelo Delights
Popcorn Delights
Poppy Seed Delights
Pork Delights
Potato Delights
Prickly Pear Cactus Delights
Prune Delights
Pumpkin Delights
Quince Delights
Quinoa Delights
Radish Delights
Raisin Delights
Raspberry Delights
Rhubarb Delights
Rice Delights
Rose Delights
Rosemary Delights
Rutabaga Delights
Salmon Delights
Salmonberry Delights
Salsify Delights
Savory Delights
Scallop Delights
Seaweed Delights
Serviceberry Delights
Sesame Delights
Shallot Delights
Shrimp Delights
Soybean Delights
Spinach Delights
Squash Delights
Star Fruit Delights
Strawberry Delights
Sunflower Seed Delights
Sweet Potato Delights
Swiss Chard Delights
Tangerine Delights
Tapioca Delights
Tayberry Delights

Tea Delights
Teaberry Delights
Thimbleberry Delights
Tofu Delights
Tomatillo Delights
Tomato Delights
Trout Delights
Truffle Delights
Tuna Delights
Turkey Delights
Turmeric Delights
Turnip Delights
Vanilla Delights
Walnut Delights
Wasabi Delights
Watermelon Delights
Wheat Delights
Wild Rice Delights
Yam Delights
Yogurt Delights
Zucchini Delights

CITY DELIGHTS

Chicago Delights
Coeur d'Alene Delights
Great Falls Delights
Honolulu Delights
Minneapolis Delights
Phoenix Delights
Portland Delights
Sandpoint Delights
Scottsdale Delights
Seattle Delights
Spokane Delights
St. Cloud Delights

FOSTER CARE

Foster Children Cookbook and
   Activity Book
Foster Children's Favorite Recipes
Holiday Cookbook for Foster Families

GENERAL THEME DELIGHTS

Appetizer Delights
Baby Food Delights

Barbeque Delights
Beer-Making Delights
Beverage Delights
Biscotti Delights
Bisque Delights
Blender Delights
Bread Delights
Bread Maker Delights
Breakfast Delights
Brunch Delights
Cake Delights
Campfire Food Delights
Candy Delights
Canned Food Delights
Cast Iron Delights
Cheesecake Delights
Chili Delights
Chowder Delights
Cocktail Delights
College Cooking Delights
Comfort Food Delights
Cookie Delights
Cooking for One Delights
Cooking for Two Delights
Cracker Delights
Crepe Delights
Crockpot Delights
Dairy Delights
Dehydrated Food Delights
Dessert Delights
Dinner Delights
Dutch Oven Delights
Foil Delights
Fondue Delights
Food Processor Delights
Fried Food Delights
Frozen Food Delights
Fruit Delights
Gelatin Delights
Grilled Delights
Hiking Food Delights
Ice Cream Delights
Juice Delights
Kid's Delights

Kosher Diet Delights
Liqueur-Making Delights
Liqueurs and Spirits Delights
Lunch Delights
Marinade Delights
Microwave Delights
Milk Shake and Malt Delights
Panini Delights
Pasta Delights
Pesto Delights
Phyllo Delights
Pickled Food Delights
Picnic Food Delights
Pizza Delights
Preserved Delights
Pudding and Custard Delights
Quiche Delights
Quick Mix Delights
Rainbow Delights
Salad Delights
Salsa Delights
Sandwich Delights
Sea Vegetable Delights
Seafood Delights
Smoothie Delights
Snack Delights
Soup Delights
Supper Delights
Tart Delights
Torte Delights
Tropical Delights
Vegan Delights
Vegetable Delights
Vegetarian Delights
Vinegar Delights
Wildflower Delights
Wine Delights
Winemaking Delights
Wok Delights

GIFTS-IN-A-JAR SERIES

Beverage Gifts-in-a-Jar
Christmas Gifts-in-a-Jar
Cookie Gifts-in-a-Jar

Gifts-in-a-Jar
Gifts-in-a-Jar Catholic
Gifts-in-a-Jar Christian
Holiday Gifts-in-a-Jar
Soup Gifts-in-a-Jar

HEALTH-RELATED DELIGHTS

Achalasia Diet Delights
Adrenal Health Diet Delights
Anti-Acid Reflux Diet Delights
Anti-Cancer Diet Delights
Anti-Inflammation Diet Delights
Anti-Stress Diet Delights
Arthritis Delights
Bone Health Diet Delights
Diabetic Diet Delights
Fibromyalgia Diet Delights
Gluten-Free Diet Delights
Healthy Breath Diet Delights
Healthy Digestion Diet Delights
Healthy Heart Diet Delights
Healthy Skin Diet Delights
Healthy Teeth Diet Delights
High-Fiber Diet Delights
High-Iodine Diet Delights
High-Protein Diet Delights
Immune Health Diet Delights
Kidney Health Diet Delights
Lactose-Free Diet Delights
Liquid Diet Delights
Liver Health Diet Delights
Low-Calorie Diet Delights
Low-Carb Diet Delights
Low-Fat Diet Delights
Low-Sodium Diet Delights
Low-Sugar Diet Delights
Lymphoma Health Support
  Diet Delights
Multiple Sclerosis Healthy Diet Delights
No Flour No Sugar Diet Delights
Organic Food Delights
pH-Friendly Diet Delights
Pregnancy Diet Delights
Raw Food Diet Delights

Ethiopian Delights
Fijian Delights
French Delights
German Delights
Greek Delights
Hungarian Delights
Icelandic Delights
Indian Delights
Irish Delights
Italian Delights
Korean Delights
Mexican Delights
Native American Delights
Polish Delights
Russian Delights
Scottish Delights
Slovenian Delights
Swedish Delights
Thai Delights
The Netherlands Delights
Yugoslavian Delights
Zambian Delights

REGIONAL DELIGHTS

Glacier National Park Delights
Northwest Regional Delights
Oregon Coast Delights
Schweitzer Mountain Delights
Southwest Regional Delights
Tropical Delights
Washington Wine Country Delights
Wine Delights of Walla Walla Wineries
Yellowstone National Park Delights

SEASONAL DELIGHTS

Autumn Harvest Delights
Spring Harvest Delights
Summer Harvest Delights
Winter Harvest Delights

SPECIAL EVENTS DELIGHTS

Birthday Delights
Coffee Klatch Delights
Super Bowl Delights
Tea Time Delights

STATE DELIGHTS

Alaska Delights
Arizona Delights
Georgia Delights
Hawaii Delights
Idaho Delights
Illinois Delights
Iowa Delights
Louisiana Delights
Minnesota Delights
Montana Delights
North Dakota Delights
Oregon Delights
South Dakota Delights
Texas Delights
Washington Delights

U.S. TERRITORIES DELIGHTS

Cruzan Delights
U.S. Virgin Island Delights

MISCELLANEOUS COOKBOOKS

Getaway Studio Cookbook
The Soup Doctor's Cookbook

BILINGUAL DELIGHTS SERIES

Apple Delights, English-French
    Edition
Apple Delights, English- Spanish
    Edition
Huckleberry Delights, English-French
    Edition
Huckleberry Delights, English-
    Spanish Edition

CATHOLIC DELIGHTS SERIES

Apple Delights Catholic
Coffee Delights Catholic
Easter Delights Catholic
Huckleberry Delights Catholic
Tea Delights Catholic

CATHOLIC BILINGUAL
DELIGHTS SERIES

Apple Delights Catholic,

English-French Edition
Apple Delights Catholic,
English-Spanish Edition
Huckleberry Delights Catholic,
English-French Edition
Huckleberry Delights Catholic,
English-Spanish Edition

CHRISTIAN DELIGHTS SERIES

Apple Delights Christian
Coffee Delights Christian
Easter Delights Christian
Huckleberry Delights Christian
Tea Delights Christian

CHRISTIAN BILINGUAL DELIGHTS SERIES

Apple Delights Christian,
English-French Edition
Apple Delights Christian, English-
Russian Edition Apple Delights
Christian, English-Spanish Edition
Huckleberry Delights Christian,
English-Spanish Edition

FUNDRAISING COOKBOOKS

Ask about our fundraising
cookbooks to help raise
funds for your organization.

The above books are also available in bilingual versions. Please contact Whispering Pine Press International, Inc., for details.

Please note that some books are future books and are currently in production. Please contact us for availability date. Prices are subject to change without notice.

The above list of books is not all-inclusive. For a complete list please visit our website or contact us at:

Whispering Pine Press International, Inc.
Your Northwest Book Publishing Company
P.O. Box 214
Spokane Valley, WA 99037-0214 USA
Phone: (509) 928-8700 | Fax: (509) 922-9949
Email: sales@whisperingpinepress.com
Publisher Websites: www.WhisperingPinePress.com
www.WhisperingPinePressBookstore.com
Blog: www.WhisperingPinePressBlog.com

Halloween Delights

A Collection of Halloween Recipes
Cookbook Delights Series

Karen Jean Matsko Hood

Published by:

Whispering Pine Press International, Inc.
Your Northwest Book Publishing Company
P.O. Box 214
Spokane Valley, WA 99037-0214 USA
Phone: (509) 928-8700 | Fax: (509) 922-9949
Email: sales@whisperingpinepress.com
Websites: www.whisperingpinepress.com
www.whisperingpinepressbookstore.com
Blog: www.whisperingpinepressblog.com
SAN 253-200X
Printed in the U.S.A.

Published by Whispering Pine Press International, Inc.
P.O. Box 214
Spokane Valley, Washington 99037-0214 USA

For sales outside the United States, please contact the Whispering Pine Press International, Inc., International Sales Department.

Book and Cover Design by Artistic Design Service, Inc.
P.O. Box 1782
Spokane Valley, WA 99037-1782 USA
www.ArtisticDesignService.com

Library of Congress Number (LCCN): 2014 pending

Hood, Karen Jean Matsko
    Title: Halloween Delights Cookbook: A Collection of Halloween Recipes: Cookbook Delights Series

    p.   cm.

ISBN: 978-1-59434-181-6   case bound
ISBN: 978-1-59434-182-3   perfect bound
ISBN: 978-1-59434-183-0   spiral bound
ISBN: 978-1-59434-184-7   comb bound
ISBN: 978-1-59434-187-8   E-PDF
ISBN: 978-1-59434-079-6   E-PUB
ISBN: 978-1-59434-853-2   E-PRC

First Edition: January 2014
1. Cookery (Halloween)   1. Title

Halloween Delights Cookbook

A Collection of Halloween Recipes
Cookbook Delights Series

Gift Inscription

To: _____

From:_____

Date: _____

Special Message:_____

_____

_____

_____

_____

_____

_____

_____

*It is always nice to receive a personal note to
create a special memory.*

www.HalloweenDelights.com
www.WhisperingPinePress.com
www.WhisperingPinePressBookstore.com

Dedications

To my husband and best friend, Jim.

To our seventeen children: Gabriel, Brianne Kristina and her husband Moulik Vinodkumar Kothari, Marissa Kimberly and her husband Kevin Matthew Franck, Janelle Karina and her husband Paul Joseph Turcotte, Mikayla Karlene, Kyler James, Kelsey Katrina, Corbin Joel, Caleb Jerome, Keisha Kalani Hiwot, Devontay Joshua, Kianna Karielle Selam, Rosy Kiara, Mercedes Katherine, Jasmine Khalia Wengel, Cheyenne Krystal, and Annalise Kaylee Marie.

To our grandchildren and foster grandchildren, Courtney and Lorenzo.

To my brother, Stephen, and his wife, Karen.

To my husband's ten siblings: Gary, Colleen, John, Dan, Mary, Ray, Ann, Teresa, Barbara, Agnes, and their families.

In loving memory of my mom, who passed away in 2007; my dad, who passed away in 1976; and my sister, Sandy, who passed away due to multiple sclerosis in 1999.

To Sandy's three sons: Monte, Bradley, and Derek. To Monte's wife, Sarah, and their children: Liam, Alice, Charlie, and Samuel. To Bradley's wife, Shawnda, and their children: Anton, Isaac, and Isabel.

To our foster children past and present: Krystal, Sara, Rebecca, Janice, Devontay Joshua, Mercedes Katherine, Zha'Nell, Makia, Onna, Cheyenne Krystal, Onna Marie, Nevaeh, and Zada, our future foster children, and all foster children everywhere.

To the Court Appointed Special Advocate (CASA) Volunteer Program in the judicial system which benefits abused and neglected children.

To the Literacy Campaign dedicated to promoting literacy throughout the world.

Acknowledgements

The author would like to acknowledge all those individuals who helped me during my time in writing this book. Appreciation is extended for all their support and effort they put into this project.

Deep gratitude and profound thanks are owed to my husband, Jim, for giving freely of his time and encouragement during this project. Also, thanks are owed to my children Gabriel, Brianne Kristina and her husband Moulik Vinodkumar Kothari, Marissa Kimberly and her husband Kevin Matthew Franck, Janelle Karina and her husband Paul Joseph Turcotte, Mikayla Karlene, Kyler James, Kelsey Katrina, Corbin Joel, Caleb Jerome, Keisha Kalani Hiwot, Devontay Joshua, Kianna Karielle Selam, Rosy Kiara, Mercedes Katherine, Jasmine Khalia Wengel, Cheyenne Krystal, and Annalise Kaylee Marie. All of these persons inspire my writing.

Thanks are due to Beverly Koerperich and Sharron Thompson for their assistance in editing and typing this manuscript for publication. Thanks go to Artistic Design Service, Inc. for their assistance in formatting and providing a graphic design of this manuscript for publication. This project could not have been completed without them.

Many thanks are due to members of my family, all of whom were very supportive during the time it took to complete this project. Their patience and support are greatly appreciated.

Halloween Delights Cookbook

Table of Contents

Halloween Delights Cookbook

A Collection of Halloween Recipes
Cookbook Delights Series

Introduction

What a perfect occasion on which to design a cookbook! The recipes in this book have been collected around the themes and season of Halloween. These recipes are great for Halloween, but they can also be used any time of the year. We hope you enjoy reading this cookbook as well as trying out all of the recipes. This cookbook is designed for easy use and is organized into alphabetical sections: appetizers, dips, and snacks; beverages; breads and rolls; breakfasts; cakes; candies and other treats; cookies; desserts; dressings, sauces, and condiments; jams, jellies, and syrups; main dishes; pies; preserving; salads; side dishes; soups; and wines and spirits.

As a poet, I found it enjoyable to color this cookbook with poetry so that readers could savor the metaphorical richness of Halloween as well as the literal flavor.

Enjoy reading about Halloween and trying new recipes, but most importantly, have fun with those you care about while you are cooking. Be sure to look at the list of current and future cookbooks for other titles in the Delights Series of cookbooks that you might desire. If you do not find the subject you are looking for, please email us with your suggestion for consideration in our list. You may email us at sales@whisperingpinepress. com.

Following is a collection of recipes gathered and modified to bring you *Halloween Delights Cookbook: A Collection of Halloween Recipes, Cookbook Delights Series* by Karen Jean Matsko Hood.

Halloween Botanical Classification

Table of Pumpkins

Scientific Name	Common Name	Main Features
Cucurbitaceae moschata	Kentucky field or cheese group	Stem is hard, and smoothly grooved; leaf nearly round to moderately lobed, soft; skin tan color (this kind widely used in commercially canned pumpkin); seeds white to brown, often plump, and surface sometimes split and wrinkled.
C. pepo	Jack-o'-lantern group, small sugar, and miniature	Stem hard, angular, grooved, and prickly; leaf palmately lobed, often deeply cut, prickly; skin yellow, bright, and dark orange; seed dull white to tan, surface smooth.
C. argyrosperma (C. mixta)	Cushaws and related types	Stem hard, angular, grooved; leaf moderately lobed, soft; seeds usually white, may be very large, surface smooth or split.
C. maxima	Mammoth types (50 to 100 pounds)	Stem soft, round; leaf usually unlobed, nearly round and soft; seed white to brown, often are plump, and surface sometimes split or wrinkled.

Halloween Cultivation and Gardening

Growing Your Pumpkins

Pumpkin patches are so much fun! They make a delightful garden patch for the entire family without too much time involved. Pumpkins come in vining, semi-bush, or bush varieties, so whether you have a large space or a small one, you can grow your own pumpkins.

When to Plant

The pumpkin is a very tender vegetable. They should not be planted until all danger of frost is past and the soil is warm, because the seeds do not germinate in cold soil, and the seedlings are injured by frost. To have them ready for Halloween, plant pumpkins from late May in northern locations to early July in extremely southern areas. If pumpkins are planted too early, they may soften and rot before Halloween.

Spacing and Depth

Vining pumpkins

Vining pumpkins require a minimum of 50 to 100 square feet per hill. Plant seeds 1 inch deep with 4 or 5 seeds per hill. Allow 5 to 6 feet between hills, spaced in rows 10 to 15 feet apart. When the young plants are well established, thin each hill to the best 2 or 3 plants.

Semi-bush pumpkins

Plant semi-bush varieties 1 inch deep with 4 to 5 seeds per hill. Thin to the best 2 plants per hill. Allow 4 feet between hills and 8 feet between rows.

Miniature pumpkins

Plant miniature varieties 1 inch deep with 2 or 3 seeds every 2 feet in a row. Rows should be 6 to 8 feet apart, with seedlings thinned to the best plant every 2 feet when they have their first true leaves.

Bush pumpkins

Plant bush varieties 1 inch deep with 1 or 2 seeds per foot of row, thinning to a single plant every 3 feet. Allow 4 to 6 feet between rows.

Care

Pumpkin plants should be kept free from weeds by hoeing and shallow cultivation. Pumpkins can tolerate short periods of hot, dry weather fairly well, but you will need to irrigate if an extended dry period occurs in early summer.

Insecticides, if they are used, should be applied only in late afternoon or early evening when the blossoms have closed for the day and bees are no longer visiting the blossoms. Bees are necessary for pollination and may be killed by insecticides.

Harvest and Storage

Pumpkins can be harvested when they are a deep, solid orange (for most varieties) and the rind is hard. Harvest in late September or early October, before heavy frost, if vines are healthy. If the vines die early, pick only mature fruit. Pumpkins without stems do not keep well and do not work well for jack-o'-lanterns, so it is better to cut them from the vines with a sharp knife or pruning shears instead of attempting to snap the stem. Leave 3 to 4 inches of stem attached. You will want to wear gloves when harvesting pumpkins, because many varieties have sharp prickles on the stems that can be irritating to your skin. Avoid damaging the pumpkins when handling them. Pumpkins that are not fully mature, have been injured, or subjected to heavy frost do not keep well. Check to make sure the pumpkins are not blemished, have no cracks or soft spots, and are a deep orange color.

Do not store pumpkins in the refrigerator or in a damp place, since moisture causes them to deteriorate quickly. Whole, unblemished pumpkins can be stored for 3 to 6 months at 45 to 50 degrees F.

Pests and Disease

Common problems in growing pumpkins include powdery mildew and insect infestation. Powdery mildew causes a white, powdery mold growth on the upper surfaces of the leaves. This growth can kill the leaves prematurely and interfere with proper ripening.

Cucumber beetles and squash bugs attack seedlings and vines as well as immature and mature fruits. Watch for infestations of cucumber beetles and squash bugs, since populations increase in late summer. These insects can damage the mature fruits, marring their appearance, and making them less likely to keep well.

Growing Jumbo Pumpkins

To grow pumpkins that weigh more than 100 pounds, allow 150 square feet per hill for jumbo and 300 square feet for giant. Thin to one or two plants per hill. Water when needed, adding a balanced, soluble fertilizer once a week. After the plants begin blooming, remove the first two or three female blossoms so the plants will grow larger and have more leaf surface before beginning to set fruit. Only allow one fruit to develop. After this fruit has set, remove all female flowers. Prune side vines. Do not allow the vine to root down at the joints near the developing fruit. Check frequently to make sure the vine is not tight. It must be able to lift as the pumpkin grows higher. The jumbo varieties grow large quickly and may break from the vine if it is anchored to the ground. As the pumpkin grows larger, provide shade to help keep it from rotting or splitting. Also, avoid giving large doses of fertilizer and water at critical growing times. If the stem splits, treat wound sites with fungicide, keep that area dry, and give it good air circulation.

Pumpkins are the most popular members of the squash family. The large jack-o'-lantern variety, often used as an ornament, has become the national symbol for Halloween, although it is very edible. The smaller sweet pumpkin or pie pumpkin is best for cooking. The flavor and texture are much more suitable for baking, and it is served up annually in pumpkin pie at Thanksgiving.

Enjoy trying your hand at growing your own jack-o'-lanterns for Halloween and pumpkins to use for your Thanksgiving pies!

Halloween Delights Cookbook

A Collection of Halloween Recipes
Cookbook Delights Series

Halloween Facts

Halloween Facts

Early national attention to trick-or-treating was given in October 1947 issues of the children's magazines *Jack and Jill* and *Children's Activities* and by Halloween episodes of the network radio programs *The Baby Snooks Show* in 1946 and *The Jack Benny Show* and *The Adventures of Ozzie and Harriet* in 1948. The custom had become firmly established in popular culture by 1952 when Walt Disney portrayed it in the cartoon "Trick or Treat" and UNICEF first conducted a national campaign for children to raise funds for the charity while trick-or-treating.

Objections to celebrating Halloween are not always limited to Christianity. Some Wiccans feel that the tradition is offensive to "real witches" for promoting a stereotypical caricature of a wicked witch. Some Neopagans and Wiccans also object to Halloween because they perceive it to be a "vulgarized, commercialized mockery" of the original Samhain rituals. However, other Neopagans, perhaps most of them, see it as a harmless holiday in which some of the old traditions are celebrated by the mainstream culture, albeit in a different way.

In Scotland, children or guisers are more likely to recite "The sky is blue, the grass is green, may we have our Halloween" instead of "trick or treat!" They visit neighbors in groups and must impress the members of the houses they visit with a song, poem, trick, joke, or dance in order to earn their treats. Traditionally, nuts, oranges, apples, and dried fruit were offered, though sometimes children would also earn a small amount of cash, usually a sixpence.

A Halloween custom which has survived to this day in Ireland is the baking (or more often nowadays the purchase) of a barmbrack. This is a light fruit cake into which a plain ring is placed before baking. It is said that whoever finds this ring will find his or her true love during the following year.

Halloween Delights Cookbook

A Collection of Halloween Recipes
Cookbook Delights Series

Halloween Folklore

Halloween Folklore

Bobbing for apples is a well-established custom on Halloween, synonymous with the Scottish "dukin." Apples were put into a barrel that had been filled to the brim with water, and an individual would have to catch an apple in their mouth without using their hands. Once an apple had been caught, it was traditional to peel the apple and toss it over one's shoulder in the hope that the strips would fall into the shape of a letter. Whatever letter the peelings arranged into would be the first initial of the participant's true love. According to another superstition, the longer the peel, the longer the peeler's life would be. Some say that the first to get an apple would be the first to marry.

The jack-o'-lantern element of the Halloween tradition can be traced back to the Irish story of Stingy Jack, a greedy, gambling, hard-drinking old farmer who tricked the devil into climbing a tree and trapped him by carving a cross into the trunk of the tree. Jack refused to free him unless the Devil agreed never to let Jack into Hell. The Devil agreed. When Jack died, the Devil would not let him into Hell, but neither could he gain access to heaven. So Jack carved out one of his turnips, put a candle inside of it, and began endlessly wandering the earth searching for a resting place. He was known as "Jack of the lantern" or Jack-o'-lantern. For centuries this bedtime parable was told by Irish parents to their children. At Halloween time the children carved out turnips, placing a candle inside to symbolize Jack's curse. The carved pumpkin was associated generally with harvest time in America and did not become specifically associated with Halloween until the mid to late 19th century.

In North America, unmarried women were frequently told that if they sat in a darkened room and gazed into a mirror on Halloween night, the face of their future husband would appear in the mirror. However, if they were destined to die before they married, a skull would appear. The custom was widespread enough to be commemorated on greeting cards from the late 19th and early 20th centuries.

Halloween Delights Cookbook
A Collection of Halloween Recipes
Cookbook Delights Series

Halloween History

Halloween History

Halloween had its beginnings in an ancient pre-Christian Celtic festival of the dead. According to what can be reconstructed of the beliefs of the ancient Celts, the bright half of the year ended around November 1 or on a moon-phase near that date or at the time of the first frost. The festival they observed at that time was called Samhain (pronounced Sah-ween or Sow-in). After the adoption of the Roman calendar with its fixed months, the date began to be celebrated independently of the moon's phases.

Since October 31st was the last day of the bright half of the year, the next day also meant the beginning of winter. The Celts often associated winter with human death and with the slaughter of livestock to provide meat for the coming winter.

The Celtic people believed Samhain was a time when the boundaries between the world of the living and the world of the dead become thinner, at times even fading away completely, allowing spirits and other supernatural entities to pass between the worlds to socialize with humans. It was the time of the year when ancestors and other departed souls were especially honored. Often a meal would be prepared of favorite foods of the family's and community's beloved dead, a place set for them at the table, and traditional songs, poetry, and dances performed to entertain them. A door or window might have been opened to the west and the beloved dead specifically invited to attend. Many would leave a candle or other light burning in a western window to guide the dead home.

Samhain is one of the eight annual holidays, often referred to as "Sabbats," observed as part of the Wiccan Wheel of the Year. It is considered by most Wiccans to be the most important of the four "greater Sabbats." Its date is not universally agreed upon, but it is generally observed on October 31 in the Northern Hemisphere. Samhain is considered by most Wiccans as a celebration of death and of the dead, and it often involves paying respect to ancestors, family members, elders of the faith, friends, pets, and other loved ones who have died. In some rituals the spirits of the departed are invited to attend the festivities. It is seen as a festival of darkness and death, which is balanced at the opposite point of the wheel by the spring festival of Beltane, which Wiccans celebrate as a festival of life and fertility.

The Anglo-Saxon invasions of the fifth and sixth centuries A.D. pushed the native Celts north and westward in Britain to present-day Wales, Cornwall, and northern England, taking the festival of All Hallows' Eve with them. The term Halloween is shortened from All-hallow-even, as it is the evening of/before "All Hallows' Day" (also known as "All Saints' Day"). The holiday was a day of religious festivities in various northern European pagan traditions, until Popes Gregory III and Gregory IV moved the old Christian feast of All Saints' Day from May 13 to November 1. All Saints' Day (All Hallows' Day) became fixed on the 1st of November in 835 and All Souls' Day on the 2nd of November circa 998. On All Souls' Eve families sat up, and little "soul cakes" were eaten by everyone. At the stroke of midnight there was silence with candles burning in every room to guide the souls back to visit their earthly homes and a glass of wine on the table to refresh them. The tradition continued in some areas of northern England as late as the 1930s, with children going from door to door "souling" for cakes or money by singing a song. The English Reformation in the 16th century de-emphasized holidays like All Hallows' Day and its associated eve.

Halloween is celebrated in most parts of the Western world, most commonly in the United States, Canada, Puerto Rico, Ireland, the United Kingdom, Peru, and with increasing popularity in Australia and New Zealand. Many European cultural traditions hold that Halloween is one of the times of the year when spirits can make contact with the physical world and when magic is most potent.

Halloween did not become a holiday in America until the 19th century, where lingering Puritan tradition meant even Christmas was scarcely observed before the 1800s. North American almanacs of the late 18th and early 19th centuries make no mention of Halloween in their lists of holidays. The transatlantic migration of nearly two million Irish following the Irish Potato Famine (1845–1849) brought the holiday and its customs to America. Scottish emigration from the British Isles, primarily to Canada before 1870 and to the United States thereafter, brought that country's own version of the holiday to North America.

When the holiday was observed in 19th-century America, it was generally in three ways. Scottish-American and Irish-American societies held dinners and balls that celebrated their heritages, with perhaps a recitation of Robert Burns's poem "Halloween" or a telling of Irish legends, much as Columbus Day celebrations were more about Italian-American heritage than Columbus. Home parties would center around children's activities, such as bobbing for apples and various divination games, particularly about future romance. And finally, pranks and mischief were common on Halloween.

The commercialization of Halloween in America did not begin until the 20th century, beginning perhaps with Halloween postcards, which were most popular between 1905 and 1915 and featured hundreds of different designs.

"Trick-or-Treat for UNICEF" has become a common sight during Halloween in North America. It started as a local event in a Philadelphia suburb in 1950 and expanded nationally in 1952.

As you can see, the Halloween tradition has a rich history and blend of cultures.

Did You Know? . . . .

Did you know that other names for Halloween are All Hallows' Eve, All Saints' Eve, Samhain, Spooky Day, Snap-Apple Night, Costume Day, and Pooky Night?

Did You Know? . . . .

Did you know that according to the U.S. Census Bureau, the first recorded Halloween celebration in the United States took place in Anoka, Minnesota, in 1921?

Halloween Delights Cookbook

A Collection of Halloween Recipes
Cookbook Delights Series

Halloween Nutrition and Health

Halloween Nutrition and Health

Halloween celebrations include pumpkin, and fortunately, it is rich in vitamins and nutrients. The orange flesh of the pumpkin is an excellent source of beta carotene, which is a powerful antioxidant. Beta carotene is converted to vitamin A in the body. vitamin A is essential for healthy skin, vision, bone development, and many other functions. Pumpkin is also a tasty source of carbohydrates and potassium.

Nutrition Facts

1 cup cooked, mashed pumpkin contains the following:

Calories	24
Protein	1 gram
Carbohydrates	5.98 grams
Dietary Fiber	1 gram
Potassium	280.6 mg
Phosphorus	36.6 mg
Vitamin A	1320 IU
Vitamin C	5.73 mg

Halloween is a holiday that has many sugary treats—candy, as well as cookies, cake, and other treats—so children get plenty of sweets. You can keep from adding to this sugar overload by handing out tasty and nutritious low-carb snacks or other "treats." Some options could be:

- Single-serving packets of peanuts, cashews, or mixed nuts.
- Party favors.
- Sugar-free gum.
- Novelty pencils and erasers.
- Small boxes of crayons.
- Individually-wrapped string cheese snacks.
- Beef sticks or beef jerky.
- Sugar-free hard candy or chocolates.

Halloween Delights Cookbook

A Collection of Halloween Recipes
Cookbook Delights Series

Poetry

A Collection of Poetry with Halloween Themes

Table of Contents

Sunflowers Sleeping

Did you know that summer is almost past?
The bright yellow sunflowers begin to look tired,

and their brown centers droop. The hummingbirds long
gone while the common sparrow remains.

The tree roots reach deeper for moisture
seeking to quench their thirst after a long

drought of the summer waiting for rain,
last spring's summer sprouts now forgotten.

Karen Jean Matsko Hood ©2014
Published in *Halloween Delights Cookbook*, 2014
By Whispering Pine Press International, Inc., 2014

Announcing Frost

Do you hear the smell of pumpkins that ripen and
talk to apples red in autumn air?

Notice that the hummingbirds left
to rest away from the cool breeze.

Frost arrives
to paint brown landscape white.

Wait for the drop of acorns,
to feed the busy squirrels.

It is a gentle time for maple leaves that
fall on tired grass.

Karen Jean Matsko Hood ©2014
Published in *Halloween Delights Cookbook*, 2014
By Whispering Pine Press International, Inc., 2014

Demon Deep Within

Demon deep within myself
nightly sighing, sleeping, silent.
Mysterious demon awakens in wheel's center,
blackness stirs within,
spokes splinter from the core
as the peel shrivels, dry.
Decay crawls under mold,
while the stench covers
skin and perfume.
Dormant bones rest
while warm heartbeats awaken.
Dawn drives away the darkness and
fills the remains
with light.

Karen Jean Matsko Hood ©2014

Published in *Halloween Delights Cookbook*, 2014
By Whispering Pine Press International, Inc., 2014

Fallen Apples

Remember that special October day?
The air was cold and crisp.
The sky was azure blue,
punctuated with autumn's auburn tones.

Crunchy Macintosh, crispy Jonathans,
and tart Grannies
savored by the morsel.
Piquant cider spiced
to perfection,
Transparents saved for sauce.

Green orchard grasses wave in
plumes as we walk over clumps
between barren spots of soil.
Rotting apples lay upon the

ground. Time has come and
gone. Neglected,
bruised, battered
and worn,
no one wants these fallen apples.
Our calico children

frolic in the fall day.
They do make
delightful cider,
even bruised.

Karen Jean Matsko Hood ©2014

Published in *Halloween Delights Cookbook*, 2014
By Whispering Pine Press International, Inc., 2014

Fallen Leaves

I look down at golden leaves
of the tree of life above them.
Veins map out the story of their origin.
They are crunchy and smell of age
mixed with rain.
Yet rain cannot bathe
gold leaves enough.
An aroma of life mixes with
mold and remains below my feet.
I gaze upon the veins of former
life and feel the fragileness of all.
Seasons bring a sense of cycles.
Soon it will be time for

Karen Jean Matsko Hood ©2014

Published in *Halloween Delights Cookbook*, 2014
By Whispering Pine Press International, Inc., 2014

Full Moon

Midnight blue sleeps and
awakens the full moon that
glows bright with a halo and
circles magnetic light.

Ocean waves crash on craggy rocks
as grains of sand rest in sea salt
cool and still as the earth
spins under the magic of the moon.

A single soul looks up
silent in awe at the enormous
size of the radiant ball
and realizes it is the tiny ant

that prevails in size under
the magic of the moon.

Karen Jean Matsko Hood ©2014

Published in *Halloween Delights Cookbook*, 2014
By Whispering Pine Press International, Inc., 2014

Head Bone

Head bone is connected to
the neck bone but how is
that connected to the toe bone?
Coordination and production
line. Up and down
the line. How can we use
that signal to flush out
this mystery? Bones
are the core,
organic infrastructure
within the skull.
Clandestine brio.
Yet
they fall apart
without the new ones.
What does it all mean?

Karen Jean Matsko Hood ©2014

Published in *Halloween Delights Cookbook*, 2014
By Whispering Pine Press International, Inc., 2014

Here Comes November

But wait.
Whatever happened to October?
Fresh with the smell
of pumpkins that ripen
while apples, once crisp,
drop to the ground.
Sunflower heads,
tired of smiling,
droop their heads,
a bit weary from the daystar.
Gardeners gather
every fruit they can find
as denuded trees replace
foliage with an occasional frost.
The final rose of summer,
with rosehips attached,
finally snaps in the wind.

Karen Jean Matsko Hood ©2014

Published in *Halloween Delights Cookbook*, 2014
By Whispering Pine Press International, Inc., 2014

October Winds

The noise awakes me in the middle of the night
before my sleep ends in rest.

Droplets of water tap on my roof
to create the beat of an uneven dance,

that tiptoes on the clay tiles
then throws pebbles against the windows.

It reminds me of others
that have no refuge,

those that huddle in shelters,
of cardboard huts on dirty streets.

Cold and wet yet no blanket
feels their touch while the last

maple leaves cling
to autumn stems.

Naked under the
glare before winter.

Karen Jean Matsko Hood ©2014

Published in *Halloween Delights Cookbook*, 2014
By Whispering Pine Press International, Inc., 2014

Happy Halloween

The air is cool, the season is fall
Soon Halloween will come to us all.
The ghosts are after things to do
In fact, a ghost brought this to you!

"Boo" is a shield from the witching hour.
Just leave it up and watch its power.
In your house is where it works.
It wards off the creepy and scary who lurk.

These yummy treats are for your pleasure.
We've even included a little treasure.
Make two copies to give your friends
They'll have warm fuzzies that never end.

We'll all have a smile upon our face
No one will know who Boo'd this place
Just one short day, your spell to cast
Or a big "ZAP" will strike you fast.

And don't forget a nifty treat
Like something cute or something sweet.
Please join the fun, let's really hear it.
And spread some Boo's and Halloween Spirit!

Directions:

- Enjoy treats!
- Leave the "BOO" on your front door.
- Now you have 24 hours to copy this twice, make two "BOO" signs and two treat bags.
- Deliver them to two neighbors who do not have a "BOO" sign.

Watch how far it goes!

Halloween Delights Cookbook
A Collection of Halloween Recipes
Cookbook Delights Series

Halloween Symbols

Halloween Symbols

Bat: In folklore bats are closely associated with vampires, who are said to be able to transform into bats. Bats are also a symbol of ghosts, death, and disease.

Black Cat: Black cats are traditionally associated with witches or demons. Cats have always been thought of as having powers. The Egyptians used them as protectors in their grain storehouses. The Druids hated cats and felt they were once humans who were transformed by supernatural forces.

Bobbing for Apples: Dipping for apples was a way of divination among the Druids and is still done today in the folk life of those who live by Celtic cultures. For thousands of years, the apple has been considered a symbol of love and fertility.

Bonfire: Bonfires played a large part in the festivities celebrated down through the last several centuries and up through the present day in some rural areas of the Celtic nations. With the bonfire ablaze, the villagers extinguished all other fires. Each family then solemnly lit its hearth from the common flame, thus bonding the families of the village together. Often two bonfires would be built side by side, and the people would walk between the fires as a ritual of purification. Sometimes the cattle and other livestock would be driven between the fires, as well.

Candy Apples: Because the holiday comes in the wake of the annual apple harvest, candy apples (also known as toffee, taffy, or caramel apples) are a treat associated with Halloween. At one time candy apples were a common treat given to children, but this practice rapidly waned after widespread rumors that some individuals were embedding items like pins and razor blades in the apples that they would pass out to children.

Costumes: Originally, costumes and masks were worn to frighten off demons and avoid potential disasters like droughts, epidemics, etc. Even after Samhain was changed to the Christian All Hallows' Eve, people in Europe were still nervous about leaving their homes at night, so they often disguised themselves with costumes and masks so that the evil spirits who were out roaming would not recognize them.

Colcannon: A traditional dish made of cabbage, mashed potatoes, parsnips, and onions that is still served on Halloween in Ireland today. Placed in the dish are a ring, a thimble, a doll, and a coin. If your serving contains the ring, you will marry within a year. If it contains the thimble, you will never marry. If it contains the doll, you will have many children. If it contains the coin, you will be wealthy.

Dracula: The world's most famous vampire character, created by author Bram Stoker.

Frankenstein's Monster: A creature first appearing in Mary Shelley's novel *Frankenstein, or The Modern Prometheus*. After the novel was adapted to film, the monster became best known in popular imagination as "Frankenstein."

Ghost: A ghost is allegedly a noncorporeal manifestation of a dead person. It is often thought to be a manifestation of the spirit or soul of a person which has remained on earth after death. Every culture and region in the world carries stories about ghosts.

Ghoul: A monster that dwells in graveyards and other uninhabited places.

Goblin: An evil or merely mischievous creature, often described as a grotesquely disfigured or elf-like phantom. Goblin means "little people."

Haunted House: A building that is supposedly the center for supernatural occurrences or paranormal phenomena. Based largely in North America, it is an attraction that uses illusions and special effects to frighten those who visit.

Jack-O'-Lantern: Jack-o'-lanterns were traditionally made from hollowed out turnips with a face carved into them, but in recent years the pumpkin has become more popular. Often the face is made to appear frightful or humorous. A candle is placed inside the lantern to illuminate it.

Masks: Since the earliest days, masks were worn to ward off evil and to coerce the gods for favors. Also, people of all classes attended Witches' Sabbaths. Since this was frowned upon, people wore masks to hide their identity.

Mummy: A corpse whose skin and dried flesh have been preserved by either intentional or accidental exposure to chemicals, extreme cold or dryness, or airlessness. A Halloween mummy is inspired by the 1932 movie, *The Mummy*. This is an Egyptian mummy that comes back to life and is malevolent.

Orange and Black: Halloween's traditional colors. Orange is for the pumpkin and black is for death and darkness. In modern Halloween images and products, purple, green, and red are also prominent.

Skeleton: Skeletons are used to symbolize death.

Trick-or-Treating: In England the poor went begging for "soul cakes" on the Eve of All Saints' Day. In Spain they bribed the evil spirits by putting cakes and nuts on graves. In Belgium the children stood in front of homes begging for money to buy cakes. Then they would eat as many cakes as they could, because they believed that for each cake eaten, the suffering of one soul would be relieved. In Ireland Druid priests would put on masks and go around to homes and farms begging for food and tithes for the Celtic House of Worship. The farmers feared that if they did not tithe, the god Muck Olla would do something to their farms. Trick-or-treating as a threat by children to get candy is an American variation and relatively new to the holiday. It is an activity for children on Halloween in which they proceed from house to house in costumes, asking for treats such as candy with the question, "Trick or treat?"

Vampire: An animated corpse, one of the undead. For it to continue to live it must drink human blood.

Werewolf: In folklore a werewolf is a person who changes into a wolfman after being placed under a curse, usually by being bitten by another werewolf, and during a full moon they turn into werewolves.

Witch: Traditionally a person who engages in magic and casts spells. Witch means "wise one." A witch usually refers to a female. A male is called a warlock.

Did You Know? . . . .

Did you know that people in Scotland believed that if nuts or stones they would put in the ashes of the hearth before going to bed at night were disturbed, that person was destined to die during the coming year?

Halloween Delights Cookbook
A Collection of Halloween Recipes
Cookbook Delights Series

Recipes

Halloween Delights Cookbook

A Collection of Halloween Recipes
Cookbook Delights Series

Appetizers, Dips, and Snacks

Table of Contents

Did You Know? . . . .

Did you know that samhainophobia is the fear of Halloween?

Bat Wings with Swamp Dip

These wings taste delicious, and my sons love them. Tell the children they are eating bat wings, and they are sure to request them even when it is not Halloween! This is one of the recipes I presented on "Good Morning Northwest" on KXLY Spokane.

Ingredients for bat wings:

    20 chicken wings (3½ lb.)
    ¾ c. soy sauce
    2 tsp. grated fresh ginger or ½ tsp. ground ginger
    ¼ tsp. crushed red pepper
    1 tsp. five-spice powder (Chinese spice mix)
    2 cloves garlic, minced

Ingredients for swamp dip:

    8 oz. dairy sour cream
    3 Tbs. coarse ground mustard
      fresh whole chives, for garnish
      paprika

Directions for bat wings:

1. Place wings in plastic bag and place in shallow dish.
2. In small bowl, stir together soy sauce, ginger, crushed red pepper, five-spice powder, and garlic.
3. Pour over wings, close bag, and toss to coat.
4. Chill in refrigerator several hours or overnight, turning bag occasionally.
5. Preheat oven to 450 degrees F.
6. Remove wings from bag, reserving marinade.
7. Place wings on foil-lined, 15 × 10 × 1-inch baking pan.
8. Bake, uncovered, for 10 minutes.
9. Brush with reserved marinade; discard remaining marinade.
10. Bake 15 to 20 minutes longer or until chicken is tender and no longer pink.

Directions for swamp dip:

1. In small bowl stir together sour cream and mustard.
2. Garnish with chives.
3. Sprinkle with paprika to add some Halloween orange color.
4. Serve with bat wings.

Yields: 20 appetizers.

Green Pond Slime

You may have to convince your Halloween party guests that this dish really is not pond slime, but once they taste it, they are sure to love it.

Ingredients:

    10 oz. frozen broccoli
    10 oz. frozen baby peas
    2 Tbs. minced chives
    ½ c. butter
    ¼ c. heavy cream
    salt and pepper
    pinch of nutmeg
    chives for garnish

Directions:

1. Microwave or boil frozen vegetables until tender.
2. Drain vegetables and place in blender or food processor.
3. Process in batches if using small blender or processor.
4. Add butter, chives, and heavy cream.
5. Purée until mixture is smooth but still flecked with dark green bits of vegetables.
6. Refrigerate if desired; before serving, place mixture in saucepan and gently heat until warmed through.
7. Add nutmeg, salt, and pepper.
8. Place in serving bowl and garnish with chives.

Eyes of Newt

These make an easy appetizer that is fun for Halloween.

Ingredients:
- 2   cans sliced ripe olives (2½ oz. each), divided
- ⅓   c. chopped roasted red pepper, divided
- 1   pkg. cream cheese (8 oz.), softened
- 1   clove garlic, minced
- 8   flour tortillas (6- to 7-inch)
- 16 slices deli roast beef

Directions:
1. Reserve 48 olive slices, 48 pieces red pepper, and 1 tablespoon cream cheese.
2. Chop remaining olives.
3. Combine remaining cream cheese, olives, red pepper, and garlic in small bowl; mix well.
4. Spread about 2 tablespoons cream cheese mixture on each tortilla and roll up.
5. Trim off uneven ends of each rolled tortilla; discard.
6. Slice each tortilla roll into eight ¾-inch pieces.
7. Using reserved cream cheese, attach reserved olives and red peppers to make roll-ups look like eyes.

Yields: 4 dozen pieces.

Brain Shrimp Spread

As the name implies, this will look rather disgusting, but that is the fun in this Halloween appetizer.

Ingredients:
- 1   can cream of mushroom soup (10¾ oz.)
- 1   pkg. cream cheese (8 oz.), softened
- 1   env. unflavored gelatin (¼ oz.) softened in ¼ c. water

1　bunch green onions, chopped
3　lb. cooked shrimp, coarsely chopped, or 1 lb. crab meat
1　c. mayonnaise
1　Tbs. lemon juice
　　red pepper sauce or Creole seasoning to taste
　　brain mold
　　crackers of your choice

Directions:
1. Heat soup, undiluted; mix in cream cheese.
2. Stir in softened gelatin; blend well.
3. Fold in remaining ingredients and pour into lightly oiled mold.
4. Chill until firm and serve with your favorite crackers.
5. To use in 3-cup brain mold: halve this recipe except for gelatin, leave out green onions, and finely chop shrimp into more of a paste so it will look more smooth-textured like a real brain.

Critter Munch

Delight your Halloween guests with this fun snack.

Ingredients:
1¾ c. animal cracker cookies
1¾ c. goldfish crackers, cheddar or any flavor
1　c. dried tart cherries
1　c. plain candy-coated chocolate pieces
1¼ c. roasted peanuts

Directions:
1. Put animal crackers, goldfish crackers, dried cherries, candy pieces, and peanuts in large mixing bowl; mix well.
2. Store in tightly covered container at room temperature.

Goblin Dip with Bone Crackers

This is another party favorite in my family around Halloween.

Ingredients for dip:

- 1 can chili without beans (16 oz.)
- 1 can refried beans (16 oz.)
- 1 pkg. cream cheese (8 oz.)
- 1 jar chunky pico de gallo (8 oz.)
- 1 can chopped green chilies (4.5 oz.), undrained
- ½ tsp. ground cumin
  - toppings: shredded cheddar or Monterey Jack cheese with peppers, chopped black olives, sliced green onions
  - bone crackers (recipe follows)

Ingredients for bone crackers:

- 2 pkg. 9-inch flour tortillas (13.5 oz. each)
- ½ c. butter, melted
- ¼ tsp. garlic salt

Directions for dip:

1. Cook first 6 ingredients in heavy saucepan over low heat, stirring often, 15 minutes or until cream cheese is melted.
2. Sprinkle with desired toppings and serve warm with Bone Crackers.

Directions for bone crackers:

1. Preheat oven to 250 degrees F.
2. Cut tortillas with 3½-inch bone-shaped cutter and place on baking sheets, or cut bone shapes with kitchen shears.
3. Stir together butter and garlic salt; brush mixture on tortillas.
4. Bake for 30 minutes or until crisp.

Devilish Dip

Ham adds flavor to this easy-to-make dip that is good any time of year.

Ingredients:
- 4   oz. cream cheese
- ½   c. finely chopped cooked ham
- 2   Tbs. prepared horseradish or to taste
- 1½   Tbs. Dijon mustard
- ¼   c. dairy sour cream

Directions:
1. Mix ingredients together until well combined.
2. Warm in microwave for 30 to 60 seconds; stir and serve with crackers, cubes of toasted sourdough, or slices of party rye.

Halloween Bugs in Bed

These are very simple to make, and the children will love these buggy treats.

Ingredients:
- 4   green apples
- 1   c. chunky peanut butter
- ½   c. chopped peanuts
- ⅔   c. crispy rice cereal
- ⅓   c. raisins

Directions:
1. Cut apples into quarters and remove core, leaving hollow for filling.
2. Mix peanut butter, chopped peanuts, cereal, and raisins.
3. Spoon into apple hollows and serve.

Halloween Haunted Forest Platter

This imaginative forest is completely edible, fun to make, and a healthy Halloween treat.

Ingredients:

- 3　stalks broccoli
- 3　med. beets
- 3　hard-boiled eggs
- 1　oz. spaghetti, cooked and drained
- wooden toothpicks
- assorted vegetables such as cherry tomatoes, pea pods, kohlrabi, radishes, sweet red peppers, sweet yellow peppers, and shredded carrot
- ripe olives, pimiento-stuffed olives, and/or tiny sweet pickles
- liquid green food coloring

Directions:

1. Create trees by cutting bottoms from stalks of broccoli to make 6-inch broccoli trees.
2. Slice beets about ½ to ¾ inch thick to make base for broccoli trees.
3. Break toothpicks in half.
4. Insert 3 to 4 toothpick pieces into bottom of each broccoli stalk, and then insert into beet slice.
5. Stand broccoli upright; cover to keep moist.
6. To make egg ghosts use small knife or ½-inch aspic cutter to hollow out eyes and mouth to form face.
7. Cut small pieces of ripe olive to press into hollowed-out areas for eyes or mouth if desired; cover to keep moist.
8. Using your imagination, create creepy creatures with tomatoes, sweet peppers, pickles, olives, and radishes.
9. Place broccoli trees on serving platter.
10. Cover surface of platter with shredded carrot.
11. Hide egg ghosts in forest along with creepy creatures.

12. Scatter piles of vegetables such as pea pods, beet slices, kohlrabi slices, olives, pickles, and/or any other desired vegetables.
13. Add strips of red pepper to broccoli branches.
14. To make moss add a few drops of green food coloring to small amount of water in medium bowl; add cooked spaghetti and let stand about 5 minutes.
15. Drain and place over broccoli trees.
16. Keep platter covered until serving time.
17. If necessary, spritz platter with water to keep moist.

Mold and Mildew Halloween Dip

Despite its name, this recipe is really quite tasty and will disappear quickly. Serve hot with crackers.

Ingredients:

2 boxes frozen artichoke hearts, defrosted, drained
2 c. mayonnaise
1 bunch scallions, thinly sliced
10 oz. frozen chopped spinach, thawed, squeezed dry
2 c. grated Parmesan cheese
1 tsp. white pepper
1 tsp. Hungarian paprika
green food coloring

Directions:

1. Preheat oven to 350 degrees F.
2. Coarsely chop artichoke hearts, and place in medium ovenproof serving dish.
3. Add mayonnaise, scallions, spinach, grated cheese, and spices.
4. Add as much green food coloring as desired.
5. Bake for 30 minutes.
6. Serve with sturdy crackers, bread rounds, or tortilla chips.

Pickled Dragon Eggs

Use your imagination as you create this fun appetizer. If you cannot find fresh dragon eggs, you may use chicken eggs in this recipe.

Ingredients:

12 dragon eggs
4 c. water
1 c. beet juice
1 c. vinegar
1 clove garlic
1 bay leaf
2 tsp. pickling spice
½ tsp. salt
1 sm. onion, cut into rings
   food coloring (colors of your choice)

Directions:

1. Place eggs in saucepan and cover with water.
2. Cook eggs until hard boiled, about 8 to 10 minutes.
3. Slowly add lukewarm water to eggs to help them cool.
4. Mix 4 cups water, beet juice, vinegar, garlic, spices, and food coloring in cauldron (bowl); mix well.
5. Use tongs to remove eggs from saucepan.
6. Gently crack shells all the way around egg.
7. Place cracked eggs into cauldron; cover with onion rings.
8. Cover cauldron with plastic wrap and let brew in refrigerator for 2 days, making sure to turn eggs in morning and at night.
9. After brewing for 2 days, pickled dragon eggs are ready for eating.
10. Peel shells and amaze your friends.

Spiced Pumpkin Seeds

These seeds have the popular flavors of Worcestershire sauce and garlic. Enjoy.

Ingredients:

1½ Tbs. butter, melted
½   tsp. salt
⅛   tsp. garlic salt
2   tsp. Worcestershire sauce
2   c. raw whole pumpkin seeds

Directions:

1. Rinse pumpkin seeds under cold water to remove pulp and strings. This is easiest just after removing from pumpkin.
2. Preheat oven to 275 degrees F.
3. Combine all ingredients; mix thoroughly and place in shallow baking dish.
4. Bake for 1 hour, stirring occasionally.

Yields: 2 cups.

Did You Know? . . . .

Did you know that in 2000 the United States Library of Congress deemed the 1931 film version of Dracula "culturally significant" and selected it for preservation in the National Film Registry?

Monster Mash Party Mix

This easy mix is always a hit at Halloween parties. It is a good idea to keep extra ingredients on hand to make more.

Ingredients:

   10 c. popped popcorn
    1   bag plain candy-coated chocolate pieces (16 oz.)
    1   jar dry-roasted peanuts (14 oz.)
    1   c. golden raisins
    1   c. candy-coated peanut butter pieces

Directions:

   1. Mix all ingredients together in large serving bowl.

Yields: 15 cups.

Halloween Witches' Corn

This sweet and salty snack is quick and easy to make. You have your choice of using regular popcorn or kettlecorn.

Ingredients:

    1   bag microwave popcorn (3.5 oz.), 12 c. popped
    2   c. bugle-shaped corn snacks
    2   c. braided twist pretzels, broken in half
    1   c. roasted pistachios
   ⅓   c. butter, melted
    3   Tbs. sugar
    1   c. candy corn

Directions:

   1. Place popped popcorn, corn snacks, pretzels, and pistachios in very large bowl; set aside.
   2. Melt butter on high in microwave-safe bowl for 30 to 45 seconds.

3. Add sugar; stir.
4. Pour butter mixture over popcorn mixture; stir to coat.
5. Carefully stir in candy corn.
6. Substitute: 1 bag microwave kettlecorn popcorn (3.5 oz.); omit butter and sugar.
7. Serve in black cauldron for a festive flair.

Shining Monster Eyes

These are actually very tasty and make a great appetizer.

Ingredients:

4	Tbs. butter, softened
1½	tsp. paprika
1	c. extra-sharp cheddar cheese
1	c. mild cheddar cheese
1	c. all-purpose flour
50	whole black olives
50	small chunks pepperoni
	dash cayenne pepper

Directions:
1. Preheat oven to 400 degrees F.
2. In medium bowl beat butter until very soft and smooth.
3. Add paprika and cayenne and blend.
4. Add cheeses and mix well.
5. Stir in flour.
6. Insert chunk of pepperoni in each olive.
7. With fingers, wrap about 1½ teaspoons of dough around each olive, leaving small part of olive outside of dough to form iris on eye, using pepperoni-stuffed opening for part that is seen for best effect.
8. Roll mixture into smooth balls, and place 1 inch apart on ungreased baking sheet.
9. Bake until cheddar pastry is firm and crispy but not browned, about 12 minutes.
10. Serve hot or cold.

Spiced Bat Wings

The sweet, savory spice of curry adds a new flavor twist to a party favorite. Season the chicken ahead of time, and then serve it hot from the oven with a chutney dip. Mango chutney is called for in this recipe, but apple, peach, and ginger chutneys would be equally delicious with this chicken.

Ingredients:

4	tsp. curry powder
2	tsp. ground ginger
1	tsp. ground cinnamon
¼	tsp. salt
2	lb. chicken wing drummettes (20 to 24)
3	Tbs. butter, melted
1	c. mango chutney

Directions:

1. Place curry powder, ginger, cinnamon, and salt in large resealable plastic food storage bag.
2. Add chicken; seal.
3. Shake bag until chicken is evenly coated with spices.
4. Refrigerate for at least 3 hours or overnight.
5. Preheat oven to 350 degrees F.
6. Arrange chicken on aluminum foil-lined 15 x 10 x 1-inch jellyroll pan.
7. Drizzle with butter.
8. Bake for 30 to 35 minutes or until chicken is golden brown and juices run clear when pierced with fork.
9. Serve chicken hot from oven with chutney.

Yields: 20 drummettes.

Halloween Delights Cookbook
A Collection of Halloween Recipes
Cookbook Delights Series

Beverages

Table of Contents

Bile Brew

Despite its appearance, this drink is very tasty. You may have to be the brave one to try it first so your guests are willing to drink it.

Ingredients:

- 2 bananas, ripe
- 2 c. water, divided
- 1 c. sugar
- 1 can frozen orange juice concentrate, thawed
- ½ can frozen lemonade concentrate, thawed
- 2 c. unsweetened pineapple juice
- 1 c. cranberry juice
- 2 liters lemon-lime soda, chilled
- 1 c. miniature marshmallows

Directions:

1. Cut ripe bananas into chunks.
2. Put banana chunks, 1 cup water, and 1 cup sugar into blender; blend until bananas are smooth but a little chunky, about 15 to 20 seconds.
3. Pour banana mixture into cauldron (bowl).
4. Add orange juice, lemonade, pineapple juice, cranberry juice, and 1 cup water to cauldron.
5. Stir with long-handled spoon while chanting, "Bile brew, Up-chuck stew, Makes me sick, How about you?"
6. Wrap cauldron tightly with plastic wrap, and carefully place into freezer to curdle and brew.
7. Freeze for at least 3 hours, but it is best if brewed overnight.
8. Remove brew from freezer about 1 hour before serving.
9. Just before serving, mash brew into chunky concoction using potato masher.
10. Add chilled lemon-lime soda and 1 cup mini marshmallows for that disgusting, chunky look.
11. Stir brew and serve.

Blood Bath

This can be served in Halloween-decorated serving dishes for added effect.

Ingredients:

    64 oz. cran-raspberry cocktail
    4 c. apple juice
    4 c. vanilla ice cream

Directions:

1. Mix together cran-raspberry cocktail and apple juice; chill.
2. Pour into punch bowl or other serving container.
3. Scoop vanilla ice cream into punch and serve immediately.

Bloody Blast

This drink is actually healthy. Using Halloween-decorated glasses or mugs will give added effect to this beverage, too.

Ingredients:

    3 cans tomato or vegetable juice (12 oz. each)
    2 Tbs. Worcestershire sauce
    1 Tbs. prepared horseradish
    1 Tbs. lemon juice
    ¼ tsp. hot red pepper sauce, or to taste
      celery ribs and olives for garnish

Directions:

1. Combine tomato juice, Worcestershire, horseradish, lemon juice, and hot pepper sauce in pitcher.
2. Chill at least 1 hour.
3. Pour into ice-filled glasses.
4. Garnish with celery stalks and olives for "eyes," if desired.

Blue Slime Sipper

Berries, citrus, and magic combine in a sweet and tasty (and colorful) potion. This makes a thick drink that has the consistency and look of slime.

Ingredients:
- 1   pkg. blueberry-flavored gelatin (6 oz.)
- 2   c. boiling water
- 4   c. cold water
- 3   c. lemonade, chilled
- 3   c. lemon-lime carbonated beverage, chilled

Directions:
1. In large mixing bowl combine gelatin and 2 cups boiling water; stir until dissolved.
2. Stir in 4 cups cold water.
3. Cover and chill at least 4 hours (gelatin will be partially set).
4. To serve, stir gelatin with large spoon, fork, or wire whisk until broken into small pieces.
5. Place ¼ cup of lemonade in large, clear glass or plastic tumbler.
6. Add ½ cup of gelatin to lemonade, then add ¼ cup of carbonated beverage.
7. Stir slightly, and you are ready to slurp some slime.

Yields: 12 servings.

Fruit Punch with Worms

Have fun with this one. The punch actually tastes good and is decorated with candy worms for fun.

Ingredients:
- 1   can frozen pineapple-orange juice concentrate (6 oz.)
- 1   can frozen pineapple-orange juice concentrate (12 oz.)

1   can apricot nectar (12 oz.), chilled
2   cans lemon-lime carbonated beverage (12 oz. each),
     chilled
     chewy, fruit-flavored candy worms

Directions:
1. For ice prepare 1 six-ounce can frozen pineapple-orange juice concentrate according to package directions.
2. Arrange chewy worms in bottom of 4-cup ring mold.
3. Pour juice into mold to almost cover worms; do not allow worms to float.
4. Cover and place in freezer for 1 hour or until frozen.
5. Add any remaining juice to mold.
6. Cover and freeze until firm.
7. In small punch bowl, prepare 12-ounce can of pineapple-orange juice concentrate according to package directions using cold water.
8. Stir in apricot nectar.
9. Add carbonated beverage, stirring gently to mix.
10. Unmold ice ring by running cool water over outside of mold; carefully add ring to punch.

Yields. 10 servings (8 ounces each).

Melted Witch

This drink is green, and you can make it spooky.

Ingredients:
1   bottle lemon-lime sports drink (32 oz.)
1   bottle lemon-lime flavored carbonated beverage (32 oz.)

Directions:
1. In punch bowl combine sports drink and lemon-lime soda.
2. Stir gently and serve over ice.

Scary Witch's Brew

A smoking cauldron of punch made with grapes and orange peel imitating eyeballs and worms. Dry ice makes a great presentation, but handle with care. This is one the recipes I presented on "Good Morning Northwest" on KXLY Spokane, and it made a fun presentation. My kids like the unique taste.

Ingredients:

4	c. cranberry juice cocktail, divided
½-1	c. chopped candied ginger
3	med. oranges
1	can frozen apple juice concentrate (12 oz.), thawed
1	can frozen limeade concentrate (6 oz.), thawed
2	c. seedless grapes
4	c. water
2	bottles ginger ale (32 oz. each)
1-2	lb. dry ice (CAUTION: never touch dry ice; use tongs to handle.)

Directions:

1. *Please note:* Use extreme caution when working with dry ice. Never let anyone directly touch the dry ice.
2. In 2-quart saucepan bring 1 cup cranberry juice and candied ginger to a boil over high heat.
3. Boil, uncovered, about 2 minutes; set aside.
4. With vegetable peeler, pare colored part only of peel from oranges; cut into thin 2-inch-long worms or use oriental shredder to make long shreds.
5. Add orange peel to cranberry-ginger mixture.
6. Cover and chill at least 4 hours or as long as overnight.
7. Juice oranges; put juice in 6- to 8-quart pan or heavy bowl.
8. Stir in cranberry-ginger mixture, remaining 3 cups cranberry juice, apple concentrate, limeade, grapes, and water.
9. If made ahead, cover and chill up to 2 hours.
10. Add ginger ale and about a 1-pound piece of dry ice.
11. Keep dry ice in one large mass, taking care not to let any small pieces come in direct contact with anyone. DO NOT put small pieces of dry ice in punch or cups.
12. Let ice smolder at least 30 minutes; ladle into cups.
13. Add any remaining ice when bubbling ceases.

Witch's Brew for Kids

It is all in fun. Squiggly gelatin hands and eyeballs float spookily to create a just-for-fun Halloween brew.

Ingredients:

    2   pkg. black cherry-flavored gelatin (3.25 oz. each)
    1½ c. boiling water
    1   pkg. orange-flavored gelatin (3.25 oz.)
    ¾   c. boiling water
    ¼   c. blueberries
    12 c. prepared orange-flavored, sugar-sweetened soft drink mix, chilled

Directions:

1. For hand: Dissolve black cherry gelatin in 1½ cups boiling water, stirring 2 minutes until completely dissolved.
2. Pour into greased 8-inch square pan.
3. Refrigerate 2 hours or until firm.
4. For eyeballs: Dissolve orange gelatin in ¾ cup boiling water, stirring 2 minutes until completely dissolved.
5. Pour into round or square ice cube trays.
6. Refrigerate until thickened but not set.
7. Insert blueberry into center of each gelatin eyeball, then refrigerate until completely set.
8. To assemble: Trace outline of small hand on piece of paper.
9. Cut out pattern, then place on top of cherry gelatin.
10. Cut around pattern with small sharp knife.
11. Carefully pull hand away from pan.
12. Place hand in punch bowl, allowing fingers to hang over side of bowl.
13. Arrange eyeballs around inside edge of punch bowl.
14. Gradually pour in prepared drink.
15. Serve immediately.

Frozen Witch's Hand

This one can be made to look very creepy. They say a witch's hand is as cold as her heart. A floating, frozen hand adds just the right decorative touch to this witch's brew in your Halloween punch bowl.

Ingredients:

food coloring
medical/cooking safety glove
water

Directions:

1. Fill latex glove with cold water.
2. Add a couple drops of food coloring, selecting colors to contrast with color of punch in bowl.
3. Tie end of glove tightly.
4. Place in freezer 2 to 3 days before party.
5. When ready to use, cut glove where it is tied, and carefully peel away latex glove.
6. Float hand in punch bowl along with your favorite witch's brew.
7. Note: Some people are allergic to latex, so let your guests know.

Yields: 1 witch's hand.

Ghoulish Punch

This makes an interesting Halloween punch that also tastes delicious.

Ingredients:

2   c. boiling water
1   pkg. lime-flavored gelatin (6 oz.)
2   c. cold orange juice
1   bottle seltzer (1 liter), chilled

2   c. orange sherbet, slightly softened
1   orange, thinly sliced
1   lime, thinly sliced
    ice cubes

Directions:

1. Stir boiling water into dry gelatin in large bowl at least 2 minutes, until completely dissolved.
2. Stir in juice; cool to room temperature.
3. Pour into punch bowl just before serving.
4. Add seltzer and ice; stir.
5. Add scoops of sherbet and fruit slices.

Yields: 10 servings.

Booberry Brew

This is a flavorful blueberry drink. Serve it in your Halloween-decorated glasses or mugs.

Ingredients:

1   pkg. frozen thawed blueberries (12 oz.) or 2½ c. fresh
1¼ c. apple juice
1   c. vanilla ice cream
¼   c. milk
¾   tsp. ground cinnamon

Directions:

1. In blender combine blueberries, apple juice, ice cream, milk, and cinnamon until smooth.
2. Serve immediately.

Yields: 4 servings.

Halloween Fruit Punch

Sparkling water and lime juice are added to cranberry juice for a refreshing non-alcoholic punch.

Ingredients:
- 4 c. ice cubes
- 1½ c. water
- ½ c. fresh lime juice (about 2 limes)
- 1 can frozen cranberry juice cocktail concentrate (12 oz.)
- 2 cans lemon or lime-flavored sparkling mineral water (12 oz. each)
  lime slices

Directions:
1. Combine ice cubes, water, lime juice, and cranberry juice concentrate in 5-cup blender container.
2. Cover; blend at high speed until ice cubes are finely chopped, 20 to 30 seconds.
3. Pour fruit mixture into serving bowl; add sparkling water.
4. Garnish with lime slices.

Lime Chiller and Blood Drippings

This punch is fun to serve in the red decorated glasses.

Ingredients:
- ¼ c. honey or corn syrup
- 12 drops red food coloring
- 4 c. chilled pineapple juice
- 6 oz. frozen limeade concentrate
- 3 c. chilled ginger ale

Directions:

1. Add honey and food coloring to shallow pan; mix until well blended.
2. Dip rims of wine goblets into mixture one at a time, coating rims of glasses.
3. Turn upright and let stand to allow mixture to drip down, resembling blood.
4. Place paper towel around base of glass to catch drips.
5. At time of serving combine pineapple juice with limeade in serving bowl or punch bowl, and stir until limeade dissolves; stir in ginger ale.
6. Tip: Instead of using ice that can water down the drinks, freeze seedless red grapes to keep punch cold. Fill baking sheet in single layer with grapes and freeze until frozen solid. Store in freezer in resealable bag until time of serving.

Ghostly Green Brew

This is a refreshing drink and fun where you need a spot of green.

Ingredients:

½ gal. lime sherbet
1 bottle lemon-lime soda (2 liters), chilled

Directions:

1. Allow sherbet to soften for about 1 hour in bottom of punch bowl.
2. Pour lemon-lime soda over and stir until all sherbet is dissolved.
3. Note: For a fun Halloween treat, serve in large, well-cleaned pumpkin with a face painted on it.

Yields: 16 servings (½ cup each).

Witch's Brew

This is a fun Halloween attention-getter that is great for parties. A fake hand is frozen in a latex glove and then slipped into the punch bowl!

Ingredients:

1   pkg. frozen raspberries (10 oz.), thawed
2½ c. cranberry juice
2   env. unflavored gelatin
2   liters ginger ale
2   liters sparkling apple cider, non-alcoholic
6   gummy worms candy
    latex dishwashing glove

Directions:

1. To make frozen hand, wash and rinse outside of latex dishwashing glove.
2. Turn glove inside out and set aside.
3. In 4-cup measuring cup, combine thawed raspberries and cranberry juice.
4. Pour 2 cups raspberry mixture into small saucepan.
5. Sprinkle gelatin over and let stand 2 minutes.
6. Warm over low heat, stirring constantly, just until gelatin dissolves.
7. Mix back into reserved raspberry mixture in measuring cup; pour raspberry mixture into inverted glove.
8. Gather top of glove together, and tie securely with kitchen twine.
9. Freeze until solid or several days if possible.
10. To serve, carefully cut latex glove away from frozen hand.
11. Place frozen hand, palm side up, leaning against side of large punch bowl.
12. Pour in ginger ale and sparkling cider.
13. Garnish with gummy worms.

Mucous Membrane Milkshake

This drink is perfect for the season, and it actually tastes great, too, despite its name.

Ingred ients:

- 2 c. buttermilk
- 2 scoops vanilla ice cream
- ½ c. pineapple juice
- 4 Tbs. brown sugar
- 2 c. milk
  - pineapple chunks (optional)
  - red cherries (optional)

Directions:

1. Measure all ingredients except milk, pineapple chunks, and red cherries into blender.
2. Blend on medium speed until smooth and creamy.
3. Add more ice cream if you like your mucus extra thick.
4. Fill tall glasses with mixture and refrigerate.
5. Heat milk in small pan over medium heat until it begins to boil
6. Remove from heat and let cool until film develops on surface.
7. Using wooden spoon, carefully scoop off film and place some on top of each milkshake.
8. If you need more mucus, just reheat remaining milk and repeat steps 6 and 7.
9. Blend chunks of pineapple into milkshake (for phlegm balls) or red cherries (for blood clots).

Yields: 4 servings.

***Did You Know?* . . . .**

Did you know that it is estimated that children have collected more than $119 million (U.S.) for UNICEF since its inception?

Spook 'n Cider

This is very easy to make. Your little spooks will love this tasty witch's brew.

Ingredients:

- 10 c. apple cider or apple juice
- 1 pkg. lightly sweetened frozen red raspberries (12 oz.)
- 1 stick cinnamon (5 in. length)

Directions:

1. In large saucepan combine apple cider or juice, raspberries, and cinnamon.
2. Bring to boiling; reduce heat.
3. Cover and simmer for 10 minutes.
4. Remove mixture from heat.
5. Strain berries and cinnamon from mixture through piece of cheesecloth.
6. Cover until serving time.
7. To serve, heat cider mixture until warm.

Yields: 16 servings (5 ounces each).

Magic Brew Refreshers

For a scientific presentation, pour into clean beakers and flasks to serve.

Ingredients:

- 8 oz. vanilla yogurt
- 1 c. orange juice
- 4 c. orange soda, divided

Directions:

1. Put vanilla yogurt, orange juice, and 2 cups orange soda in blender container.
2. Cover blender with lid; blend on high speed until combined.
3. Pour mixture into 2 ice cube trays; cover with plastic wrap.
4. Put ice cube trays in freezer; freeze for 6 hours or overnight.
5. Just before serving, remove frozen cubes from 1 ice cube tray.
6. Put cubes in blender container; add 1 cup of orange soda.
7. Cover and blend on high speed until slushy.
8. Pour into 6 glasses.
9. Repeat with remaining frozen cubes and orange soda.

Yields: 12 servings.

Halloween Ghost Drink

This beverage is fun to make since it has ghosts on top. Enjoy.

Ingredients:

- 2   c. orange juice
- 2   c. milk
- 2   pt. orange sherbet
- 4   med. ripe bananas
- 2   c. Sweetened Whipped Cream (recipe page 193)
- 18 miniature chocolate chips

Directions:

1. In batches, process orange juice, milk, sherbet, and bananas in blender until smooth.
2. Pour into glasses.
3. Fill pastry bag with whipped cream.
4. Pipe ghost shape on top of each beverage.
5. Place chocolate chips on top for eyes.

Sulfuric Acid Swig

This is an easy-to-make, great-looking punch. It makes a totally toxic-looking treat.

Ingredients:

- 6 oz. frozen lemonade concentrate, partially thawed
- ½ c. lemon juice
- 1 c. grapefruit juice, chilled
- 2 qt. lemon sherbet
- 1 qt. club soda, chilled
- lemon or lime-flavored powdered drink mix for garnish

Directions:

1. In large pitcher mix together lemonade concentrate, lemon juice, and grapefruit juice.
2. Add amount of water required on lemonade can.
3. Pour liquid into tall glasses, filling halfway, and add scoop of lemon sherbet to each.
4. Fill glasses with club soda, sprinkle top of each glass with pinch of lemon or lime-flavored powdered drink mix, and serve immediately.

Hand Ice Mold and Dragon's Blood Punch

This is another version of a spooky hand in the punch.

Ingredients:

- 1 new rubber glove, washed well and rinsed
- 1 lb. coffee can, washed and rinsed
- 1 bottle apple juice (64 oz.), chilled
- 1 bottle cranberry juice (64 oz.), chilled
- 2 bottles ginger ale (32 oz. each), chilled
- red food coloring (optional)

Directions:

1. To make hand fill rubber glove with water.
2. Tie at wrist with string and freeze 1 or 2 days; unmold.
3. Sometimes a finger will fall off when unmolding, but this only adds to the ghoulish effect.
4. To make base for hand, fill coffee can about ⅓ full with water; insert hand and freeze until firm.
5. To remove, run water on outside of can.
6. When ready to serve pour half the chilled juices and ginger ale into punch bowl.
7. Insert hand ice mold in center.
8. Fill bowl with remaining juices and soda.
9. For added effect place a few drops of red food coloring on tips of fingers just before serving.

Yields: 20 servings (1 cup each).

Warm Witch's Blood

The decorations you serve with this punch will add a Halloween look to your menu.

Ingredients:

4   c. apple-cranberry juice
2   c. orange juice
1   tsp. whole cloves
1   stick cinnamon
3-4 allspice berries
1-2 Tbs. sugar to taste
    orange slices for garnish

Directions:

1. Bring all ingredients to a boil in saucepan; reduce heat to simmer.
2. Simmer gently for 15 minutes, stirring and muttering appropriate incantations.
3. Serve in ghoulish glasses and garnish with orange slice if desired.

Witch's Brew Punch

This is another tasty variation for a Halloween punch.

Ingredients:

1	can frozen lemonade concentrate (12 oz.)
1	can frozen orange juice concentrate (6 oz.)
6	c. water
4	c. apple cider
8	whole cloves
4	whole allspice
2	cinnamon sticks
	orange sherbet

Directions for serving cold:

1. Combine all ingredients except sherbet in 5-quart saucepan; mix well.
2. Cook over medium-high heat until mixture comes to a boil, 15 to 20 minutes.
3. Reduce heat to low; cook 10 minutes.
4. Remove from heat; remove spices.
5. Cool 30 minutes at room temperature.
6. Cover; refrigerate until chilled, 2 to 4 hours.
7. At serving time, pour into serving bowl; float scoops of sherbet in punch.

Directions for serving hot:

1. Follow recipe above, adding 2 tablespoons butter.
2. Pour into heatproof pitcher.
3. Garnish with lemon slices if desired.

Yields: 12 servings (1 cup each).

Did You Know? . . . .

Did you know that bobbing for apples dates back to ancient Roman times in honor of the Roman goddess of fruits and apples?

Breads and Rolls

Table of Contents

Did You Know? . . . .

Did you know that Knott's Scary Farm in California, featuring a dozen different mazes, roving costumed performers, and amusement park rides re-themed for Halloween, is the largest Halloween attraction in the United States?

Hot Cross Black Widows

These are fun muffins to decorate and enjoy.

Ingredients for muffins:

- 1   Tbs. butter
- 1   egg
- ¼   c. vegetable oil
- 1   c. milk
- 2   c. all-purpose flour
- 3   tsp. baking powder
- 1   tsp. salt
- ¼   c. sugar

Ingredients for frosting:

- 4   oz. cream cheese, softened
- 3   Tbs. unsalted butter, room temperature
- 1½ c. confectioners' sugar
- ½   tsp. vanilla extract
  juice of ¼ lemon or 1 tsp. bottled lemon juice
  red, yellow, green, and blue food coloring
  black licorice strings

Directions for muffins:

1. Preheat oven to 400 degrees F.
2. Butter bottoms but not sides of 12 medium-size muffin cups.
3. Beat egg in large bowl with fork; stir in vegetable oil and milk.
4. Combine flour, baking powder, salt, and sugar in small mixing bowl.
5. Add to egg mixture, stirring lightly until dry ingredients are barely moistened; batter should be lumpy.
6. Fill muffin cups ¾ full of batter.
7. Bake for 20 to 30 minutes or until muffins turn golden brown.
8. Carefully remove from oven, turn out of pan, and set on rack to cool.

Directions for frosting:
1. Mix cream cheese and butter together with electric mixer.
2. Slowly add confectioners' sugar and continue beating.
3. Add vanilla extract and lemon juice; mix thoroughly.
4. Put small portion of frosting in separate bowl, and mix in a few drops of red food coloring; set aside.
5. Color remaining frosting, drop by drop, with red, yellow, green, and blue food coloring until it is black.
6. With rubber spatula spread black frosting on top of each muffin.
7. Add small, red Black Widow hourglass to each one.
8. Add legs to spiders using licorice whip strings.
9. Place arachnids on platter and serve.
10. Tip: Decorate platter with fake spider webs.

Halloween Green Bread

This "ugly monster bread" is a good way to get your children to eat their fruit servings for the day. It goes well with hotdogs and beans for a rustic autumn taste.

Ingredients:
- ¼ c. butter
- 2 c. cornmeal
- 2 eggs
- 2 c. all-purpose flour
- 2 Tbs. baking powder
- ½ c. milk
- 2 Tbs. sugar
- 1 can blueberries (16½ oz.), do not drain

Directions:
1. Preheat oven to 425 degrees F.
2. Grease cast-iron frying pan.
3. Mix together all ingredients; put into prepared pan.
4. Bake for 20 to 25 minutes. (Bread will crack and pull away from side of pan.)
5. Note: Use canned strawberries to make red bread.

Yields: 4 to 6 servings.

Mexican Pan de Muerto
(Bread of the Dead)

Anise adds flavor to this skeleton-shaped bread.

Ingredients:

½	c. unsalted butter
½	c. milk
½	c. water
5–5½	c. all-purpose flour
2	pkg. dry yeast
1	tsp. salt
1	Tbs. whole anise seed
1	c. sugar, divided
4	eggs
⅓	c. freshly squeezed orange juice
2	Tbs. grated orange zest

Directions:

1. Over medium heat in saucepan, heat butter, milk, and water until butter melts.
2. In large mixing bowl combine 1½ cups flour, yeast, salt, anise seed, and ½ cup sugar.
3. Add butter and milk mixture and stir until well combined.
4. Add eggs and beat in another cup of flour.
5. Continue to add more flour until dough is soft but not sticky.
6. Knead dough on lightly floured surface for 10 minutes or until smooth and elastic.
7. Lightly grease large mixing bowl and place dough in it.
8. Cover with plastic wrap and let rise in warm place until doubled in bulk, about 1½ hours.
9. Punch dough down and shape into 2 loaves resembling skulls or skeletons; place on baking sheet.
10. Let rise in warm place for 1 hour.
11. Preheat oven to 350 degrees F.
12. Bake loaves for 40 minutes or until tops are golden brown.
13. While bread is baking, prepare glaze.

14. In small saucepan mix remaining ½ cup sugar, orange juice, and zest over high heat.
15. Bring to a boil, stirring constantly for 2 minutes, then remove from heat and keep warm.
16. When bread is done, apply glaze to hot loaves with pastry brush.

Apple Donut Balls

These donut balls make a warm autumn treat.

Ingredients:

4	Tbs. butter, softened
1½	c. sugar
3	eggs
3	tsp. baking powder
1	tsp. salt
2	tsp. ground nutmeg
2	tsp. ground cinnamon
¾	c. milk
1	c. applesauce
5	c. sifted all-purpose flour
	canola or vegetable oil for deep-fat frying

Directions:

1. Cream butter and sugar together.
2. Add eggs 1 at a time, beating well after each egg.
3. Add baking powder, salt, nutmeg, and cinnamon; mix well.
4. Mix in milk and applesauce.
5. Add flour 1 cup at a time, mixing well after each addition.
6. Drop by ½ teaspoonfuls into oil heated to 350 to 375 degrees F., cooking until golden brown. (Use new oil for best flavor.)
7. Drain on paper towels with paper sacks underneath.
8. Roll in mixture of cinnamon and sugar.

Biscuits with the Look of Mold

Moldy biscuits do not sound appealing, but these moldy look-a-likes add fun to your Halloween party.

Ingredients:

- 3 Tbs. butter
- 2 scallions, thinly sliced
- 2 c. all-purpose flour
- 3 tsp. baking powder
- ½ tsp. baking soda
- ½ tsp. salt
- ½ c. butter
- ¾ c. buttermilk
- 1 Tbs. melted butter
- 1 Tbs. buttermilk
-    green food coloring

Directions:

1. Preheat oven to 425 degrees F.
2. Sauté scallions in 3 tablespoons butter until soft; set aside and let cool.
3. Sift flour, baking powder, baking soda, and salt into large mixing bowl.
4. Cut ½ cup butter into small pieces, and cut into dry ingredients until mixture resembles coarse crumbs.
5. In small bowl mix together ¾ cup buttermilk and green food coloring until it is very dark shade of green.
6. Make well in center of flour mixture; add scallions and green buttermilk.
7. Mix until very sticky dough just holds together.
8. Turn out onto floured surface and knead 20 times.
9. Pat out until ½ inch thick; cut with 2-inch cutter.
10. Place biscuits on baking sheet about 3 inches apart.
11. Mix melted butter and 1 tablespoon buttermilk; brush on biscuits.
12. Bake until golden brown, 12 to 15 minutes.
13. Note: Leave out green food coloring for regular biscuits.

Pizza Dough

This pizza dough is simple to make and decorate with your favorite Halloween decorations. Try making jack-o'-lantern faces with your favorite meat toppings or use white Alfredo sauce for ghost faces.

Ingredients:

- 1 env. active dry yeast
- 1 c. warm water
- ½ tsp. sugar
- 3½ c. all-purpose flour
- 1 tsp. salt

Directions:

1. Put warm water in cup; sprinkle yeast over water and stir in sugar.
2. Let yeast stand for about 10 minutes or until it begins to bubble.
3. Sift flour and salt into large bowl; pour in yeast mixture and beat until stiff dough forms.
4. Turn dough out onto floured surface; knead about 5 minutes or until smooth and elastic.
5. Add extra flour as necessary to keep dough from sticking to hands and board.
6. Place in large greased bowl; turn dough to coat other side.
7. Cover with towel; let rise in warm place away from drafts for about 30 minutes, until dough doubles in bulk.
8. Punch dough down and divide in half.
9. Grease two 14-inch pizza pans and grease hands lightly.
10. Place half the dough in each pan and stretch to fit bottom and up sides of pan.
11. Keep dough slightly thick around edges.
12. Fill with favorite filling and toppings, and bake according to pizza recipe directions or about 15 to 20 minutes at 425 degrees F.

Yields: Enough for 2 pizzas (14 inches each).

Halloween Cinnamon Twists

Everyone seems to enjoy cinnamon twists every now and then. Enjoy.

Ingredients:

- ¼ c. warm water (105 to 115 degrees F.)
- 2 pkg. active dry yeast
- 1½ c. milk
- ½ c. sugar
- ½ tsp. salt
- 2 tsp. ground cinnamon
- 6 Tbs. butter
- 2 eggs
- 5 c. all-purpose flour
- 1 c. sugar
- 1 tsp. ground cinnamon
- 1 tsp. ground nutmeg
- oil for frying

Directions:

1. Dissolve yeast in warm water in large bowl.
2. In saucepan combine milk, sugar, salt, cinnamon, and butter.
3. Heat to 110 degrees F. or lukewarm but not too hot for yeast mixture.
4. Add milk mixture with eggs and 2 cups flour to dissolved yeast.
5. Beat until smooth.
6. Beat in remaining flour. (Dough will be soft and sticky.)
7. Let rise for about 1 hour; stir down.
8. Turn dough out onto well-floured surface.
9. Roll in flour to coat.
10. Gently roll into 8 x 24-inch rectangle.
11. With sharp, floured knife, cut into 1-inch crosswise strips.
12. Bring ends of strips together and twist strands loosely.
13. Let rise on floured board or pan for 20 to 30 minutes until almost doubled.
14. Heat 1 inch of oil in skillet to 350 degrees F.
15. Fry on both sides, about 3 minutes total; drain.
16. Mix together 1 cup sugar, cinnamon and nutmeg.
17. Coat twists with sugar/spice mixture.

Yields: 2 dozen.

Pumpkin-Black Walnut Biscuits

A batch of these pumpkin-flavored biscuits is a nice addition to any meal. This biscuit has a tendency to get too brown on the bottom, so use a light-colored metal baking sheet instead of a nonstick sheet. Serve biscuits hot with butter.

Ingredients:

2	c. unbleached all-purpose flour
2	Tbs. sugar
1	Tbs. baking powder
1	tsp. baking soda
¼	tsp. salt
¼	tsp. ground allspice
¼	tsp. ground cinnamon
¼	tsp. grated nutmeg
½	c. butter, cold
⅓	c. finely chopped black walnuts
⅔	c. canned or mashed cooked pumpkin
½	c. buttermilk

Directions:

1. Sift together flour, sugar, baking powder, soda, salt, and spices into large bowl.
2. Cut in butter until mixture resembles coarse crumbs.
3. Add nuts.
4. In small bowl whisk together pumpkin and buttermilk.
5. Add to flour mixture and stir to combine. (Dough will be quite stiff and not all flour will be incorporated.)
6. Turn dough out onto lightly floured cloth, and knead gently a few times to work in remaining flour.
7. Roll out dough to ½-inch thickness, and cut with 2-inch round cutter.
8. Transfer biscuits to lightly oiled, shiny baking sheet, and sprinkle tops with sugar.
9. Bake for 10 minutes. (Do not let them get too brown.)
10. Serve immediately with butter.

Yields: 6 servings.

Pumpkin Dumplings

Pumpkin adds great flavor and color to these dumplings.

Ingredients:

- ½ c. canned solid-pack pumpkin
- 1 lg. egg
- ½ tsp. salt
- ⅛ tsp. grated nutmeg
- ⅛ tsp. (generous) baking powder
- ½ c. all-purpose flour
- 3 Tbs. butter
- ½ c. grated Parmesan cheese

Directions:

1. Bring large pot of salted water to a boil.
2. Whisk pumpkin, egg, salt, nutmeg, and baking powder in large bowl to blend.
3. Mix in flour (dough will be soft).
4. Dip ½-teaspoon measuring spoon into boiling water to moisten.
5. Scoop up generous ½ teaspoonful of dough and return spoon to water, allowing dough to drop.
6. Working in 2 batches, repeat dropping ½ teaspoonfuls of dough into water, first dipping spoon into water to moisten each time.
7. Boil dumplings until cooked through, about 10 minutes.
8. Using slotted spoon, transfer to colander and drain.
9. Melt butter in heavy, large skillet over medium heat; add dumplings.
10. Sauté until beginning to brown, about 8 minutes.
11. Transfer dumplings to bowl.
12. Sprinkle with cheese and serve.

Yields: 4 side-dish servings.

Fiesta Pumpkin Corn Muffins

These muffins make a nice addition to your Halloween meals.

Ingredients:

- 1¼ c. yellow cornmeal
- 1 c. all-purpose flour
- ½ tsp. chili powder
- 2 Tbs. sugar
- 4 tsp. baking powder
- ½ tsp. salt
- 3 eggs
- 1 c. cooked puréed pumpkin
- 1 c. milk
- 3 Tbs. vegetable oil
- 1 can chopped green chilies (4 oz.)
- 1 sm. tomato, diced and seeded
- 1¼ c. shredded cheddar cheese

Directions:

1. Preheat oven to 400 degrees F.
2. In large bowl mix dry ingredients together.
3. In smaller bowl beat eggs.
4. Blend in pumpkin, milk, and oil; fold in chilies and tomato.
5. Blend wet ingredients into dry until batter is just barely moistened.
6. Spoon into greased or papered muffin cups.
7. Sprinkle with cheese, and bake for 20 to 25 minutes or until wooden pick inserted in center comes out clean.
8. Remove from pan immediately and serve warm.
9. May be baked ahead and reheated before serving.

***Did You Know?* . . . .**

Did you know that to this day the Frankenstein's Monster is the only true rival for Dracula in terms of fame and reputation?

Porcupine Bread

Oats and seeds add flavor to this easy-to-make yeast bread.

Ingredients:

5-5½	c. bread flour
1	c. rolled oats
2	pkg. active dry yeast or quick-rising yeast
1	Tbs. salt
¼	c. sugar
1½	c. buttermilk
½	c. water
2	Tbs. vegetable oil
¼	c. raisins
⅔	c. sunflower seeds
½	c. sesame seeds
1	egg
1	Tbs. water

Directions:

1. In large mixer bowl combine 2 cups bread flour, rolled oats, yeast, salt, and sugar; mix well.
2. Heat buttermilk, water, and oil until very warm (120 to 130 degrees F.); add to flour mixture.
3. Blend at low speed until moistened; beat 3 minutes at medium speed.
4. By hand with spoon, gradually stir in raisins, sunflower seeds, sesame seeds, and enough remaining flour to make firm dough.
5. Knead on floured surface until smooth and elastic, 5 to 8 minutes. (Dough may be slightly sticky.)
6. Place in greased bowl, rotating to grease top.
7. Cover with cloth; let rise until double in size, about 1 hour (30 minutes if quick-rising yeast).
8. Punch down dough.
9. Divide into 2 parts; shape into loaves and place in greased 9 x 5-inch bread or loaf pans.
10. Cover; let rise in warm place again until double in size, about 1 hour (½ hour if quick-rising yeast).
11. Preheat oven to 375 degrees F.

12. Whisk together 1 egg and 1 tablespoon water to make egg wash; brush tops of loaves.
13. Sprinkle additional sunflower and sesame seeds on loaves.
14. Bake until golden brown.
15. Remove from pans while still warm; cool on cooling rack.

Yields: 2 loaves.

Pumpkin Spice Quick Bread

This pumpkin bread is easy to make.

Ingredients:

1¾   c. all-purpose flour
1   c. pumpkin purée
¾   c. firmly packed brown sugar
½   c. butter, softened
2   lg. eggs
1   tsp. ground cinnamon
½   tsp. ground ginger
¼   tsp. ground nutmeg
¼   tsp. ground cloves
1   tsp. baking soda
½   tsp. salt
¼   tsp. baking powder

Directions:

1. Preheat oven to 350 degrees F.
2. Grease 9 x 5-inch loaf pan.
3. Combine all ingredients in large mixing bowl.
4. Beat at medium speed, scraping bowl often, for 1 to 2 minutes until well mixed.
5. Spoon batter into prepared pan.
6. Bake 45 to 55 minutes or until wooden pick inserted in center comes out clean.
7. Cool in pan on wire rack 10 minutes; remove to wire rack to cool completely.
8. Tip: Wrap bread in plastic food wrap or aluminum foil, and refrigerate up to 3 days or freeze up to 3 months.

Maple-Nutmeg Pumpkin Rolls

These golden-orange dinner rolls are wonderful for fall and winter. They are also wonderful left over, toasted, and spread with butter and jam. Give yourself plenty of time for this recipe, as it is a yeast bread that starts off with a "sponge."

Ingredients:

¼	c. warm water
2½	tsp. dry yeast (1 env.)
¼	c. all-purpose flour
1	Tbs. sugar
½	c. milk
2	Tbs. butter
¾	c. canned solid-pack pumpkin
¼	c. pure maple syrup
2	lg. eggs
1	tsp. salt
¾	tsp. ground nutmeg
¼	c. plus 1 Tbs. sugar
4	c. all-purpose flour

Directions:

1. For sponge, dissolve yeast in warm water in large mixing bowl.
2. Add ¼ cup flour and 1 Tbs. sugar.
3. Mix together, cover with plastic, and let rise in warm place for 45 minutes or until very foamy.
4. When sponge is almost ready, bring milk and butter just to a simmer, then remove from heat and stir to melt butter; cool 10 minutes.
5. Into milk/butter mixture, whisk pumpkin, syrup, eggs, salt, nutmeg, and ¼ cup plus 1 tablespoon sugar.
6. Whisk pumpkin mixture into sponge.
7. Using mixer with dough hook, mix in flour 1 cup at a time until dough forms.
8. Mix until smooth and elastic, adding more flour if sticky, about 5 minutes.
9. Cover bowl with plastic and a clean kitchen towel; let dough rise in warm, draft-free area until doubled in volume, about 1½ hours.
10. When dough has risen, grease 2 heavy baking sheets.

11. Punch dough down and transfer to floured surface; knead until smooth.
12. Divide dough into 18 equal pieces.
13. Shape each piece into desired shape and arrange on prepared baking sheets, spacing 2 inches apart.
14. Cover with clean kitchen towels and let rise until doubled, about 45 minutes.
15. Preheat oven to 425 degrees F.
16. Bake rolls until golden brown, about 15 minutes.
17. Transfer to racks and cool slightly, then serve.

Yields: 18 rolls.

Applesauce Pumpkin Bread

This pumpkin bread is moist and delicious.

Ingredients:

⅔ c. butter
4 c. brown sugar
4 eggs
1 c. applesauce
1 c. cooked pumpkin, mashed
3½ c. all-purpose flour
½ tsp. ground nutmeg
1½ tsp. ground cinnamon
½ tsp. baking powder
2 Tbs. baking soda
1 c. apple juice
1½ c. chopped nuts (walnuts or pecans)

Directions:

1. Preheat oven to 350 degrees F.
2. Cream butter and sugar together.
3. Add eggs 1 at a time, beating well after each addition.
4. Stir in applesauce and pumpkin.
5. Sift dry ingredients together and add with apple juice.
6. Stir in nuts.
7. Pour into 2 greased loaf pans.
8. Bake for 1 hour.

Yields: 2 loaves.

Pumpkin Gingerbread Mini Loaves

Enjoy these pumpkin mini loaves.

Ingredients:

- 2 c. all-purpose flour, divided
- ½ c. packed brown sugar
- 2 tsp. baking powder
- 1 tsp. ground cinnamon
- ½ tsp. baking soda
- 1 c. canned pumpkin purée
- ½ c. molasses
- 2 eggs
- ⅓ c. butter
- ¼ c. milk
- 1 Tbs. grated fresh gingerroot or 1 tsp. ground ginger
- ⅓ c. finely chopped walnuts
- 2 Tbs. sugar

Directions:

1. Preheat oven to 350 degrees F.
2. Grease bottom and sides of four 4½ x 2½ x 1½-inch loaf pans; set aside. (Grease only halfway up sides. That way loaves will have nicely rounded tops and no unwanted rims around edges.)
3. Stir together 1 cup flour, brown sugar, baking powder, cinnamon, and baking soda.
4. Add pumpkin, molasses, eggs, butter, milk, and gingerroot or ginger.
5. Beat with electric mixer on low to medium speed until combined, about 30 seconds.
6. Beat on medium to high speed for 2 minutes, scraping sides of bowl occasionally.
7. Add remaining flour; beat for 2 minutes or until mixed.
8. Divide batter evenly among prepared pans.
9. Stir together walnuts and sugar; sprinkle evenly over batter in pans.
10. Bake for 40 to 50 minutes or until wooden pick inserted near center of each loaf comes out clean.
11. Cool loaves in pans on wire racks for 10 minutes.
12. Remove loaves from pans; cool thoroughly on wire racks.
13. To freeze, wrap each loaf tightly in moisture- and vapor-proof wrap.
14. Seal, label, and freeze for up to 6 months.
15. To thaw, let stand, loosely covered, at room temperature for 1 hour.

Halloween Delights Cookbook

A Collection of Halloween Recipes
Cookbook Delights Series

Breakfasts

Table of Contents

Did You Know? . . .

Did you know that according to the National Retail Federation's 2006 Halloween Consumer Intentions and Actions Survey, the top Halloween costumes for children were Princess, Pirate, Witch, Spider-Man, Superman, Disney Princess, Power Ranger, Pumpkin, Cat, and Vampire?

Monster Muffins

Have fun decorating these pumpkin muffins.

Ingredients:

1½ c. all-purpose flour
2　tsp. baking powder
¾　tsp. salt
⅔　c. sugar
¼　c. firmly packed brown sugar
½　tsp. ground cinnamon
½　tsp. ground nutmeg
1　egg
1　can crushed pineapple (8 oz.), drained
¾　c. canned pumpkin
½　c. cold milk
¼　c. butter, melted
　　creamy peanut butter
　　decorations: assorted candies, pretzels, mints, pipe
　　cleaners

Directions:

1. Preheat oven to 425 degrees F.
2. Combine first 7 ingredients in large bowl; make well in center of mixture.
3. Combine egg and next 4 ingredients.
4. Add to dry ingredients, stirring just until moistened. (Batter will be stiff.)
5. Place paper baking cups in muffin pans and spoon batter into cups, filling each ⅔ full.
6. Bake for 20 minutes or until golden.
7. Remove from pan immediately, and cool on wire racks.
8. Decorate if desired.
9. Tip: Spread muffins with peanut butter and decorate as desired using assorted candies, pretzels, mints, and pipe cleaners to transform these muffins into devils, cats, spiders, and aliens.

Yields: 1 dozen muffins.

Pumpkin Apple Streusel Muffins

Be sure to make a double batch, because your family will beg for more of these moist muffins.

Ingredients muffins:

2½ c. all-purpose flour
2 c. sugar
1½ tsp. ground cinnamon
¾ tsp. ground ginger
½ tsp. ground nutmeg
¼ tsp. ground cloves
1 tsp. baking soda
½ tsp. salt
2 eggs, slightly beaten
1 c. canned pumpkin
½ c. vegetable oil
2 c. apples, peeled, cored and finely chopped

Ingredients for streusel topping:

2 Tbs. all-purpose flour
½ c. sugar
½ tsp. ground cinnamon
4 tsp. butter

Directions for muffins:

1. Preheat oven to 350 degrees F.
2. In large bowl combine first 8 ingredients.
3. In medium bowl combine eggs, pumpkin, and oil.
4. Add liquid ingredients to dry ingredients.
5. Stir until just moistened.
6. Stir in apples.
7. Spoon batter into greased or paper-lined muffin cups, filling ¾ full.
8. Sprinkle streusel topping over batter.
9. Bake for 35 to 40 minutes or until wooden pick comes out clean.

Directions for streusel topping:

1. In small bowl combine flour, sugar, and cinnamon.
2. Cut in butter until mixture is crumbly.

Pumpkin Crepes with Brandied Butter Sauce

Our family loves crepes and these are delicious.

Ingredients for filling:

　¾　c. pumpkin purée, canned or homemade

Ingredients for crepes:

　3　eggs
　1　c. milk
　1　tsp. vanilla extract
　1　Tbs. brandy
　¾　c. cornstarch
　2　Tbs. sugar
　3　Tbs. pumpkin purée
　1　pinch salt
　4　Tbs. unsalted butter, melted

Ingredients for sauce:

　½　c. unsalted butter
　1　c. sugar
　¼　c. water
　3　Tbs. brandy
　2　Tbs. orange juice
　½　tsp. orange zest
　⅛　tsp. freshly grated nutmeg
　　　toasted pine nuts or fried sage leaves (optional garnish)

Directions for filling:

1. When using fresh pumpkin, cut 2½-pound sugar pumpkin in half and scoop out seeds.
2. Roast in oven at 375 degrees F. for 1 hour or steam in microwave until soft.
3. Cool; process flesh in blender or food processor.

Directions for crepes:

1. Combine eggs, milk, vanilla, brandy, cornstarch, sugar, pumpkin, and salt.
2. Whisk until smooth.
3. Brush nonstick, 6-inch crepe pan or skillet with melted butter.
4. Place over moderate heat until pan begins to smoke.
5. Remove from heat and ladle about 3 tablespoons batter into center of pan.
6. Quickly tilt pan in all directions to spread batter.
7. Return pan to heat; cook until crepe is set and underside is lightly browned.
8. Flip crepe and cook 2 to 3 seconds longer.
9. Slide crepe out onto parchment paper or cooling rack.
10. Repeat, making about 15 crepes.
11. Crepes may be made ahead and refrigerated or frozen; separate crepes with wax paper if refrigerating or freezing to keep them from sticking together.

Directions for sauce:

1. Melt butter in skillet over low heat.
2. Stir in remaining ingredients, whisking until smooth and sugar dissolves.
3. Sauce may be made in advance and reheated gently.

Directions to assemble:

1. Cool crepes or, if made ahead, warm to room temperature.
2. Lay out crepes with brown side down.
3. Spread each crepe with very thin layer of pumpkin purée, about 2 teaspoons.
4. Fold crepe in half and then in half again.
5. Heat crepes in sauce until warmed through.
6. Place 2 on each plate.
7. If desired, garnish with toasted pine nuts or fried sage leaves.

Pumpkin Cheese-Filled Pecan Muffins

These pumpkin muffins have cream cheese in the middle for a tasty surprise.

Ingredients:

- 2 c. all-purpose flour
- ¾ c. sugar
- 1 c. chopped pecans
- 1 Tbs. baking powder
- ¾ tsp. ground cinnamon
- ½ tsp. ground ginger
- ⅛ tsp. ground nutmeg
- ⅛ tsp. ground cloves
- ½ tsp. salt
- 2 eggs, beaten
- ¾ c. pumpkin purée
- ¼ c. dairy sour cream
- ½ c. butter, melted
- 1 pkg. cream cheese (3 oz.), cut into cubes

Directions:

1. Preheat oven to 400 degrees F.
2. In large bowl mix flour, sugar, pecans, spices, baking powder, and salt.
3. In small bowl mix eggs, pumpkin, sour cream, and melted butter.
4. Add to flour mixture; stir until blended only.
5. Fill greased muffin tins half full.
6. Place cream cheese cube in middle; top with more batter.
7. Bake for approximately 20 minutes.

Yields: 1 dozen muffins.

***Did You Know?* . . . .**

Did you know that Halloween dates back 2000 years ago to the Celtic celebration of the dead?

Pumpkin Fritters

My mom used to make apple fritters for us when we were kids, and these are a delicious variation.

Ingredients:

1	lg. egg
½	c. sugar
½	tsp. salt
1½	c. canned pumpkin purée
1	c. all-purpose flour
¼	tsp. baking soda
1	Tbs. butter, softened
1	tsp. ground cinnamon
½	tsp. ground nutmeg
¼	tsp. ground allspice
¼	tsp. ground cloves
½	tsp. ground ginger
¾	tsp. vanilla extract
	additional butter and confectioners' sugar for topping

Directions:

1. In small mixing bowl whisk together egg, sugar, and salt until well blended.
2. Add pumpkin purée and continue to mix until well blended.
3. In separate larger bowl sift together flour and baking soda.
4. Add egg mixture to larger bowl along with butter, spices, and vanilla; mix until well combined.
5. Spoon ¼-cup amounts onto greased griddle over medium-high heat.
6. Cook until golden on both sides.
7. Serve warm with pat of butter and sprinkling of confectioners' sugar.

Yields: 12 servings.

Pumpkin Oat Muffins

Oats add a nice texture to these pumpkin muffins.

Ingredients for muffins:

- 1 c. all-purpose flour
- 2 tsp. baking powder
- ¼ tsp. baking soda
- ½ tsp. ground cinnamon
- ¼ tsp. ground nutmeg
- ⅛ tsp. ground allspice
- ⅛ tsp. ground cloves
- ½ tsp. salt
- 1 c. quick-cooking oats
- 1 lg. egg
- ¾ c. canned mashed pumpkin
- ½ c. brown sugar, firmly packed
- ¼ c. milk
- ¼ c. vegetable oil
- ½ c. raisins

Ingredients for crumb topping:

- ½ c. brown sugar, firmly packed
- 1 Tbs. all-purpose flour
- ¼ tsp. pumpkin pie spice (recipe page 207)
- 2 Tbs. butter

Directions for muffins:

1. Preheat oven to 400 degrees F.
2. Prepare 12 regular muffin cups with muffin papers or light coating of cooking spray.
3. In large bowl sift together flour, baking powder, baking soda, spices, and salt; mix in oats.
4. In separate medium bowl beat egg slightly.
5. Add pumpkin, brown sugar, milk, and oil; mix well.
6. Add wet ingredients to dry ingredients, and mix until just moistened.

7. Fold in raisins.
8. Spoon batter into prepared muffin cups, filling each about ⅔ full.

Directions for crumb topping:
1. Mix all topping ingredients together in bowl.
2. Sprinkle mixture evenly over muffins.
3. Bake for 18 to 20 minutes or until golden brown or when wooden pick inserted into center comes out clean.

Boo-Banana

It used to be difficult to make your children eat their bananas and multi-vitamins. Not anymore. The only thing scary about this Halloween treat is how delicious it is. Make sure they do not eat more than the proper vitamin dose.

Ingredients:
    1   banana
    2   grapes
    1   candy-coated chocolate piece
    1   multi-vitamin
        chocolate sauce
        toothpick

Directions:
1. Peel banana halfway down.
2. Break toothpick in half, and poke each half in where eyes will go.
3. Place grapes on each toothpick half for eyes.
4. Press candy-coated chocolate piece in for nose.
5. Push in vitamin pill to make mouth.
6. Give your banana a full head of hair with chocolate sauce.

Yields: 1 serving.

Pumpkin Mini Soufflés

These pumpkin soufflés are delicious and will disappear quickly.

Ingredients:

- 2 mini pumpkins, cut across top, seeded, and cleaned
- 2 Tbs. brown sugar
- 1 c. heavy cream
- 1 egg
- 2 Tbs. confectioners' sugar
- ¼ tsp. ground cinnamon
- 1 pinch of ground nutmeg
- 1 Tbs. butter
- ½ c. chopped pecans
- ½ c. graham cracker crumbs

Directions:

1. Preheat oven to 325 degrees F.
2. Rub inside of each pumpkin with 1 tablespoon brown sugar mixed with pinch of cinnamon and pinch of nutmeg.
3. Mix together cream, egg, confectioners' sugar, cinnamon, and nutmeg; pour into pumpkins.
4. Place filled pumpkins on cookie sheet and bake for 50 minutes; remove from oven.
5. Mix together butter, pecans, and graham cracker crumbs; sprinkle on top of soufflés.
6. Return pumpkins to oven and bake 10 minutes more.

Yields: 2 servings.

Did You Know? . . . .

Did you know that in Ireland salt was once sprinkled in the hair of the children to protect against evil spirits?

Pumpkin Oat Pancakes

These pancakes make a unique breakfast for Halloween time. Have fun decorating these tasty cakes.

Ingredients:

    1   c. all-purpose flour
    1   c. quick-cooking oats
    2   Tbs. wheat germ
    2   tsp. sugar
    2   tsp. baking powder
    ½   tsp. salt
    1   pinch ground cinnamon
    1   c. milk
    1   egg, lightly beaten
    ¾   c. canned pumpkin
    2   Tbs. vegetable oil
        chocolate chips or raisins (optional)

Directions:

1. In bowl combine flour, oats, wheat germ, sugar, baking powder, salt, and cinnamon.
2. In separate bowl combine milk, egg, pumpkin, and oil; stir into dry ingredients just until moistened.
3. Pour batter by ¼ cupfuls onto hot greased griddle; turn when bubbles form on top of pancakes.
4. Cook until second side is golden brown.
5. Decorate with chocolate chips and raisins if desired.

Yields: 10 to 12 pancakes.

Did You Know? . . . .

Did you know that in popular culture a werewolf can be killed if shot by a silver bullet, although this was not a feature of the folk legends?

Chocolate Crepes with Orange Cream Cheese Filling

I have a friend who loves the combination of orange and chocolate, and these crepes are very tasty.

Ingredients for crepes:

- 1 pkg. chocolate chips (6 oz.)
- 3 Tbs. butter
- 1 c. all-purpose flour
- 1 c. sifted confectioners' sugar
- 4 eggs
- ½ c. milk
- ½ c. water
- 1 Tbs. vanilla extract
- 1 tsp. salt
- melted butter
- confectioners' sugar

Ingredients for filling:

- 3 pkg. cream cheese (8 oz. each), softened
- ¾ c. sifted confectioners' sugar
- ½ c. milk
- 2 Tbs. grated orange rind

Directions for crepes:

1. Over hot (not boiling) water, combine chocolate chips and butter.
2. Heat until chips melt and mixture is smooth.
3. Remove from heat; cool slightly.
4. In blender container combine cooled chocolate mixture, flour, sugar, eggs, milk, water, vanilla, and salt.
5. Blend at medium speed until smooth, about 2 minutes, scraping sides of container when necessary.
6. Brush 6- to 8-inch crepe pan or skillet with melted butter.
7. When butter begins to sizzle, pour about 3 tablespoons batter into pan.

8. Turn and tip pan immediately to coat bottom.
9. Cook until top of crepe begins to dry, about 20 seconds; turn and cook a few seconds more.
10. Remove from pan.
11. Repeat with remaining batter.

Directions for filling:
1. In large bowl combine cream cheese, sugar, milk, and grated orange rind.
2. Beat until smooth and creamy.

Directions to assemble:
1. Spread 2 level tablespoonfuls orange cream cheese filling over each crepe.
2. Roll up jelly-roll fashion; place on platter.
3. Dust with confectioners' sugar.

Pumpkin Spread English Muffins

This is a simple topping to add to your toasted English muffins. Enjoy decorating these into jack-o'-lanterns for Halloween.

Ingredients:
cream cheese
canned pumpkin
confectioners' sugar
English muffins
raisins

Directions:
1. Whip cream cheese, pumpkin, and confectioners' sugar together to taste.
2. Toast English muffins.
3. Spread cream cheese mixture on English muffin halves, and let children make jack-o'-lantern faces with raisins.

Cranberry Pumpkin Waffles

These waffles add a nice variety of color and flavor to your Halloween breakfast.

Ingredients:

2   c. all-purpose flour
2   Tbs. sugar
4   tsp. baking powder
1   tsp. salt
1   tsp. ground cinnamon
1   tsp. ground ginger
1½ c. milk
4   Tbs. unsalted butter
¼ c. vegetable oil
2   lg. eggs
1   c. canned puréed pumpkin
½ c. dried cranberries, plumped in hot water to cover for 10 minutes and drained

Directions:

1. Place flour, sugar, baking powder, salt, and spices in large mixing bowl; stir with fork until blended.
2. Place milk, butter, and oil in small saucepan, and heat over low heat until butter has melted; cool slightly.
3. In separate bowl beat eggs with pumpkin purée.
4. Stir in cooled milk mixture.
5. Add to dry ingredients, and stir with wooden spoon until well combined.
6. Stir in cranberries.
7. Preheat waffle iron, and spray with nonstick cooking spray.
8. Add about ½ cup batter. (It takes from ½ cup to ⅔ cup batter to make 1 waffle, depending on size of your waffle iron.)
9. Bake waffles until golden and crisp.
10. Serve hot.

Yields: 4 servings.

Pumpkin Spice Breakfast Casserole

This is an unusual surprise for a tasty casserole.

Ingredients:

- 6   English muffins, torn into 1-inch pieces
- 1   tart apple, peeled and sliced
- 1   c. half-and-half
- 3   eggs
- ¼   cup plus 2 Tbs. sugar, divided
- ½   tsp. ground cinnamon
- ¼   tsp. ground nutmeg
- ⅛   tsp. ground allspice
- ⅛   tsp. ground cloves
- ½   c. pumpkin purée
- 2   Tbs. butter, cut into small pieces

Directions:

1. Preheat oven to 350 degrees F.
2. Butter bottom of 8 x 8-inch casserole, and scatter half of English muffin pieces on bottom.
3. Place half of apple slices over muffin pieces.
4. Whip together half-and-half, eggs, ¼ cup sugar, spices, and pumpkin purée in small bowl.
5. Pour half of pumpkin cream mixture over apples and muffins.
6. Repeat process, layering muffin pieces and apple slices, then covering with remaining pumpkin cream.
7. Sprinkle with 2 tablespoons sugar and butter pieces.
8. Cover with aluminum foil.
9. Bake for 1 hour, or refrigerate overnight and bake before serving.
10. Serve warm.

Yields: 6 servings.

Pumpkin Spice Bagels

Homemade bagels are extra delicious.

Ingredients:

3	c. white bread flour
3¼	tsp. active dry yeast
½	c. plus 2 Tbs. lukewarm water
6	Tbs. brown sugar
1	tsp. salt
½	c. canned pumpkin
1½	tsp. ground cinnamon
1	tsp. ground cloves
1½	tsp. ground nutmeg
¾	tsp. ground allspice
3	qt. boiling water
1	Tbs. sugar
1	egg, beaten, for wash
	poppy seeds or sesame seeds for garnish

Directions:

1. In mixer bowl combine 1½ cups flour and yeast.
2. Combine warm water, sugar, salt, pumpkin, and spices; pour over flour mixture.
3. Beat at low speed for 30 seconds, scraping sides of bowl constantly.
4. Beat 3 minutes on high speed.
5. Stir in as much remaining flour as can be mixed in with a spoon.
6. Turn out onto lightly floured surface; knead in enough remaining flour to make a moderately stiff dough.
7. Continue kneading until smooth and elastic, 6 to 8 minutes.
8. Cover; let dough rest 10 to 15 minutes.
9. Divide into 8 portions.
10. Form balls; gently press thumb through center of ball and slowly stretch into bagel shape.
11. Cover; let rise 20 minutes.
12. While bagels rise, bring 3 quarts water and 1 tablespoon sugar to a rapid boil in large saucepan.

13. Test dough by dropping piece of dough into boiling water; when bagels are ready to cook, dough will pop up to surface of water right away.
14. Using slotted spoon, drop 2 to 3 bagels into rapidly boiling water; boil on each side for 30 seconds.
15. Remove and cool on rack 1 minute; brush with egg and sprinkle with sesame or poppy seeds if desired.
16. Bake at 400 degrees F. on baking sheet sprinkled with cornmeal, until golden, approximately 15 minutes.

Yields: 8 bagels.

Pumpkin Pecan Oatmeal

Pumpkin and pecans make a nice addition to your morning oatmeal.

Ingredients:

3	c. water
½	tsp. ground cinnamon
¼	tsp. ground nutmeg
⅛	tsp. ground allspice
⅛	tsp. ground cloves
2	c. old-fashioned oats, uncooked
1	c. canned puréed pumpkin
⅓	c. firmly packed brown sugar
8	oz. vanilla yogurt
3	Tbs. coarsely chopped, toasted pecans

Directions:
1. In medium saucepan bring water and spices to a boil; stir in oats.
2. Return to boil; reduce heat to medium.
3. Cook 5 minutes or until most of liquid is absorbed, stirring occasionally.
4. Stir in pumpkin and brown sugar; cook 1 minute.
5. Let stand until desired consistency is reached.
6. Spoon oatmeal into bowls; top with yogurt and pecans.

Yields: 4 servings.

Scary Egg Man

A little army of scary egg men is perfect for your Halloween breakfast or any Halloween party.

Ingredients:

  1   hard-boiled egg
  1   thick slice tomato
  2   pimento-stuffed olives
  1   peppercorn
      twigs of cilantro
      mustard
      toothpicks

Directions:

1. Peel shell off egg and cut in half the short way.
2. If egg does not stand by itself, cut thin slice from bottom so it does.
3. Place tomato slice between the two halves and put toothpick through egg to hold it together.
4. Leave part of toothpick sticking out of top to hold hair.
5. Break a toothpick in half and stick ½ in each eye socket.
6. Place olive eyes over toothpicks.
7. Poke peppercorn in place for nose.
8. Dab mustard on tomato slice to make dirty yellow teeth.
9. Place cilantro on top for green hair.

Yields: 1 serving.

Did You Know? . . . .

Did you know that Americans spend over $14 billion on costumes, decorations, party supplies, and other Halloween paraphernalia—second only to Christmas in spending?

Halloween Delights Cookbook
A Collection of Halloween Recipes
Cookbook Delights Series

Cakes

Table of Contents

Did You Know? . . . .

Did you know that according to the National Retail Federation's 2006 Halloween Consumer Intentions and Actions Survey, the top Halloween costumes for adults were Witch, Pirate, Vampire, Cat, Clown, Fairy, Gypsy, Superhero, Ghost, and Ghoul?

Ant Hill Cake

This ant hill cake is fun to make and tastes good, too.

Ingredients:

30	chocolate sandwich cookies
1	bag small peppermint chocolate patties (13 oz.)
2	pt. vanilla bean ice cream
20	vanilla wafers
8-10	round chocolate covered almonds
8-10	round chocolate covered caramels
1	tube black gel icing
	candy corn for garnish

Directions:

1. Place chocolate sandwich cookies in food processor, and process to coarse texture.
2. Add peppermint patties and process to coarse texture.
3. Coat 10-inch springform pan with cooking spray.
4. Add cookie mixture and press down gently to coat bottom and up ½ inch on sides.
5. By spoonfuls, add ice cream.
6. Use back of spoon to smooth ice cream evenly on top.
7. Cover with foil and freeze overnight.
8. Place vanilla wafers in food processor, and blend until smooth.
9. Place in sealed bag until needed, and store at room temperature.
10. Remove rim of springform pan, and place cake on serving platter.
11. On one side of cake, slowly pour vanilla wafer crumbs to form a mound for the anthill.
12. Arrange "ants" on cake using 1 chocolate covered almond for each body and 1 chocolate covered caramel for each head.
13. Pipe on eyes and legs with gel.
14. Garnish with candy corn.

Boogers and Slugs Halloween Cake

Top this cake off with a little confectioners' sugar (for that mildewed look) or try cream cheese frosting or caramel topping. Children, and most adults, will get a good laugh out of it. Have fun, and use up those green tomatoes hanging around in the garden.

Ingredients:

　　4½　c. chopped green tomatoes, ¼-inch dice
　　½　　c. butter, softened
　　2　　c. sugar
　　2　　lg. eggs
　　2　　c. all-purpose flour
　　½　　tsp. ground cinnamon or to taste
　　½　　tsp. ground nutmeg
　　½　　tsp. ground allspice
　　1　　tsp. baking soda
　　½　　tsp. salt
　　¾　　c. golden raisins
　　½　　c. chopped walnuts

Directions:

1. Preheat oven to 350 degrees F.
2. Grease and flour 9 x 13-inch cake pan.
3. Wash and dice green tomatoes.
4. Place tomatoes in strainer and let drain at least 10 to 15 minutes.
5. Cream butter with sugar until light.
6. Add eggs 1 at a time, until thoroughly mixed and fluffy.
7. Mix all dry ingredients together.
8. Toss in raisins and nuts to coat them.
9. Slowly incorporate dry ingredients into creamed mixture, then add chopped tomatoes and mix well.
10. Pour batter into prepared baking pan.
11. Bake for about 40 to 45 minutes.
12. Check with wooden pick for doneness at 40 minutes.
13. When wooden pick comes out clean, remove from oven and allow to cool on rack.
14. The boogers will be visible.
15. Dust with confectioners' sugar or frost with your favorite frosting.

Yields: 24 servings.

Candy Corn Chocolate Cakes

This chocolate cake is fun to decorate for Halloween treats.

Ingredients for cake:

- 2 c. sugar
- 2 c. all-purpose flour
- 1 c. baking cocoa
- 1 c. vegetable oil
- 1 tsp. salt
- 2 lg. eggs
- 1 c. buttermilk
- 1 c. hot water
- 2 tsp. baking soda
- 2 tsp. vanilla extract

Ingredients for buttercream frosting:

- 1 c. butter, softened
- 1 pkg. confectioners' sugar (2 lb.)
- ⅓ c. milk
- 1 tsp. vanilla extract
- orange paste food coloring
- yellow paste food coloring

Directions for cake:

1. Preheat oven to 350 degrees F.
2. Beat first 6 ingredients in large bowl at medium speed with electric mixer until blended.
3. Stir in buttermilk.
4. Stir together 1 cup hot water and baking soda; stir into batter.
5. Stir in vanilla.
6. Pour into 2 greased and floured 9-inch round cake pans.
7. Bake for 30 to 40 minutes or until wooden pick inserted in center comes out clean.
8. Cool in pans on wire racks for 10 minutes; remove from pans, and cool completely on wire racks.
9. Freeze layers 30 minutes.
10. Cut each layer into 8 wedges.

Directions for buttercream frosting:

1. Beat butter at medium speed with electric mixer until fluffy.

2. Gradually add confectioners' sugar, beating until light and fluffy.
3. Add milk, beating until spreading consistency.
4. Stir in vanilla.
5. Stir orange food coloring into 1½ cups frosting.
6. Stir yellow food coloring into 1¼ cups frosting.
7. Pipe frosting on top and sides of cake wedges to resemble candy corn.
8. Using medium star tip, pipe white frosting on small end of each cake, yellow frosting on center, and orange on wide end.

Yields: 16 servings; 3½ cups frosting.

Pumpkin Pudding Cake

This is a rich, moist cake that becomes a welcome autumn treat. It also freezes well.

Ingredients:
- 1   c. chopped walnuts
- 2   c. self-rising flour
- ⅓   c. sugar
- ½   tsp. ground cinnamon
- ¼   tsp. ground cloves
- ½   c. pumpkin purée
- ⅓   c. vegetable oil
- 1   egg
- ¾   c. raisins
- 1   c. orange juice
      Sweetened Whipped Cream (recipe page 193)

Directions:
1. Preheat oven to 350 degrees F.
2. Spray 10-inch bundt pan with nonstick cooking spray; sprinkle walnuts evenly in bottom.
3. In large mixing bowl combine flour, sugar, cinnamon, and cloves.
4. Add pumpkin, oil, egg, raisins, and orange juice; beat until smooth then pour into prepared bundt pan.
5. Bake 40 to 50 minutes or until wooden pick inserted in center comes out clean.
6. Cool in pan for 20 minutes; remove from pan.
7. Serve warm, topped with whipped cream.

Chocolate Spider Web Cake

This chocolate cake tastes great and is fun to decorate.

Ingredients for cake:

    1⅔ c. all-purpose flour
    1½ c. sugar
    ⅔   c. baking cocoa
    1½ tsp. baking soda
    1   tsp. salt
    ½   tsp. baking powder
    2   lg. eggs
    ½   c. butter, softened
    1½ c. buttermilk
    2   tsp. vanilla extract
    buttercream frosting (recipe follows)
    spider web (recipe follows) or white decorating icing

Ingredients for buttercream frosting:

    6   Tbs. butter, softened
    2⅔ c. confectioners' sugar
    ½   c. baking cocoa
    4-6 Tbs. milk
    1   tsp. vanilla extract

Ingredients for spider web:

    ½ c. white chocolate chips
    ½ tsp. shortening (no substitutes)

Directions for cake:

1. Preheat oven to 350 degrees F.
2. Thoroughly butter and flour two 9-inch round baking pans.
3. Combine dry ingredients in large bowl; add eggs, butter, buttermilk, and vanilla.

4. Beat on low speed of mixer 1 minute, scraping bowl constantly.
5. Beat on high speed 3 minutes, scraping bowl occasionally.
6. Pour batter into prepared pans.
7. Bake 30 to 35 minutes or until wooden pick inserted in center comes out clean.
8. Cool 10 minutes; remove from pans to wire racks.
9. Cool completely.

Directions for buttercream frosting:

1. Beat butter.
2. Add confectioners' sugar and cocoa alternately with milk, beating to spreading consistency.
3. Stir in vanilla.

Directions for spider web:

1. Place chips and shortening in small heavy seal-top plastic bag.
2. Microwave on high 45 seconds.
3. Squeeze gently.
4. If necessary, microwave additional 10 to 15 seconds; squeeze until chips are melted.
5. Make small diagonal cut in one bottom corner of bag; squeeze mixture onto cake as directed.
6. Frost 1 cake with buttercream frosting.
7. Immediately pipe or drizzle spider web in 4 or 5 concentric circles on top of cake.
8. Using knife or wooden pick, immediately draw 8 to 10 lines from center to edges of cake at regular intervals to form web.
9. Garnish with "spider," using a caramel, licorice, and other candies.

Yields: 12 servings.

Halloween Chocolate Cupcakes

These cupcakes are fun to decorate and great for children to take to a party.

Ingredients for cupcakes:

- 2   c. all-purpose flour
- 2   c. sugar
- ¾   c. baking cocoa
- 1   tsp. baking soda
- 1   tsp. salt
- ½   tsp. baking powder
- ¾   c. butter, softened
- ¾   c. buttermilk
- ¾   c. water
- 2   lg. eggs
- 1   tsp. vanilla extract
     peanut butter cream filling (recipe follows)
     assorted candies (optional)

Ingredients for peanut butter cream filling:

- 2   pkg. cream cheese (3 oz. each), softened
- ⅔   c. creamy peanut butter
- ¼   c. milk
- 1   tsp. vanilla extract
- 3   c. confectioners' sugar

Directions for cupcakes:

1. Preheat oven to 350 degrees F.
2. Line 2½-inch-diameter muffin cups with paper bake cups.
3. Stir together dry ingredients in large bowl.
4. Add butter, buttermilk, water, eggs, and vanilla.
5. Beat on low speed of electric mixer 30 seconds, scraping bowl constantly.
6. Beat on high speed 3 minutes, scraping bowl occasionally.
7. Fill muffin cups ½ full with batter.

8. Bake 20 minutes or until wooden pick inserted in center comes out clean.
9. Remove from pan to wire rack; cool completely.
10. Prepare Peanut Butter Cream Filling.

Directions for peanut butter cream filling:
1. Beat cream cheese and peanut butter in large bowl until blended.
2. Add milk and vanilla; beat well.
3. Gradually add confectioners' sugar, beating until smooth.
4. Beat in additional milk 1 teaspoon at a time, if necessary, until desired consistency is reached.
5. Place into pastry bag fitted with large star tip.
6. Insert tip into center of cupcakes; pipe filling into cake.
7. Remove tip from cake; garnish top with swirl of filling.
8. Decorate with candies if desired.
9. Cover; refrigerate leftover cupcakes.

Yields: 3 dozen cupcakes; about 2¾ cups filling.

Did You Know? . . . .

Did you know that as of 2004 an estimated 160 films feature Dracula in a major role, a number second only to Sherlock Holmes?

Did You Know? . . . .

Did you know that as of October 2006 Boston, Massachusetts, holds the record for the most lit jack-o'-lanterns at one time and place?

Halloween Graveyard Cake

Underneath tasty "tombstones," ghosts, pumpkins, "worms," and "soil" that make this dessert a conversation piece, you will find a delectable chocolate cake made from scratch in a few simple steps.

Ingredients for cake:

- 2 c. all-purpose flour
- 2 c. sugar
- 1 tsp. baking soda
- ½ tsp. salt
- 1 c. butter
- 1 c. water
- ¼ c. baking cocoa
- ½ c. dairy sour cream
- 2 eggs

Ingredients for frosting:

- ¼ c. butter
- 3 Tbs. milk
- 2 Tbs. baking cocoa
- 2 c. confectioners' sugar
- ½ tsp. vanilla extract
- 18 cream-filled chocolate sandwich cookies
- 9 cream-filled oval vanilla sandwich cookies
- 1 c. whipped cream
  green and brown decorator's icing or gel
  pumpkin candies and gummy worms (optional)

Directions for cake:

1. Preheat oven to 350 degrees F.
2. In mixing bowl combine flour, sugar, baking soda, and salt; set aside.
3. In saucepan combine butter, water, and cocoa; bring to boil over medium heat.
4. Add to flour mixture; beat well.

5. Beat in sour cream and eggs.
6. Pour into greased 13 x 9 x 2-inch baking pan.
7. Bake for 35 to 38 minutes or until wooden pick inserted near center comes out clean.
8. Cool on wire rack for 5 minutes.

Directions for frosting:
1. In saucepan combine butter, milk, and cocoa; bring to boil.
2. Remove from heat; stir in sugar and vanilla.
3. Pour over warm cake.
4. Crumble chocolate cookies; sprinkle over frosting while still warm.
5. Cool completely.
6. For tombstones, use icing to decorate vanilla cookies with words or faces; place on cake.
7. For ghosts, make mounds of whipped cream; use icing to add eyes and mouths as desired.
8. Refrigerate for at least 1 hour.
9. Just before serving, add pumpkins and gummy worms if desired.

Yields: 16 servings.

Did You Know? . . . .

Did you know that the Village Halloween Parade in New York City is the largest Halloween celebration in the United States, as well as the largest annual parade held at night, attracting over two million spectators and participants and about four million television viewers each year?

Halloween Chocolate Cake

This delicious chocolate cake is decorated to look like a pumpkin.

Ingredients for cake:
    1   milk chocolate bar (6 oz.), broken into pieces
    ½   c. butter, softened
    1   c. boiling water
    2   c. all-purpose flour
    1½   c. sugar
    ½   c. baking cocoa
    2   tsp. baking soda
    1   tsp. salt
    2   lg. eggs
    ½   c. dairy sour cream
    1   tsp. vanilla extract
         chocolate-coated ice cream cone (recipe follows)
         orange frosting (recipe follows)
         decorator frosting (recipe follows)

Ingredients for ice cream cone:
    1 c. semisweet chocolate chips
    1 Tbs. shortening (no substitutions)
    1 flat-bottom ice cream cone

Ingredients for orange frosting:
    ⅓   c. butter
    2   c. confectioners' sugar
    2   tsp. freshly grated orange peel
    1½   tsp. vanilla extract
    2-4 Tbs. hot water
         red and yellow food color

Ingredients for decorator frosting:
    3   Tbs. water
    1   Tbs. meringue powder
    1½   c. confectioners' sugar
    ⅛   tsp. vanilla extract
         green food coloring

Directions for cake:

1. Preheat oven to 350 degrees F.
2. Grease and flour 12-cup fluted tube pan.
3. Stir together chocolate bar pieces, butter, and water in medium bowl until chocolate is melted.
4. Stir together flour, sugar, cocoa, baking soda, and salt in large bowl; gradually add butter mixture, beating until well blended.
5. Add eggs, sour cream, and vanilla; beat on medium speed for 1 minute.
6. Pour batter into prepared pan.
7. Bake 50 to 55 minutes or until wooden pick inserted in center of cake comes out clean.
8. Cool 10 minutes; remove from pan to wire rack and cool completely.

Directions for ice cream cone:

1. Place chocolate chips and shortening in small microwave-safe bowl.
2. Microwave on high (100%) for 1 to 1½ minutes or just until chips are melted and mixture is smooth when stirred.
3. Spoon melted chocolate over outside of flat-bottom ice cream cone.
4. Refrigerate until chocolate is firm, about 30 minutes.

Directions for orange frosting:

1. Place butter in microwave-safe bowl.
2. Microwave on high (100%) for 1 minute or until melted.
3. Stir in confectioners' sugar, orange peel, and vanilla.
4. Stir in 2 to 4 tablespoons hot water for desired consistency.
5. Stir in red and yellow food color for desired color.
6. Drizzle over cooled cake.

Directions for decorator frosting:

1. Combine water and meringue powder in small bowl.
2. Add confectioners' sugar and vanilla extract; beat on high speed of mixer until stiff.
3. Stir in green food color for desired color.
4. Place ice cream cone into center of cake for pumpkin stem.
5. Using leaf decorating tip, pipe leaves onto "pumpkin" with decorator icing.

Orange-Ooze Cupcakes

These cupcakes ooze a delicious cream cheese filling.

Ingredients for filling:

   8   oz. cream cheese; softened
   1   egg
   ⅓   c. sugar
   6   oz. chocolate chips
       yellow and red food coloring

Ingredients for cupcakes:

   3   c. all-purpose flour
   2   c. sugar
   ½   c. baking cocoa
   2   tsp. baking soda
   ½   tsp. salt
   2   c. water
   ½   c. plus 2 Tbs. vegetable oil
   2   Tbs. cider vinegar
   2   tsp. vanilla extract

Directions for filling:

   1. In small mixing bowl use electric mixer to combine cream cheese, egg, and sugar.
   2. Blend in 2 drops yellow food coloring and 1 drop red food coloring, adding more coloring if necessary to reach desired shade of orange.
   3. Use spoon to stir in chocolate chips; set filling aside.

Directions for cupcakes:

   1. Preheat oven to 350 degrees F.
   2. Line cupcake baking pans with paper cupcake liners.
   3. In large mixing bowl combine flour, sugar, cocoa, baking soda, and salt; set aside.
   4. In second small mixing bowl, combine water, vegetable oil, vinegar, and vanilla.

5. Add contents of small mixing bowl to large mixing bowl, and stir with spoon to combine.
6. Using spoon, fill cupcake liners half full with cupcake batter then place 1 teaspoon filling at center of each.
7. As cupcake bakes, batter will rise to surround filling.
8. Bake approximately 25 minutes or until cupcakes test done.
9. Cool on wire rack.
10. If desired, frost with orange icing—or just let orange filling ooze out as a surprise.

Black Death Cake

This makes a moist and delicious chocolate cake.

Ingredients:

1	lb. butter, softened
3	c. sugar
6	eggs
3½	c. all-purpose flour
1	c. dairy sour cream
2	tsp. vanilla extract
1	c. baking cocoa
2	tsp. baking powder

Directions:

1. Preheat oven to 350 degrees F.
2. Cream butter and sugar.
3. Add eggs and beat well.
4. Add 2 cups flour and beat well.
5. Mix in sour cream and vanilla.
6. Combine remaining flour, cocoa, and baking powder; mix well.
7. Butter 10-inch bundt pan and dust with cocoa powder.
8. Pour batter into pan.
9. Bake for about 1 hour or until cake pulls away from edges of pan.
10. Cool in pan for 20 minutes; remove and finish cooling.

Pumpkin Spice Cake with Orange Sauce

My father used to enjoy spice cake, and this pumpkin version is a nice variety.

Ingredients for cake:

½   c. butter, softened
¾   c. sugar
2   lg. eggs
¾   c. mashed cooked pumpkin
1   tsp. vanilla extract
1½ c. all-purpose flour
1½ tsp. baking powder
¼   tsp. salt
¼   tsp. ground cinnamon
⅛   tsp. ground nutmeg
1   dash of ground allspice
1   dash of ground cloves
     confectioners' sugar
     orange sauce (recipe follows)
     orange rind strips for garnish

Ingredients for orange sauce:

⅓   c. light brown sugar
1   Tbs. cornstarch
1½ c. orange juice
1   tsp. lemon juice

Directions for cake:

1. Preheat oven to 350 degrees F.
2. Beat butter at medium speed with electric mixer until creamy.
3. Gradually add sugar, beating well.
4. Add eggs 1 at a time, beating until blended after each addition.
5. Stir in pumpkin and vanilla.
6. Combine flour, baking powder, salt, and spices.

7. Gradually add to sugar mixture, beating at low speed until blended after each addition.
8. Pour into greased and floured 9-inch round cake pan.
9. Bake for 20 minutes or until wooden pick inserted in center comes out clean.
10. Cool in pan on wire rack 10 minutes; remove from pan and cool on wire rack.
11. Place paper doily over cake; sift confectioners' sugar through wire-mesh strainer over doily.
12. Remove doily, and serve with orange sauce.
13. Garnish if desired.

Directions for orange sauce:
1. Whisk together all ingredients in heavy saucepan until blended.
2. Bring mixture to a boil over medium heat, whisking constantly.
3. Boil, whisking constantly, 1 minute.
4. Serve warm or cool.

Yields: 8 servings cake; 1¾ cups sauce.

Did You Know? . . . .

Did you know that ghoul is also the name for a mythical desert-dwelling, shape-shifting demon that can assume the guise of an animal, especially a hyena? It lures unwary travelers into the desert wastes to slay and devour them. The creature also robs graves and eats the dead.

Witch's Hat Chocolate Cupcakes

Have fun making these decorative chocolate cupcakes.
They taste good and make great-looking witch's caps.

Ingredients for cupcakes:

  ¾   c. butter, softened
  1⅔ c. sugar
  3   lg. eggs
  1   tsp. vanilla extract
  2   c. all-purpose flour
  ⅔   c. baking cocoa
  1¼ tsp. baking soda
  1   tsp. salt
  ¼   tsp. baking powder
  1⅓ c. water
      orange cream filling (recipe follows)

Ingredients for filling:

  ½   c. butter, softened
  1   c. marshmallow cream
  1¼   c. confectioners' sugar
  ½-1 tsp. freshly grated orange peel
  ½   tsp. vanilla extract
  2-3 tsp. orange juice
       red and yellow food color (optional)

Directions for cupcakes:

1. Preheat oven to 350 degrees F.
2. Line 2½-inch-diameter muffin cups with paper bake cups.
3. Beat butter, sugar, eggs, and vanilla in large bowl on high speed of mixer for 3 minutes.
4. Stir together flour, cocoa, baking soda, salt, and baking powder; add alternately with water to butter mixture, beating just until blended.
5. Fill muffin cups ⅔ full with batter.

6. Bake 20 to 25 minutes or until wooden pick inserted in center comes out clean.
7. Remove from pan to wire rack; cool completely.
8. Prepare orange cream filling.

Directions for filling:
1. Beat butter in small bowl; gradually beat in marshmallow creme.
2. Add confectioners' sugar, orange peel, and vanilla, beating until blended.
3. Gradually add orange juice and food color if desired, beating to desired consistency.
4. Cut 1½-inch cone-shaped piece from center of each cupcake; reserve.
5. Fill each cavity with scant tablespoon filling.
6. Place reserved cake pieces on filling, pointed side up.
7. Refrigerate before serving.

Yields: 2½ dozen cupcakes; 1⅓ cups filling.

Did You Know? . . . .

Did you know that in Sweden children dress up as witches and go trick-or-treating on Maundy Thursday (the Thursday before Easter), while Danish children dress up in various attires and go trick-or-treating on Fastelavn, the Sunday before Ash Wednesday?

Did You Know? . . . .

Did you know that growing pumpkins is a serious hobby for some people, especially since the prize money for the largest pumpkin can be as much as $25,000 at some fall festivals?

Autumn Cake

This cake is actually an upside-down apple cake. It is very delicious.

Ingredients for fruit bottom:

2	Tbs. butter
¾	c. brown sugar, firmly packed
5	apples, peeled, cored, sliced
1	c. nuts, chopped

Ingredients for cake:

½	c. butter, softened
½	c. sugar
1	egg, beaten
1	c. light molasses
2½	c. all-purpose flour
1	tsp. ground cinnamon
½	tsp. ground cloves
1½	tsp. baking soda
1	tsp. ground ginger
1	tsp. salt
1	c. hot water

Directions for fruit bottom:

1. Preheat oven to 350 degrees F.
2. Coat 12 x 8 x 2-inch pan with 2 tablespoons butter.
3. Sprinkle brown sugar evenly over butter.
4. Arrange apple slices over sugar mixture.
5. Sprinkle nuts over all.
6. Place pan on bottom shelf of oven, and let apples cook while mixing remaining ingredients.

Directions for cake:

1. Cream together butter and sugar.
2. Add egg and molasses; mix well.
3. Sift dry ingredients and stir into creamed mixture.
4. Pour in hot water and mix to thin batter.
5. Remove pan from oven and pour batter over apples.
6. Return to oven and bake for 35 minutes.
7. Remove from oven and loosen cake around edges.
8. Let stand 5 minutes and turn out onto serving tray.

Yields: 8 to 10 servings.

Halloween Delights Cookbook

A Collection of Halloween Recipes
Cookbook Delights Series

Candies and Other Treats

Table of Contents

Candy Corn Popcorn Balls

Children can help make these seasonal treats for a Halloween party and choose their flavor.

Ingredients:

- ¼ c. butter
- 1 pkg. miniature marshmallows (10.5 oz.)
- 1 pkg. gelatin (3.25 oz.), any flavor
- 12 c. popped popcorn
- 1 c. candy corn

Directions:

1. Microwave butter and marshmallows in large microwave-safe bowl on high for 1½ to 2 minutes or until marshmallows are puffed.
2. Stir in gelatin until well blended.
3. Pour marshmallow mixture over combined popcorn and candy corn in large bowl.
4. Mix lightly until well coated.
5. Shape into sixteen 2-inch balls or other shapes with greased or wet hands.

Yields: 16 servings.

Halloween Spiders

Add these decorative spiders to your Halloween treats.

Ingredients:

- 2 Tbs. peanut butter
- 2 Tbs. confectioners' sugar
- 2 Tbs. graham cracker crumbs
- 2 Tbs. coconut
-   licorice
-   raisins

Directions:
1. Mix peanut butter, sugar, and crumbs together and form into ball.
2. Divide ball into 2 parts and form into 2 balls, one slightly smaller than the other.
3. Roll balls in coconut and place smaller ball (head) on top of larger one (abdomen).
4. Add 8 licorice legs and 8 raisin eyes.

Yields: 1 scary spider.

Creepy Crawly Spiders

These are easy to make, and it is fun to see how creepy you can make your spiders.

Ingredients:
2   c. miniature marshmallows
1   pkg. semisweet baking chocolate, melted (8 squares)
24   pieces black shoestring licorice (12 inches each)
48   assorted miniature round candies

Directions:
1. Mix marshmallows and melted chocolate until marshmallows are completely coated.
2. Drop by spoonfuls onto sheets of wax paper to make 24 clusters for "bodies" of "spiders."
3. Cut each 12-inch piece of licorice into 8 pieces.
4. Decorate each spider with 8 pieces of licorice for "legs" and 2 candies for "eyes."
5. Let stand at room temperature or refrigerate until firm.
6. Store in airtight container at room temperature.

Yields: 12 servings.

Candy Corn Fudge

This makes a decorative Halloween fudge.

Ingredients:

- 1 pkg. vanilla or white chocolate chips (12 oz.), melted
- 2 containers vanilla frosting (16 oz. each)
- 1 pkg. butterscotch-flavored chips (10 oz.), melted
- ⅛ tsp. or more yellow food coloring, divided
- ⅛ tsp. or more red food coloring
- 48 pieces candy corn

Directions:

1. Line 13 x 9 x 2-inch pan with foil, leaving a couple inches of overhang on each end; butter foil.
2. In large bowl combine melted vanilla chips and half of frosting; mix well.
3. Spread ⅓ of mixture in prepared pan.
4. Combine melted butterscotch chips and remaining frosting in another large bowl; mix well.
5. Add enough yellow and red food coloring to turn mixture orange.
6. Stir until well blended.
7. Spread orange mixture over white layer in pan.
8. If remaining white mixture has hardened, heat in microwave until just melted and smooth, stirring occasionally.
9. Add enough yellow food coloring to turn mixture yellow; stir until well blended.
10. Spread over orange layer in pan.
11. Refrigerate 1 hour or until firm.
12. Use foil to lift fudge from pan.
13. Turn white side up and carefully peel off foil.
14. Cut into 48 pieces.
15. Press a candy corn into center of each piece.
16. Store in refrigerator.

Yields: 48 pieces.

Candy Peanut Butter Worms

Have fun making these giant worms. They are a treat for children and adults who love peanut butter. These go perfect in a dirt cake instead of the usual store-bought gummy worms.

Ingredients:

    1   c. smooth peanut butter
    ½   c. honey
    1½ c. powdered milk
    ½   c. confectioners' sugar
        raisins
        peanuts

Directions:

1. Put peanut butter and honey in food processor or mixer and combine well.
2. Add dry milk powder and confectioners' sugar, and mix again until smooth and well blended.
3. Take out, make into 1 long log roll, and divide into about 20 pieces.
4. Roll each piece into a thick worm and place 2 peanuts or raisins at the end to look like 2 eyes.
5. Chill at least 30 minutes before serving.

Yields: 20 worms.

***Did You Know?* . . . .**

Did you know that the largest pumpkin in the world weighed 1,446 pounds. It was weighed at a pumpkin festival in Port Elgin, Ontario, Canada, in October 2004.

Huge Scary Spiders

These spiders can look pretty scary with their giant red eyes.

Ingredients:

2	squares unsweetened chocolate (1 oz. each)
1¼	c. all-purpose flour
1½	tsp. baking powder
¼	tsp. salt
¼	c. butter, softened
1	c. sugar
1	egg
1	tsp. vanilla extract
40	cinnamon red hot candies

Directions:

1. Preheat oven to 375 degrees F.
2. Lightly grease baking sheet.
3. In saucepan melt chocolate over low heat; let cool.
4. In small bowl mix flour, baking powder, and salt.
5. In medium bowl beat butter on low speed until smooth.
6. Add sugar and beat until creamy.
7. Stir in egg, vanilla, and melted chocolate.
8. Add flour mixture and mix well, forming stiff dough.
9. To make spider, shape 2-inch flat oval for body.
10. Make spider's head by flattening circle about ½ inch wide.
11. Shape dough for legs, making each about 2 inches long and less than ¼ inch wide.
12. Attach head and legs to body.
13. Put 2 red candies into head for eyes.
14. Bake for 5 to 8 minutes.
15. Let spiders cool on baking sheet to avoid breaking when moving.

Yields: 10 spiders.

Cemetery Crunch

This is a simple, sweet candy to make for Halloween.

Ingredients:

¼ c. maple-flavored or pancake syrup
2 Tbs. butter
¼ tsp. ground cinnamon
4 c. cocoa, fruit-flavored, or cinnamon puffed cereal
1 c. dry-roasted peanuts
2 c. miniature marshmallows
1 c. candy corn
1 c. candy-coated chocolate pieces

Directions:

1. Preheat oven to 300 degrees F.
2. Mix syrup, butter, and cinnamon in large microwave-safe bowl.
3. Microwave on high for 1 minute; stir until butter is completely melted.
4. Add cereal and peanuts; mix lightly.
5. Spread into lightly greased 15 x 10 x 1 inch baking pan.
6. Bake 30 minutes, stirring after 15 minutes; cool completely.
7. Break into pieces.
8. Toss with marshmallows and candies.
9. Store in airtight container at room temperature.

Yields: 18 servings.

Did You Know? . . . .

Did you know that there really are vampire bats? They are not from Transylvania but are from Central and South America and feed on the blood of horses, cattle, and birds.

Halloween Kitty

This will make a great popcorn treat in the shape of a cat.

Ingredients:

2   c. sugar
1½ c. water
½   tsp. salt
½   c. light corn syrup
1   tsp. vinegar
1   tsp. vanilla extract
6   c. popped popcorn, unsalted (unpopped kernels removed)
2   oval paper plates (8½ x 11-in.)
1   dessert paper plate (6 in.)
     aluminum foil
     licorice strings (six 2-in. strips) or colored toothpicks
     licorice rope (one 15-in. strip)
     light corn syrup for assembly

Directions:

1. Combine sugar, water, salt, ½ cup corn syrup, and vinegar; cook to hard-ball stage, 250 degrees F.
2. Add vanilla.
3. Pour over popped corn and mix well.
4. Line paper plates with foil and press popcorn mixture firmly into them.
5. Allow to cool; unmold.
6. With sharp knife, cut a wedge from one end of each large oval to form legs of cat.
7. Trim each small round (head) popcorn shape to fit other end of oval (body).
8. Cut licorice strings into six 2-inch strips and rope licorice into 15-inch strip.
9. To assemble, heat corn syrup to a boil and brush over body and head shapes where they fit together; press together to form cat.

10. Brush flat side of one cat with hot syrup; arrange 2-inch strips of licorice to make whiskers.
11. Press second cat over first to give a three-dimensional effect.
12. Cut ears from popcorn wedge scraps and attach to head with hot syrup.
13. Shape licorice rope into tail and attach to body.

Yields: 6 servings.

Cow Pies

These look like their name but make a tasty candy.

Ingredients:
- 2 c. milk chocolate chips (12 oz.)
- 1 Tbs. vegetable shortening
- ½ c. raisins
- ½ c. toasted slivered almonds, chopped
- ½ c. toasted shredded coconut

Directions:
1. In double boiler over simmering water, melt chocolate chips and shortening, stirring until smooth.
2. Remove from heat.
3. Stir in raisins, almonds, and coconut; mix well.
4. Drop by tablespoonfuls onto foil, wax paper, or plastic wrap-lined baking sheet.
5. Chill until ready to serve.
6. Variation: Leave out coconut if desired.

Yields: About 2 dozen.

Did You Know? . . . .

Did you know that you can restore a shriveled jack-o'-lantern by soaking it in water overnight?

Chocolate Mice

These are fun to make. Decorate these black and white mice to the artistic design of your choice.

Ingredients:

 4   squares semisweet chocolate (1 oz. each)
 ⅓   c. dairy sour cream
 1   c. finely crushed chocolate wafer cookies
 ⅓   c. chocolate cookie crumbs
 ⅓   c. confectioners' sugar
 24 silver dragees decorating candy
 ¼   c. sliced almonds
 12 long red vine licorice

Directions:

1. Melt chocolate and combine with sour cream.
2. Stir in 1 cup chocolate wafer crumbs; mix well.
3. Cover and refrigerate until firm.
4. Roll by level tablespoonfuls into balls.
5. Mold to slight point at one end for nose.
6. Roll dough in confectioners' sugar for white mice or in chocolate cookie crumbs for dark mice.
7. On each mouse in appropriate spots, place dragees for eyes, almond slices for ears, and a licorice string for tail.
8. Refrigerate for at least two hours until firm.

Yields: 12 mice.

Did You Know? . . . .

Did you know that some people believe that if you see a spider on Halloween, it is the spirit of a loved one who is watching over you?

Chocolate Peanut Butter Coated Apples

These are delicious and easy to make. They are a nice variation of traditional caramel apples.

Ingredients:

    12 wooden ice cream sticks
    12 medium apples, stems removed
    1   pkg. peanut butter chips (10 oz.)
    ½ c. vegetable oil
    ⅔ c. confectioners' sugar
    ⅔ c. baking cocoa
        chopped peanut butter chips, chocolate chips, vanilla chips, or flaked coconut (optional)

Directions:

1. Insert wooden stick into each washed and dried apple.
2. Cover baking sheet with wax paper.
3. In medium microwave-safe bowl, stir together peanut butter chips and oil.
4. Microwave on high 1½ minutes or until chips are softened; stir until melted.
5. Stir together confectioners' sugar and cocoa.
6. Gradually add to melted chip mixture, stirring until smooth.
7. Microwave on high 1 minute or until very warm.
8. Dip apples ¼ way into mixture, twirling to remove excess coating. (If coating becomes too thick, return to microwave for a few seconds.)
9. Roll coated apple in chopped chips or coconut if desired.
10. Allow to cool on prepared baking sheet.

Yields: 1 dozen apples.

Did You Know? . . . .

Did you know that Illinois produces 457 million pounds of pumpkins a year, making it the leading producer of the 50 states?

Eat-'em-up Ghosts

An all-time favorite of children everywhere, these adorable chain rattlers have a cereal and marshmallow base and are coated with vanilla-flavored candy.

Ingredients:

- 1   bag marshmallows (10 oz.)
- ¼   c. butter
- 6   c. crispy rice cereal
- 12 oz. vanilla-flavored candy coating, melted
  - black licorice candy
  - chocolate sprinkles
  - miniature semisweet chocolate pieces

Directions:

1. In large pan combine marshmallows and butter.
2. Cook and stir over medium-low heat until mixture is melted.
3. Gradually stir in cereal until well combined.
4. Using ½ to 1 cup of cereal mixture, form into ghost shapes.
5. Set aside to cool completely.
6. Dip each ghost shape into melted candy coating.
7. Use pieces of licorice, chocolate sprinkles, and/or chocolate pieces for eyes, nose, eyebrows, and mouth.

Yields: 9 to 12 ghosts.

Did You Know? . . . .

Did you know that Jerry Ayers of Baltimore, Ohio, carved a pumpkin in 37 seconds, making him the fastest pumpkin carver in the world?

Eerie Eyeballs

These eyeballs make a disgusting decoration that is fun to eat.

Ingredients:

- 3 oz. lemon gelatin (can be sugar-free)
- 1 c. hot water
- ½ c. miniature marshmallows
- 1 c. pineapple juice
- 8 oz. cream cheese
- 1 c. mayonnaise
  - truffle candy mold or round ice cube trays
  - food coloring: black, blue, brown, and/or green

Directions:

1. Dissolve lemon gelatin in 1 cup water in double boiler.
2. Add marshmallows and stir to melt; remove from heat.
3. Add pineapple juice and cream cheese.
4. Beat until well blended; cool slightly.
5. Fold in mayonnaise.
6. Pour mixture into molds and place in refrigerator to set.
7. If you do not have truffle molds or round ice cube trays, pour mixture into deep ceramic dish and chill until thickened or firm enough to use melon baller to scoop full balls.
8. To decorate use liquid food coloring and an old detail paintbrush to paint on iris and pupil.

Yields: 9 dozen bite-size eyeballs when using truffle molds.

Did You Know? . . . .

Did you know that Halloween is the Number One season for selling humorous greeting cards?

Halloween Popcorn Logs

Try these popcorn logs for a fun, decorative treat.

Ingredients:

3	qt. popped popcorn
12	candy sticks (about 4½ inches long each)
2	c. sugar
1½	c. water
½	c. light corn syrup
1	tsp. vinegar
½	tsp. salt
1	tsp. vanilla extract
	cellophane and ribbon

Directions:

1. Keep popcorn warm in oven set at 300 degree F. while preparing syrup.
2. In large saucepan combine sugar, water, corn syrup, vinegar, and salt.
3. Cook to hard-ball stage, 250 degrees F., on candy thermometer.
4. Stir in vanilla.
5. Pour over popped popcorn, stirring to coat.
6. Butter hands; shape about 1 cup popped corn around each candy stick to form logs.
7. Let stand until cool.
8. Wrap each log in clear or colored cellophane or any bright paper.
9. Secure each end with ribbon.

Yields: 12 logs.

***Did You Know?* . . . .**

Did you know that cucurbit phobia is the fear of pumpkins?

Jack-O'-Lantern Candy

This is fun to make, and it tastes delicious.

Ingredients:

- ½   c. peanut butter
- 2   Tbs. butter
- 1¼ c. confectioners' sugar, sifted
- 1   c. baking cocoa, sifted
- ½   c. evaporated milk
- 1   c. peanuts, chopped
- ⅔   c. desiccated coconut
  red and yellow food coloring
  pretzel sticks or licorice whips

Directions:

1. Combine peanut butter and butter in medium bowl.
2. Microwave on high for 45 to 60 seconds until melted; stir until blended.
3. Gradually add confectioners' sugar and cocoa, alternating with evaporated milk, until smoothly blended.
4. Stir in peanuts.
5. Chill until firm enough to shape into balls.
6. Color coconut with red and yellow food coloring to desired shade of orange by shaking coconut and food coloring together in jar with tight lid.
7. Form tablespoonfuls of chocolate mixture into balls.
8. Roll in coconut and insert small piece of pretzel or licorice into top for stem.
9. Chill well before serving.
10. Store, covered, in refrigerator.

Yields: About 2 dozen.

***Did You Know?* . . . .**

Did you know that a pumpkin is really a squash?

153

Caramel Apple Slices

These are delicious caramel apple slices to enjoy.

Ingredients:

    1   bag vanilla caramels (14 oz.), about 48
    3   Tbs. water
    3   apples, cored, peeled, and sliced
    1   c. semisweet chocolate pieces (6 oz.)
    1   Tbs. vegetable shortening
    ¾   c. walnuts or pecans, chopped fine

Directions:

1. Place unwrapped caramels and water in medium saucepan.
2. Cook until caramels are melted and smooth, stirring constantly.
3. Remove from heat.
4. Arrange apple slices on pizza plate or pan.
5. Use spoon to drizzle caramel mixture over apples.
6. Put chocolate pieces and shortening in small saucepan.
7. Cook over medium-low heat until mixture is melted and smooth, stirring constantly.
8. Use another spoon to drizzle chocolate mixture over caramel-covered apples.
9. Sprinkle with nuts.
10. Let stand at room temperature for up to 10 minutes.

Yields: 6 to 8 servings.

Did You Know? . . . .

Did you know that the color orange is associated with harvest and black is associated with death? This is thought to be the reason they were chosen for Halloween colors.

Toasted Tongues

These meringue tongues are easy to make and also fun to put together.

Ingredients:

   6   egg whites
   1   c. sugar
       red food coloring
       pink or red cake crystals
       Popsicle sticks

Directions:

   1. Position oven rack on lowest shelf, and preheat oven to 200 degrees F.
   2. Separate egg whites from yolks into 2 small bowls.
   3. Rapidly beat egg whites until stiff peaks form.
   4. Slowly stir spoonfuls of sugar into whites, and continue to beat until entire cup of sugar has been added.
   5. Whites should form stiff, shiny peaks.
   6. Stir in 2 to 3 drops red food coloring.
   7. Place sheet of parchment paper on cookie sheet.
   8. Spoon about 3 tablespoons meringue in shape of a tongue onto parchment paper.
   9. Tongues should be the length of a Popsicle stick.
   10. Press Popsicle stick gently into center of each tongue, leaving about 2 inches hanging over end.
   11. Bake about 3 hours or until tongues are completely dry to the touch.
   12. Allow to cool completely before carefully lifting off paper.

   Yields: About 12 little lickers.

Did You Know? . . . .

Did you know that pumpkins also come in white, blue, and green?

Chocolate-Covered Bugs

Have fun making these candy bugs.

Ingredients:

    1   pkg. red licorice whips
   24 soft caramel candies
    1   c. chocolate chips (6 oz.)
    1   c. colored sprinkles
    1   c. red hot candies
    1   c. sliced almonds
    1   c. assorted decors and dragees

Directions:

1. Line baking sheet with wax paper.
2. Cut licorice into small pieces.
3. Use hands to flatten each caramel into small oval.
4. Press bits of licorice onto 12 flattened caramels to make legs.
5. Top each with second caramel and press edges to seal.
6. Place on prepared baking sheet.
7. Put chocolate in microwave-safe bowl; microwave on high about 1 minute.
8. Stir and then microwave on high 1 minute longer.
9. Remove from microwave and stir until melted.
10. Spoon melted chocolate over each candy.
11. Decorate with nuts and candy.

***Did You Know?* . . . .**

Did you know that one-quarter of all the candy sold each year in the United States is purchased between September 15 and November 10?

Halloween Delights Cookbook

A Collection of Halloween Recipes
Cookbook Delights Series

Cookies

Table of Contents

Black Cat Cookies

These butter cookies are very good to eat and fun to decorate for your Halloween party.

Ingredients:

  1   c. butter (no substitutes), softened
  2   c. sugar
  2   eggs
  3   tsp. vanilla extract
  3   c. all-purpose flour
  1   c. baking cocoa
  ½   tsp. baking powder
  ½   tsp. baking soda
  ½   tsp. salt
  24 wooden craft or Popsicle sticks
  48 candy corn candies
  24 red-hot candies

Directions:

1. Preheat oven to 350 degrees F.
2. Lightly grease baking sheets and set aside. (Do not use air-cushion baking sheets on these cookies for best results.)
3. In mixing bowl cream butter and sugar.
4. Beat in eggs and vanilla.
5. In separate bowl combine flour, cocoa, baking powder, soda, and salt; gradually add to creamed mixture.
6. Using hands, roll dough into twenty-four 1½-inch balls.
7. Place balls 3 inches apart on baking sheets.
8. Insert wooden stick into each cookie (perpendicular to baking sheet).
9. Flatten cookie with glass dipped in sugar. (Do not mash so flat and thin that cookie will not hold stick properly. This should be a sturdy cookie.)
10. Pinch top edge of cookie to form ears, smoothing as needed.
11. For whiskers press tines of fork once into each side of cookie.

12. Bake for 10 to 12 minutes or until cookies are set.
13. Remove from oven.
14. Immediately press candy corn for eyes and red-hot candy for nose onto each cookie.
15. Remove to wire racks to cool.

Yields: 24 cookies.

Bewitched Crispies

Children of all ages will enjoy these chocolate-drizzled crisp cereal bars.

Ingredients:

½ c. butter, melted
2   pkg. regular-size marshmallows (10 oz. each)
3   drops orange food color
10 c. crisp rice cereal
½ c. real semisweet chocolate chips
1   tsp. shortening

Directions:
1. Lightly butter 15 x 10 x 1-inch jellyroll pan; set aside.
2. Melt ½ cup butter in 6-quart saucepan over low heat, 1 to 2 minutes.
3. Add marshmallows and food color; stir until melted, 2 to 3 minutes.
4. Add cereal; mix lightly until well coated.
5. Pat cereal mixture evenly into prepared pan.
6. Melt chocolate chips and butter in 1-quart saucepan over low heat, stirring occasionally, until smooth, 2 to 4 minutes.
7. Drizzle chocolate over bars.
8. Let stand until set, about 30 minutes.

Yields: 48 bars.

Black Widow Bars

These are easy-to-make, delicious bars to enjoy. They also freeze well, so you can make extra.

Ingredients for bars:

¼	c. unsalted butter, melted and hot
¼	c. peanut butter, preferably chunky
1	c. dark brown sugar, packed
3	lg. eggs
2	tsp. vanilla extract
1⅓	c. all-purpose flour
½	tsp. baking powder
1	c. semisweet chocolate chips, coarsely chopped

Ingredients for frosting:

½	c. unsalted butter, melted and hot
1	c. semisweet chocolate chips
2⅔	c. confectioners' sugar, divided
¾	c. dark chocolate syrup
¼	c. plus 1 Tbs. milk, divided

Directions for bars:

1. Heat oven to 350 degrees F.
2. Very lightly grease bottom of 9-inch round baking pan.
3. Line bottom with parchment or wax paper.
4. In heatproof mixing bowl whisk together melted butter and peanut butter until smooth.
5. Add brown sugar, eggs, and vanilla, whisking until smooth.
6. Add flour and baking powder; stir with spoon until moistened.
7. Stir in 1 cup chopped chocolate chips and scrape bowl well.
8. Spoon into prepared pan and bake for 25 to 30 minutes, just until tester inserted in center comes out clean.
9. Cool 15 minutes in pan.
10. Run knife around pan edge to loosen.

11. Turn onto cake plate and remove paper.
12. Cool 30 minutes before frosting.

Directions for frosting:

1. In 4-cup heatproof bowl combine hot melted butter and semisweet chips.
2. Stir continuously until chocolate melts and mixture is smooth.
3. Add 1 cup confectioners' sugar and ¼ cup chocolate syrup; stir until combined. (Mixture will thicken and become stiff.)
4. Add another cup confectioners' sugar, ¼ cup milk, and ¼ cup chocolate syrup; stir until smooth.
5. Allow frosting to stand 2 minutes.
6. Add remaining ¼ cup chocolate syrup, adjusting if too stiff. (Frosting should appear smooth and satiny.)
7. Frost top and sides of cake; set aside.
8. Work quickly to make web decoration; do not allow fudge frosting to dry.
9. For web decoration: In small bowl combine ⅔ cup confectioners' sugar, and 1 tablespoon milk.
10. Stir until smooth, adding milk until a slightly runny glaze forms.
11. Spoon into small decorating bag fitted with round writing tip. (Alternatively, pour glaze into small plastic bag and snip off corner to create a tip.)
12. Starting in center of cake using white glaze, pipe circles on top ½ inch apart.
13. Using cake tester or toothpick, lightly drag lines through frosting from outer edges to center, about 1 inch apart.
14. Decorate with spiders and cut into small wedges.
15. Store at room temperature.
16. Tip: For an enhanced chunky texture, add ½ cup chopped nuts to bar base before baking.

Yields: 20 servings.

Brain Cookies with Blood Glaze

This makes another strange-looking decoration, perfect for your Halloween party.

Ingredients for cookies:

- 2   sticks unsalted butter, softened
- 1   c. sugar
- 3   c. all-purpose flour
- ½   tsp. baking soda
- ½   tsp. salt
- 2   lg. eggs
- 1   c. walnuts or pecans, very finely chopped
- 1   tsp. vanilla extract
-    about 5 drops red food coloring
-    about 9 drops blue food coloring

Ingredients for glaze:

- 2   c. confectioners' sugar
- 35   drops red food coloring

Directions for cookies:

1. Preheat oven to 350 degrees F.
2. Line 2 large baking sheets with parchment paper and set aside.
3. In large bowl cream together butter and sugar.
4. In separate bowl sift together flour, baking soda, and salt.
5. Alternating with eggs, add flour mixture to butter mixture, beating well after each addition.
6. Fold in nuts, vanilla, and red and blue food coloring, being careful not to overmix dough. (The food coloring will make dough a grayish color, resembling the color of brains.)
7. Place dough in batches in a potato ricer and push out onto prepared baking sheets in long tubes of dough.
8. With your fingers, loosely pat and arrange dough strands into clumps resembling brains, pushing to form 2 hemispheres and shaping into a walnut-like shape.

9. Bake until golden brown on the bottom, 12 to 14 minutes.
10. Remove from oven and transfer to wire rack to cool.

Directions for glaze:
1. In small bowl combine confectioners' sugar with food coloring to make a thick glaze, whisking together.
2. Drizzle "blood" onto cookies, and serve either warm or at room temperature.

Cat Poop Cookies

This is a pretty disgusting method of serving your cookies, but it makes a great party conversation piece.

Ingredients:
½ c. honey
⅔ c. butter
1   egg
2   c. all-purpose flour
⅓ c. baking cocoa (may use ½ c.)
1   tsp. vanilla extract
    crunchy nugget cereal

Directions:
1. Microwave honey on high until bubbly, about 1 minute.
2. Add butter; mix.
3. Add egg and mix well.
4. Mix in all other ingredients except cereal.
5. Chill 1 hour in freezer or several hours in refrigerator.
6. Preheat oven to 350 degrees F.
7. Roll dough into assorted shapes of cat poop.
8. Roll in cereal.
9. Bake for 10 to 15 minutes.
10. Serve in new litter box on a bed of crunchy nugget cereal.
11. Use a new litter scoop to remove.

Candy Corn Cookies

Enjoy these candy-corn butter cookies for Halloween.

Ingredients for butter cookies:

- ¾ c. butter, softened
- ¼ c. sugar
- ¼ c. packed light brown sugar
- 1 egg yolk
- 1¾ c. all-purpose flour
- ¾ tsp. baking powder
- ⅛ tsp. salt

Ingredients for glaze:

- 4 c. confectioners' sugar
- 4 Tbs. milk, plus extra for proper consistency
   yellow and orange food coloring

Directions for cookies:

1. Combine butter, sugar, brown sugar, and egg yolk in medium bowl.
2. Add flour, baking powder, and salt; mix well.
3. Cover; refrigerate about 4 hours or until firm.
4. Preheat oven to 350 degrees F.
5. Roll dough on floured surface to ¼-inch thickness.
6. Cut out 3-inch candy corn shapes from dough.
7. Place cutouts on ungreased cookie sheets.
8. Bake 8 to 10 minutes or until edges are lightly browned.
9. Remove to wire racks to cool completely.

Directions for glaze:

1. Combine confectioners' sugar and milk.
2. Add 1 to 2 tablespoons more milk as needed to make medium-thick, pourable glaze.
3. Divide glaze into thirds; place in separate small bowls.
4. Tint ⅓ glaze with yellow food coloring and ⅓ with orange food coloring; leave remaining glaze white.
5. Place racks of cookies over wax-paper-lined baking sheets.
6. Spoon glazes over cookies to resemble candy corn.
7. Let stand until glaze is set.

Creepy Witches' Fingers

You will scare everyone with these creepy cookies.

Ingredients:
- 1 c. butter, softened
- 1 c. confectioners' sugar
- 1 egg
- 1 tsp. almond extract
- 1 tsp. vanilla extract
- 2⅔ c. all-purpose flour
- 1 tsp. baking powder
- 1 tsp. salt
- ¾ c. whole blanched almonds
- 1 tube red decorator gel

Directions:
1. Preheat oven to 325 degrees F.
2. In bowl beat together butter, sugar, egg, almond extract, and vanilla.
3. Beat in flour, baking powder, and salt.
4. Cover and refrigerate 30 minutes.
5. Working with ¼ of dough at a time and keeping remainder refrigerated, roll heaping teaspoonful of dough into finger shape for each cookie.
6. Press almond firmly into one end for nail.
7. Squeeze in center to create knuckle shape.
8. Using paring knife, make slashes in several places to form knuckle.
9. Place on lightly greased baking sheets; bake for 20 to 25 minutes or until pale golden.
10. Let cool for 3 minutes.
11. Lift up almond, squeeze red decorator gel onto nail bed, and press almond back in place so gel oozes out from underneath. (May also make slashes in finger and fill with "blood.")
12. Remove from baking sheets and let cool on racks.
13. Repeat with remaining dough.

Yields: 5 dozen.

Cyclops Cookies

My children always enjoyed imagining what a Cyclops might look like.
This recipe gives them a chance to make them according to their imagination.

Ingredients:

- ½ c. butter
- ½ c. peanut butter
- ½ c. sugar
- ½ c. packed brown sugar
- 1 egg
- 2 Tbs. milk
- 1 tsp. vanilla extract
- 1¾ c. all-purpose flour
- 1 tsp. baking powder
- ¼ tsp. salt
- ⅛ tsp. baking soda
- ⅓ c. sugar for decoration
- 48 milk chocolate candy kisses, unwrapped

Directions:

1. In large mixer bowl beat butter and peanut butter with electric mixer on medium speed for about 30 seconds.
2. Add ½ cup of sugar and the brown sugar; beat until fluffy.
3. Add egg, milk, and vanilla and beat well.
4. In medium mixing bowl stir together flour, baking powder, salt, and baking soda.
5. With mixer on low speed, gradually add flour mixture to peanut butter mixture.
6. Beat until well combined.
7. Cover and chill dough for 1 hour.
8. Preheat oven to 375 degrees F.
9. Shape dough into 1-inch balls.
10. Roll balls in additional sugar.
11. Place about 2 inches apart on ungreased cookie sheets.
12. Bake for 10 to 12 minutes or until edges are firm.
13. Immediately press a chocolate kiss atop each cookie.
14. Transfer cookies to cooling rack and let cool.

Yields: 24 cookies.

Disappearing Ghost Cookies

Enjoy making these cookies, and you will see how they earned their name.

Ingredients:

- ½ c. firmly packed brown sugar
- ½ c. butter, softened
- ¼ c. sugar
- 1 lg. egg
- 1 tsp. vanilla extract
- 1 c. all-purpose flour
- ½ tsp. baking soda
- ¼ tsp. salt
- 1 c. uncooked old-fashioned oats
- 1 c. mini real semisweet chocolate chips
- 15 regular-size marshmallows, cut in half
- 1¼ c. hot fudge ice cream topping
- Halloween decorator candies

Directions:

1. Preheat oven to 375 degrees F.
2. Combine brown sugar, butter, and sugar in large bowl.
3. Beat at medium speed, scraping bowl often, until creamy.
4. Add egg and vanilla; continue beating until well mixed.
5. Reduce speed to low; add flour, baking soda, and salt.
6. Beat, scraping bowl often, until well mixed.
7. Stir in oats and chocolate chips by hand.
8. Drop dough by rounded teaspoonfuls, 2 inches apart, onto ungreased cookie sheets; flatten in criss-cross pattern with fork.
9. Bake for 6 to 7 minutes or until lightly browned.
10. Immediately place 1 marshmallow half onto each cookie.
11. Continue baking for 1 to 2 minutes or until marshmallow is slightly puffed.
12. Cool completely.
13. Top each cookie with 2 teaspoons hot fudge; decorate with candies as desired.

Yields: 2½ dozen cookies.

Fossilized Egg Nest Chewies

Youngsters will love discovering dinosaurs in these great cookies.

Ingredients:

- ½ lb. butter (2 sticks), softened
- 1 c. firmly packed brown sugar
- 2 lg. eggs
- 1 tsp. vanilla extract
- 2 c. quick or old-fashioned oats, uncooked
- 1½ c. all-purpose flour
- 1 tsp. baking soda
- ½ tsp. salt
- 1 c. sweetened flaked coconut
- 1 c. toffee baking bits
- 1 c. semisweet chocolate mini morsels
- 1 c. yogurt-covered raisins
- 36 gummy dinosaur candies

Directions:

1. Preheat oven to 350 degrees F.
2. In large bowl beat butter and sugar with electric mixer until creamy.
3. Add eggs and vanilla; beat well.
4. Add combined oats, flour, baking soda, and salt; mix well.
5. Stir in coconut, toffee bits, and mini chocolate morsels; mix well.
6. Drop heaping tablespoons of dough 2 inches apart on ungreased cookie sheets.
7. Gently press 3 yogurt-covered raisins into top of each cookie.
8. Bake 10 to 12 minutes or until golden brown. (Cookies should be soft in center.)
9. Cool 1 minute on cookie sheets; remove to wire racks.
10. Immediately press gummy dinosaurs into top of each cookie.
11. Cool completely; store tightly covered.
12. Note: If using old-fashioned oats, add 2 tablespoons additional flour.

Yields: 3 dozen.

Glowing Jack-O'-Lantern Cookies

These cookies are fun to make and decorate into happy or scary jack-o'-lanterns.

Ingredients:

 2   c. all-purpose flour
 2   tsp. baking powder
 ¼   tsp. salt
 ½   c. butter
 1   c. sugar
 1   lg. egg
 1   tsp. vanilla extract
 1   Tbs. milk
 1   pkg. lemon drop candy (5.5 oz.), crushed
     orange and green food coloring

Directions:

1. Preheat oven to 350 degrees F.
2. Cover 3 baking sheets with foil; set aside.
3. In medium bowl combine flour, baking powder, and salt, mixing well, set aside.
4. Cream butter and sugar together until light and fluffy.
5. Add egg and vanilla and mix well.
6. Stir in flour mixture.
7. Add milk if batter is too stiff.
8. Tint all but ⅛ of dough orange; tint remaining dough green.
9. Roll 1-inch balls from orange dough, and flatten with bottom of sugar-coated glass.
10. Roll stems out of green dough and attach to top of "pumpkin."
11. Carefully cut out wide spaces for eyes, nose, and mouth with sharp knife.
12. Fill holes in with crushed lemon candy. (Candy will melt when baked.)
13. Bake 8 to 10 minutes or until done. (Do not allow to brown.)
14. Allow to cool for 10 minutes, and carefully peel off foil.
15. Tip: Crush lemon drops in food processor with a little confectioners' sugar.

Halloween Cookie Pizza

This makes a fun and delicious cookie pizza.

Ingredients for cookie:

- ¾ c. packed brown sugar
- ½ c. butter, softened
- 1 lg. egg
- 1 Tbs. water
- 1 tsp. vanilla extract
- 1¼ c. all-purpose flour
- ½ tsp. baking soda
- ¼ tsp. salt
- 1 c. peanut butter chips
- 1 c. miniature marshmallows
- ¾ c. semisweet chocolate chips
- 1 c. chopped pecans

Ingredients for chocolate drizzle:

- ¼ c. semisweet chocolate chips
- 1½ Tbs. shortening (no substitutes)

Ingredients for orange drizzle:

- ½ c. confectioners' sugar
- 1 Tbs. water
- 3 drops yellow food coloring
- 2 drops red food coloring

Directions for cookie:

1. Preheat oven to 350 degrees F.
2. Lightly grease 12-inch round pizza pan; set aside.
3. In large bowl beat sugar and butter until creamy.
4. Add egg, water, and vanilla and beat well.
5. In separate bowl combine flour, baking soda, and salt; add to sugar mixture, beating on low speed until blended.
6. Stir in peanut butter chips.

7. Spread batter in prepared pan to within ½ inch of edge.
8. Bake 11 to 13 minutes or until set.
9. Remove from oven.
10. Sprinkle marshmallows, chocolate chips, and pecans over top.
11. Return to oven; bake 5 to 7 minutes or until marshmallows are lightly browned.
12. Cool completely.

Directions for drizzles:
1. Melt chocolate drizzle ingredients together and drizzle over top of cookie pizza.
2. Blend orange drizzle ingredients, and drizzle over the chocolate.
3. Let stand 1 hour until topping is set.
4. Cut into wedges.

Yields: 16 to 20 servings.

Did You Know? . . . .

Did you know that until the 1990s Irish children said, "Help the Halloween Party," but are now more inclined to use the American "Trick or treat" due to the influence of American popular culture, movies, and television?

Did You Know? . . . .

Did you know that David Bowman of Great Britain grows two million pumpkins a year, and that Spalding, the town where he lives, claims to be the pumpkin capital of Britain?

Halloween Molasses Cut-Outs

Molasses cookies are always flavorful and a perfect match for Halloween.

Ingredients for cookies:

½ c. butter, softened
½ c. sugar
½ c. molasses
1 lg. egg
1½ tsp. white distilled vinegar
2½ c. all-purpose flour
1 tsp. baking soda
½ tsp. ground cinnamon
½ tsp. ground ginger
¼ tsp. ground nutmeg

Ingredients for frosting:

4 c. confectioners' sugar
½ c. butter, softened
2 tsp. vanilla extract
3-4 Tbs. milk
   decorator sugars

Directions for cookies:

1. Combine butter, sugar, molasses, egg, and vinegar in large bowl.
2. Beat at medium speed, scraping bowl often, until creamy.
3. Reduce speed to low; add all remaining ingredients.
4. Beat, scraping bowl often, until well mixed.
5. Divide dough into thirds; wrap in plastic food wrap.
6. Refrigerate until firm for 2 hours or overnight.
7. Preheat oven to 350 degrees F.
8. Roll out dough on surface lightly covered with equal mixture of flour and sugar, one portion at a time (keeping remaining dough refrigerated), to ¼-inch thickness.
9. Cut with assorted 2- to 3-inch cookie cutters.

10. Place 1 inch apart onto ungreased cookie sheets.
11. Bake for 8 to 10 minutes or until no indention remains when touched.
12. Let stand 1 minute; cool completely.

Directions for frosting:

1. Combine confectioners' sugar, butter, and vanilla in small mixer bowl.
2. Beat at low speed, scraping bowl often and gradually adding enough milk for desired spreading consistency.
3. Decorate cooled cookies with frosting and decorator sugars as desired.

Creepy Crisp Crunchies

These easy-to-make bars will help decorate your Halloween meal.

Ingredients:

3 Tbs. butter
4 c. miniature marshmallows or 10 oz. large marshmallows, about 40
6 c. crisp rice cereal
6 oz. orange and brown Halloween candy-coated chocolate pieces

Directions:

1. Melt butter in large saucepan over low heat.
2. Add marshmallows and stir until completely melted; remove from heat.
3. Add cereal and stir until well coated.
4. Add candy and stir until candy is evenly mixed.
5. Spray 13 x 9 x 2-inch pan with nonstick cooking spray or line with wax paper.
6. Using buttered spatula or wax paper, press mixture evenly into pan.
7. When cool, cut into squares.

Halloween Spiced and Iced
Pumpkin Cookies

Here is a pumpkin-flavored treat that you can keep in the cookie jar. Have this popular recipe on hand from October through Christmas for all of your holiday well-wishers.

Ingredients for cookies:

1   c. butter, softened
½   c. sugar
½   c. packed brown sugar
¾   tsp. ground cinnamon
¼   tsp. ground nutmeg
¼   tsp. ground allspice
¼   tsp. ground cloves
½   tsp. baking powder
¼   tsp. baking soda
1   lg. egg
1   c. canned pumpkin
2   c. all-purpose flour

Ingredients for brown sugar glaze:

½   c. packed brown sugar
3   Tbs. butter
1   Tbs. milk
1   c. sifted confectioners' sugar
1   tsp. vanilla extract

Directions for cookies:

1. Preheat oven to 375 degrees F.
2. In medium mixing bowl beat butter with electric mixer on medium to high speed for 30 seconds.
3. Add sugar, brown sugar, spices, baking powder, and baking soda.
4. Beat until combined, scraping sides of bowl.
5. Beat in egg and pumpkin.
6. Beat in as much of the flour as you can with the mixer; stir in remaining flour.

7. Drop dough by rounded teaspoonfuls 2 inches apart onto ungreased cookie sheet.
8. Bake for 8 to 10 minutes or until tops seem firm.
9. Transfer cookies to wire rack; cool.

Directions for brown sugar glaze:
1. In small saucepan combine brown sugar, butter, and milk.
2. Heat and stir until butter melts.
3. Remove saucepan from heat.
4. Stir in confectioners' sugar and vanilla.
5. Spread cooled cookies with glaze.

Yields: 42 cookies.

Brittle Meringue Bones

These meringue bones are fun to make and perfectly edible.

Ingredients:
3   lg. egg whites
¼   tsp. cream of tartar
⅛   tsp. salt
⅔   c. sugar
½   tsp. vanilla extract

Directions:
1. Preheat oven to 200 degrees F.
2. Line cookie sheets with brown paper bag or parchment.
3. In medium-size bowl at high speed, beat egg whites, cream of tartar, and salt until fluffy.
4. Gradually beat in sugar; add vanilla.
5. Place in pastry bag fitted with medium plain piping tip.
6. Pipe 3-inch bone shapes onto parchment or brown paper bag.
7. Bake 1 hour until set.
8. Turn off oven; dry in oven 1 hour.

Yields: 4 to 5 dozen small bones.

Happy Pumpkin Faces

Have fun making these happy pumpkin faces, and you will enjoy eating them, too.

Ingredients for cookies:

    2   c. all-purpose flour
    1   tsp. baking soda
    ¼   tsp. salt
    ½   tsp. ground cinnamon
    2   c. packed brown sugar
    1   c. butter
    2   lg. eggs
    2   c. quick-cooking oats
    1   c. plain candy-coated chocolate pieces
    2   c. vanilla frosting (recipe follows)
        food coloring
        plain candy-coated chocolate pieces (harvest colors)

Ingredients for frosting:

    4   c. confectioners' sugar
    ½   c. butter, softened
    2   tsp. vanilla extract
    3-4 Tbs. milk

Directions for cookies:

 1. Preheat oven to 350 degrees F.
 2. In medium bowl combine flour, baking soda, salt, and cinnamon, mixing well; set aside.
 3. In large mixing bowl cream sugar and butter together until lightly fluffy.
 4. Add eggs and beat well.
 5. Stir in flour mixture until just mixed.
 6. Fold in oats and candy-coated chocolate pieces.
 7. Roll heaping tablespoonfuls of dough into balls and place about 3 inches apart on nonstick baking sheets.
 8. Press dough into shape of a pumpkin.
 9. Add a bit of dough for stem.
10. Bake 12 to 14 minutes or until lightly browned.
11. Transfer to wire racks to cool completely.

Directions for frosting:

1. Combine confectioners' sugar, butter, and vanilla in small mixer bowl.
2. Beat at low speed, scraping bowl often and gradually adding enough milk for desired spreading consistency.
3. Tint with food coloring if desired.
4. Spread frosting on cookies, and decorate with harvest-colored candy-coated chocolate pieces for eyes and smile.

Yields: About 3 dozen cookies.

Creepy Crawly Spider Cookies

These cookies are easy to make and very delicious.

Ingredients:

2 c. semisweet chocolate chips (12 oz.), divided
½ c. crisp rice cereal
¼ c. sweetened shredded coconut
1½ c. chow mein noodles
1 small tube decorator frosting (optional)

Directions:

1. Place 1 cup chocolate chips in 2- to 4-cup glass measure.
2. Heat on high in microwave for 1 minute.
3. Remove, stir, and heat on high for 1 minute.
4. Let sit for 1 minute and stir until chips are melted. (Or heat chocolate chips in heavy saucepan over low heat until melted.)
5. Mix in cereal and coconut.
6. Drop by teaspoonfuls onto wax paper for spider bodies.
7. Melt second cup of chocolate chips.
8. Gently stir in chow mein noodles, being careful not to break noodles up.
9. Pick noodles out one by one and attach them to spider bodies for legs (8 to a spider).
10. Add dots of frosting for eyes if desired.
11. Leftover chocolate noodles can be spooned onto wax paper for additional treats.

Yields: 36 cookies.

Jack-O'-Lantern Brownie

This jack-o'-lantern is fun to make. Serve for a Halloween chocolate treat.

Ingredients for brownie:

 ¾ c. butter, melted
 1½ c. sugar
 1½ tsp. vanilla extract
 3 lg. eggs
 ¾ c. all-purpose flour
 ½ c. baking cocoa
 ½ tsp. baking powder
 ¼ tsp. salt
  vanilla frosting (recipe follows)
  garnishes of your choice

Ingredients for vanilla frosting:

 4 c. confectioners' sugar
 ½ c. butter, softened
 2 tsp. vanilla extract
 3-4 Tbs. milk
  yellow and red food color

Directions for brownie:

1. Preheat oven to 350 degrees F.
2. Grease 12-inch round pizza pan. (If using disposable pan, place on baking sheet to bake.
3. Beat melted butter, sugar, and vanilla with spoon in large bowl.
4. Beat in eggs.
5. Stir in dry ingredients; beat with spoon until well blended.
6. Spread into pan.
7. Bake 20 to 22 minutes or until top springs back when touched lightly in center.
8. Cool completely.

Directions for frosting:

1. Combine confectioners' sugar, butter, and vanilla in small mixer bowl.

2. Beat at low speed, scraping bowl often and gradually adding enough milk for desired spreading consistency.
3. Add yellow and red food color to frosting for desired shade of orange.
4. Frost brownie; garnish to resemble a jack-o'-lantern.

Yields: 12 to 16 servings.

Halloween Crisp Candy Corn Treats

Kids will love these easy-to-make cereal treats.

Ingredients:
- 10 c. crisp rice cereal
- 2 c. mixture of candy corn and Indian candy corn
- ¾ c. miniature chocolate chips
- ½ c. butter
- 9 c. miniature marshmallows
- candy pumpkins
- orange food coloring

Directions:
1. Butter 15 × 10 × 1-inch jellyroll pan; set aside.
2. In large bowl, mix rice cereal, candy corn and chocolate chips together.
3. In large saucepan melt butter and marshmallows over medium-low heat, stirring constantly until smooth.
4. Remove from heat and add 3 or 4 drops food coloring; mix until well blended.
5. Add marshmallow mixture to cereal mixture; stir quickly to combine.
6. Turn onto prepared jellyroll pan; place piece of wax paper or plastic wrap the length of the pan over mixture, and press mixture evenly into pan.
7. While warm, press on candy pumpkins spaced 1½ to 2 inches apart.
8. When firm, cut into squares.

Yields: About 4 dozen squares.

Petrifying Pumpkin Bars for a Crowd

This recipe is great for a large group, and they also freeze well.

Ingredients for bars:

- 2   c. all-purpose flour
- 2   tsp. baking powder
- 1   tsp. baking soda
- 2   c. sugar
- ½   tsp. salt
- 2   tsp. ground cinnamon
- 4   lg. eggs
- ½   c. corn oil
- ½   c. applesauce
- 2½   c. canned pumpkin
- 1½   c. chopped nuts

Ingredients for cream cheese frosting:

- 2   pkg. cream cheese (8 oz. each), softened
- ½   c. butter, softened
- 1   tsp. vanilla extract
- 2   c. sifted confectioners' sugar

Directions for bars:

1. Preheat oven to 350 degrees F.
2. Combine dry ingredients.
3. Add eggs, oil, applesauce, and pumpkin; blend well.
4. Stir in nuts.
5. Divide batter into two 13 x 9 x 2-inch ungreased pans.
6. Bake 20 to 25 minutes; cool.
7. Frost with cream cheese frosting if desired.

Directions for cream cheese frosting:

1. In medium bowl cream together cream cheese and butter.
2. Mix in vanilla, then gradually stir in confectioners' sugar.
3. Store in refrigerator after use.

Blackberry Blackheads

These thumbprint cookies are delicious. Make extra, because they will disappear quickly.

Ingredients:

- ½ lb. butter, room temperature
- ⅔ c. sugar
- 2 egg whites
- 4 c. all-purpose flour
- 1 Tbs. butter, room temperature
  blackberry jam with seeds

Directions:

1. Preheat oven to 325 degrees F.
2. Beat ½ pound butter until creamy.
3. Add sugar a little at a time until all sugar has been used.
4. Add egg whites and flour to butter and sugar mixture; beat until dough is well blended.
5. Dip pastry brush into the tablespoon of butter and lightly brush a very thin layer onto cookie sheet.
6. With clean hands roll dough into golf-ball-size balls.
7. Flatten balls slightly, and, using your thumb, press a dime-size dent into middle of each one.
8. Place cookies dent side up about 1 inch apart on cookie sheet.
9. Bake about 12 minutes or until slightly browned.
10. Allow cookies to cool on cookie sheet for a few minutes before moving to wire rack with spatula.
11. When cookies are completely cooled, use small spoon to fill dent in each cookie with jam.

Yields: About 3½ dozen blackheads.

The Purr-fect Treat

These cookies are to be decorated to look like a cat. Have fun decorating.

Ingredients for cookies:

⅓	c. butter, softened
⅓	c. vegetable shortening
1¾	c. all-purpose flour
¾	c. sugar
1½	c. baking cocoa
1	lg. egg
2	Tbs. milk
½	tsp. finely shredded orange peel
3	tsp. orange juice
1	tsp. baking powder
2	tsp. vanilla extract
	orange icing (recipe follows)

Ingredients for orange icing:

1	c. sifted confectioners' sugar
¼	tsp. vanilla extract
2-3	tsp. orange juice
	orange food color (or a combination of red and yellow)

Directions for cookies:

1. Preheat oven to 375 degrees F.
2. In large mixing bowl, beat shortening and butter with electric mixer on medium to high speed 30 seconds or until softened.
3. Add half the flour, the sugar, cocoa, egg, milk, orange peel and juice, baking powder, and vanilla.
4. Beat until combined, scraping bowl occasionally.
5. Beat or stir in remaining flour.
6. Divide in half.
7. Cover; chill for 1 to 2 hours or until easy to handle.

8. On lightly floured surface, roll each dough portion to ⅛-inch thickness.
9. Using cat-shaped cutter, cut into shapes.
10. Place shapes 1 inch apart on ungreased cookie sheet.
11. Bake for 7 to 9 minutes or until edges are firm and bottoms are light brown.
12. Remove cookies; cool thoroughly on wire rack.
13. Decorate cats with orange icing.

Directions for orange icing:
1. In small mixing bowl stir together confectioners' sugar, vanilla extract, and enough orange juice to make piping consistency.
2. Stir in enough orange food coloring to color icing orange.
3. Place icing in small, sealed plastic bag with small hole snipped in one corner or in pastry bag fitted with small round tip.
4. Decorate cookies as desired.

Yields: About 5 dozen 2- to 3-inch cookies.

Did You Know? . . . .

Did you know that of the domestically marketed pumpkins in the U.S., 99 percent are used for jack-o'-lanterns?

Did You Know? . . . .

Did you know that the first Halloween card was made in the early 1900s, and now U.S. consumers spend around $50 million on Halloween greetings?

Witches' Hats

This chocolate cookie, shaped like a witch's hat, will be bewitching on a Halloween cookie tray for your holiday-themed meal or party.

Ingredients:

- ¾ c. butter, softened
- ½ c. sugar
- ½ c. firmly packed brown sugar
- 1 lg. egg
- 1 tsp. vanilla extract
- 1¾ c. all-purpose flour
- 1 tsp. baking soda
- ¼ tsp. salt
- 4 sq. unsweetened baking chocolate (1 oz. each), melted and cooled slightly
- ½ c. chocolate decors or sugar
- 48 milk chocolate candy kisses

Directions:

1. Combine butter, sugar, and brown sugar in large bowl.
2. Beat at medium speed, scraping bowl often, until creamy.
3. Add egg and vanilla; continue beating until well mixed.
4. Reduce speed to low; add flour, baking soda, and salt.
5. Beat until well mixed.
6. Divide dough in half; wrap in plastic food wrap.
7. Refrigerate until firm, about 2 hours.
8. Preheat oven to 375 degrees F.
9. Roll teaspoonfuls of dough into 1-inch balls.
10. Place 2 inches apart onto ungreased cookie sheets.
11. Press balls to about ⅛ inch thick with glass dipped in sugar; sprinkle with chocolate decors.
12. Bake for 7 to 9 minutes or until set and cookies just begin to crack.
13. Immediately press 1 chocolate kiss in center of each cookie.
14. Cool 1 minute; remove from cookie sheets.
15. Cool completely.

Yields: 4 dozen cookies.

Halloween Delights Cookbook
A Collection of Halloween Recipes
Cookbook Delights Series

Desserts

Table of Contents

Baked Apples with Dragon Droppings

Baked apples are best served warm but are also good cold for breakfast. Serve with sweetened whipped cream or your favorite vanilla ice cream.

Ingredients:

- 4 cooking apples, medium size
- 4 Tbs. water
- 2 oz. butter
-    raisins for decoration
-    Sweetened Whipped Cream (recipe page 193)
-    sugar to taste

Directions:

1. Preheat oven to 350 degrees F.
2. Wipe and core apples, then peel off top ⅓ of skin.
3. Arrange apples in ovenproof dish, and add the water around them.
4. Fill apple cavities with sugar, and then add a chunk of butter on top.
5. Place dish in preheated oven, and cook for about 35 to 40 minutes or until apples are soft.
6. Serve apples topped with whipped cream and a sprinkling of raisins (dragon droppings).

Yields: 4 servings.

Chocolate Slime

Despite its name, this is great for dipping and tastes delicious.

Ingredients:

- 8 bars white baking chocolate (2 oz. each)
- 2 Tbs. heavy cream
-    green food coloring

bananas, sliced into 1-inch rounds
red or green apples, rinsed, cored, and sliced
oranges, peeled and divided into sections
pineapple, cut into large chunks
red and green grapes, rinsed and removed from stem
bite-size chunks of angel food cake

Directions:

1. In medium-size, microwave-safe bowl melt chocolate, uncovered, in microwave on medium-high heat for 1 minute.
2. Stir and microwave for 10- to 20-second intervals until smooth; do not overcook.
3. Add cream and food coloring to desired slime color and stir thoroughly.
4. Keep warm in double boiler or fondue pot and present with fresh fruits and cake.

Campfire Cooked Apples

A delicious and simple campfire treat, this is fun to serve as a holiday treat.

Ingredients:

one apple per person
light brown sugar

Directions:

1. Cut core out of apples.
2. Place each apple on piece of aluminum foil.
3. Fill empty core cavity with brown sugar.
4. Wrap apple in aluminum foil.
5. Place apples in campfire and cook for about 15 to 20 minutes until tender.
6. To cook at home: Preheat oven to 350 degrees F., place apples on cookie sheet, and bake for 15 to 20 minutes until tender.

Bleeding Human Heart

This is a great Halloween centerpiece for your holiday-themed meal. As your guests sip their coffee, unveil a glistening pink gelatin heart on a pedestal cake stand. Pull out a carving knife and stab it, causing dark, gooey blood to pour from the wound. Cut slices off the lobes of the heart and flip them onto dessert plates. Hold each portion under the oozing gash until it is nicely sauced with gore, and then add a dollop of whipped cream and serve.

Ingredients:

4	boxes (3 oz. each) or 2 boxes (6 oz. each) of peach (pink; think of lung tissue) or strawberry (redder; think of livers and hearts) gelatin dessert mix
4	env. unflavored gelatin
4	c. boiling water
1	can unsweetened evaporated milk (12 oz.)
1	c. light corn syrup
½	c. grenadine syrup
1	sm. bottle red food coloring (0.3 fl. oz.)
3	drops blue food coloring
6½	c. heart-shaped gelatin mold or cake pan (or a human heart mold)
1	gallon-size, zip-closure food-storage bag

Directions:

1. Place packaged gelatin and unflavored gelatin in bowl, and pour boiling water over it, stirring constantly.
2. Cool to room temperature. (This is very important or the next step may present problems.)
3. Stir in evaporated milk.
4. Pour enough mixture into mold to cover bottom (this will be the top when served) with a layer about ½-inch thick; refrigerate until it gels firmly.
5. Prepare a nice bladder of blood by stirring together corn syrup, grenadine, and food colorings.

6. For the bladder (the bag that keeps the blood together inside the mass of gelatin), take the gallon-size food-storage bag and turn it inside out.
7. Pour the blood mixture into one corner of the bag, and twist it closed so that no air bubble is caught between the sauce and the twist.
8. Tie a knot in the twisted plastic.
9. Adjust position of knot so that when bag lies on counter it is about 1½ to 2 inches high; tighten knot.
10. With a pair of scissors, snip off extra plastic outside knot.
11. When gelatin on bottom of mold is stiff and firm, position bladder of blood in mold with point of bag just inside point of heart.
12. Make sure there is at least ¾ inch of space between all sides of bag and sides of mold. (This will ensure that your guests do not see clues ahead of time.)
13. Pour in remaining gelatin until mold is as full as can be handled. (Do not worry if you see a little of the blood-bladder grazing the surface of the gelatin, as long as it does not project too much; the side you are looking at now will be the bottom when served.)
14. Refrigerate until gelled firmly to texture of fine, lean organ meat, about 4 hours.
15. To unmold put about 2½ inches of hot, but not boiling, water in sink.
16. Set mold in water so that water comes just below edge of mold for 15 to 20 seconds; the time depends on the thickness of the mold pan.
17. Remove mold from water, and run blade of knife around edge of gelatin.
18. Invert serving platter, ideally a white pedestal cake plate, on top and hold firmly in place.
19. Use both hands to turn over mold and plate.
20. Remove mold. (It may need to be tapped or slightly shaken to free gelatin.)

Presentation:
1. To serve use a nice, big psycho-style chef's knife and stab side of gelatin about ⅓ of the way up from pointed end of heart.

2. Twist knife slightly, and blood will start to ooze out.
3. Bare your teeth like a Marine jabbing with bayonet, and widen the wound.
4. When blood is coming at a good slip, grab a dessert plate (white is best for effect), and cut a slice from one of the lobes of the heart.
5. Flip it onto the plate, and drizzle it with blood by holding it under the edge of the pedestal.
6. Add whipped cream and serve.
7. Note: Be careful not to serve pieces of the food-storage bag to your guests. They could choke to death.

Black Halloween Fondue

This is popular with my children at Halloween and any time of year.

Ingredients:
    2   Tbs. light corn syrup
    ½   c. light cream
    9   oz. bar milk chocolate, broken
    ¼   c. pecans, finely chopped
    1   tsp. vanilla extract
        bite-size chunks of cake
        fruits and/or marshmallows

Directions:
1. Heat syrup and cream in microwave.
2. Add chocolate and stir until melted.
3. Mix in vanilla and pecans.
4. Place in fondue pot over flame and twirl in chocolate mixture.
5. Cool slightly before serving.

Did You Know? . . . .

Did you know that 82 percent of children and 67 percent of adults take part in Halloween festivities?

Flaming Fall Compote

Let jack-o'-lanterns and this dish briefly be the only light at the party to make a spooky entrance. Regular brandy or apricot brandy can be used in place of the apple brandy if desired. Serve this compote plain or on top of cake, ice cream, or oatmeal cookies.

Ingredients:

- 4   c. apple cider
- ¼   c. brown sugar
- 2   tsp. ground cinnamon
- 1   tsp. freshly grated nutmeg
- 1   pinch ground ginger
- 1   c. coarsely chopped, unsulphured dried apricots
- ½   c. dried figs
- 1   c. coarsely chopped prunes
- 1   c. dried cranberries
- 1   c. dried golden raisins
- 3   tart apples, peeled and cubed
- ⅓   c. apple brandy

Directions:

1. Bring apple cider to a boil in large, heavy saucepan.
2. Add sugar, cinnamon, nutmeg, and ginger; cook until sugar dissolves.
3. Add dried fruit and return to a boil.
4. Reduce heat and simmer for 15 minutes.
5. Add apples and cover; simmer for 10 minutes or until apples are tender.
6. Remove fruit and place in heat-tolerant serving dish.
7. Return cider to burner and return to a boil.
8. Boil uncovered for 5 to 7 minutes or until mixture thickens slightly.
9. Pour over fruit mixture.
10. Heat brandy in microwave or small saucepan until warm.
11. Carefully light and pour flaming brandy over compote.

Swirled Pumpkin and Caramel Cheesecake

The gingersnap and pecan crust adds wonderful texture and flavor to contrast with the pumpkin and caramel flavors in this delicious cheesecake.

Ingredients:

- 1½ c. ground gingersnap cookies
- 1½ c. toasted pecans
- ¼ c. firmly packed brown sugar
- ¼ c. unsalted butter, melted
- 4 pkg. cream cheese (8 oz. each), room temperature
- 1⅔ c. sugar
- 1½ c. canned pumpkin
- 9 Tbs. whipping cream, divided
- 1 tsp. ground cinnamon
- 1 tsp. ground allspice
- 4 lg. eggs
- 5 Tbs. caramel sauce
- 1 c. sour cream

Directions:

1. Preheat oven to 350 degrees F.
2. Finely grind crushed cookies, pecans, and brown sugar in processor.
3. Add melted butter and blend until combined.
4. Press crust mixture onto bottom and up sides of 9-inch springform pan with 2¾-inch-high sides.
5. Using electric mixer, beat cream cheese and sugar in large bowl until light.
6. Transfer ¾ cup mixture to small bowl; cover tightly and refrigerate to use for topping.
7. Add pumpkin, 4 tablespoons whipping cream, cinnamon, and allspice to mixture in large bowl, and beat until well combined.
8. Add eggs 1 at a time, beating just until combined.
9. Pour filling into crust (filling will almost fill pan).

10. Bake until cheesecake puffs, top browns, and center moves only slightly when pan is shaken, about 1 hour 15 minutes.
11. Transfer cheesecake to rack and cool 10 minutes.
12. Run small sharp knife around cake pan sides to loosen cheesecake; cool.
13. Cover tightly and refrigerate overnight.
14. Bring remaining ¾ cup cream cheese mixture to room temperature.
15. Add remaining 5 tablespoons whipping cream to cream cheese mixture and stir to combine.
16. Press down firmly on edges of cheesecake to even thickness.
17. Pour cream cheese mixture over cheesecake, spreading evenly.
18. Spoon caramel sauce in lines over cream cheese mixture.
19. Using tip of knife, swirl caramel sauce into cream cheese mixture. (Can be prepared 1 day ahead; cover and refrigerate.)
20. Release pan sides from cheesecake.
21. Spoon sour cream into pastry bag fitted with small star tip. (Do not stir before using.)
22. Pipe decorative border around cheesecake and serve.

Yields: 10 servings.

Sweetened Whipped Cream

This is a delicious topping on many desserts. Enjoy.

Ingredients:
    1   c. heavy cream
    ¼   c. sugar
    1   tsp. vanilla extract (or ½ tsp. extract, flavoring, or spice of choice)

Directions:
    1. For best results thoroughly chill cream, bowl, and beaters before whipping.
    2. Whip cream until almost stiff.
    3. Add sugar and vanilla; beat until cream holds peaks.
    4. Note: Do not overbeat or cream will separate.

Yields: About 2⅓ cups whipped cream.

Liposuctioned Lard

This dessert actually tastes good if you can get your guests to move past its name.

Ingredients:

    2   lg. eggs
    3   Tbs. sugar
    1½   c. milk
    ½   tsp. vanilla extract
    1½   c. mini marshmallows

Directions:

1. Beat eggs and sugar until well blended.
2. Add milk and vanilla; mix well.
3. Divide mixture evenly among 6 custard cups.
4. Place custard cups in large frying pan, and fill pan with water to about ½ inch from top of cups.
5. Place pan on medium heat, and bring water to a simmer.
6. Turn heat down to low, cover pan with lid, and continue to let water simmer for 10 minutes.
7. Turn off heat.
8. Carefully remove cups from water.
9. Allow custard to cool for 5 minutes.
10. Gently stir ¼ cup marshmallows (fat lumps) into each cup.
11. Make sure all the "fat" is covered with custard.
12. Refrigerate cups for 1 to 2 hours or until well chilled.

Yields: 6 servings.

Caramel Rum Fruit Dip

Caramel apples are popular on Halloween.

Ingredients:

    ½   c. butter
    1   pkg. caramels (14 oz.), unwrapped

¼ c. chopped pecans
1 Tbs. milk
1 tsp. rum extract
  fresh fruit, cut up

Directions:
1. Heat butter and caramels in 2-quart saucepan over low heat, stirring occasionally, until caramels are melted, 12 to 15 minutes.
2. Stir in pecans, milk, and rum extract.
3. Stir vigorously to incorporate butter; keep warm.
4. Use as a dip for cut-up fresh fruit.

Yields: 1½ cups.

Frozen Jack-O'-Lanterns

These are easy to make for a decorative ice cream dessert.

Ingredients:
12 navel oranges
12 cinnamon sticks
½ gal. dark chocolate ice cream

Directions:
1. Cut off tops of oranges.
2. Gently hollow out pulp (reserve for another use), leaving a thick shell; remove pulp from tops, also.
3. Carefully cut jack-o'-lantern faces into each orange.
4. Pack chocolate ice cream into shells; avoid letting ice cream come out of holes.
5. Cut center out of orange top.
6. Set tops back on over ice cream, and insert cinnamon stick stem through hole.
7. Place on baking sheet and freeze for a minimum of 3 hours or until serving time.

Yields: 12 servings.

Gingered Pumpkin Flan

My husband loves flan and this is a good one.

Ingredients:

- ¾ c. plus ⅓ c. sugar, divided
- ⅓ c. water
- 2 lg. eggs
- 4 lg. egg whites
- 1 c. canned, unseasoned pumpkin purée
- 1 tsp. grated fresh gingerroot
- 1 tsp. vanilla extract
- ¾ c. milk
- ¾ c. evaporated milk

Directions:

1. Preheat oven to 325 degrees F.
2. Put kettle of water on to heat for water bath.
3. In small, heavy saucepan combine ¾ cup sugar and ⅓ cup water.
4. Bring to simmer over low heat, stirring occasionally until sugar melts.
5. Increase heat to medium-high and cook, without stirring, until caramel turns amber, 5 to 7 minutes. (Watch so it does not burn.)
6. Carefully pour caramel into six ¾-cup ramekins, and tilt to coat insides evenly; set aside.
7. In mixing bowl whisk eggs, egg whites, and remaining ⅓ cup sugar until smooth.
8. Add pumpkin purée, ginger, and vanilla; whisk until smooth.
9. Stir in milk and evaporated milk.
10. Pour into prepared ramekins; skim off air bubbles.
11. Place folded kitchen towel in roasting pan; place ramekins on towel.
12. Add enough boiling water to pan to come halfway up outsides of ramekins.

13. Bake flans for 45 to 50 minutes, or until knife inserted in centers comes out clean.
14. Remove ramekins from water and let cool on wire rack.
15. Cover and refrigerate until chilled, at least 2 hours.
16. Flans will keep, covered, in refrigerator for up to 2 days.
17. To serve, run knife around edge of each flan and invert into shallow dessert bowls.

Yields: 6 servings.

Frozen Halloween Dessert

Orange sherbet is spread smoothly over a cookie crumb crust and then drizzled with a divine chocolate sauce. It is so good, and it maintains the spooky theme.

Ingredients:

    20 cream sandwich cookies, crushed
    ⅓ c. butter, melted
    2 qt. orange sherbet, slightly softened
    2 sq. baking chocolate (1 oz. each)
    ½ c. sugar
    1 can evaporated milk (12 oz.)
    1 c. pecans, chopped

Directions:

1. In bowl combine 20 crushed cream sandwich cookies and melted butter.
2. Press into 13 x 9-inch baking dish.
3. Spread orange sherbet over crumb layer; freeze until firm.
4. In top of double boiler, combine baking chocolate, sugar, and evaporated milk.
5. Cook, stirring constantly, until smooth; cool.
6. Drizzle over sherbet and sprinkle with chopped pecans.
7. Keep frozen until served.

Yields: 16 servings.

Graveyard Pumpkin Mousse

This smooth pumpkin mousse, smothered with "dirt," makes a fun yet elegant dessert for Halloween. Both kids and adults will have fun digging in this graveyard for this imaginative dessert!

Ingredients:

    12 chocolate sandwich cookies
    1¼ c. heavy cream
    1   pkg. cream cheese (8 oz.), softened
    ¾   c. sugar
    1   can pumpkin purée (15 oz.)
    ¼   tsp. ground cinnamon
    ¼   tsp. ground nutmeg
    ¼   tsp. ground allspice
    3   med. bananas, cut into ¼-inch slices
        gummy worms
        plastic skeletons and spiders for decorating

Directions:

1. In food processor process cookies to form fine crumbs; set aside.
2. In mixing bowl beat cream to form stiff peaks; set aside.
3. In separate mixing bowl, beat cream cheese and sugar until creamy.
4. Add pumpkin and spices; mix well.
5. Fold in whipped cream and bananas until blended.
6. Spoon ¾ cup pumpkin mousse into each of 8 stemmed dessert glasses or large custard cups; spread to even top.
7. Sprinkle 2 tablespoons cookie crumbs over top.
8. Cover and refrigerate until serving time.
9. To decorate, arrange gummy worms and plastic skeletons or spiders on "dirt" layer, placing worms so that they resemble worms crawling out of the glass.

Yields: 8 servings.

Halloween Delights Cookbook

A Collection of Halloween Recipes
Cookbook Delights Series

Dressings, Sauces, and Condiments

Table of Contents

Vegetable Salsa

This vegetable salsa is full of color and flavor.

Ingredients:

- 2 Tbs. olive oil
- 2 Tbs. red wine vinegar
- 3 cloves garlic, minced
- 1 c. chopped plum tomato
- ⅓ c. chopped green onions
- 1 tsp. chopped fresh cilantro
- 1 can black beans (15 oz.), rinsed and drained
- 1 can shoepeg white corn (11 oz.), drained
- 1 can chopped green chilies (4.5 oz.), drained

Directions:

1. Combine first 3 ingredients in large bowl; stir well with whisk.
2. Stir in tomato and remaining ingredients.

Yields: 8 (½-cup) servings.

Italian Seasoning Mix

Ingredients:

- 6 Tbs. dried basil
- 1 Tbs. dried marjoram
- 2 Tbs. dried oregano
- 1 Tbs. dried thyme

Directions:

1. Mix all ingredients together thoroughly.
2. Store in airtight container.

Pizza Sauce

Try this quick homemade pizza sauce on your favorite pizza crust recipe. Enjoy.

Ingredients:

- 1 clove garlic, mashed and minced
- ½ tsp. salt
- 1 can tomato paste (6 oz.)
- 1 can tomato sauce (8 oz.)
- ⅛ tsp. pepper
- ½ tsp. basil
- ½ tsp. oregano
- 2 Tbs. olive oil

Directions:

1. Combine all ingredients.

Yields: 1½ cups (enough for 2 pizzas).

Dill Butter

This butter has an excellent flavor. Enjoy.

Ingredients:

- ½ c. butter, softened
- 2 tsp. dill weed, dried
- 2 tsp. chives, chopped
- ½ tsp. lemon juice

Directions:

1. Combine all ingredients with softened butter.

Pumpkin Vinaigrette

This tasty pumpkin vinaigrette will go great on salad for your Halloween or autumn meals.

Ingredients:

- 4 Tbs. pumpkin purée
- ¼ c. cider or balsamic vinegar
- 1 clove garlic, finely minced
- 1 tsp. sugar
- ½ tsp. salt
- ⅛ tsp. black pepper
- ½ c. olive oil

Directions:

1. Place all ingredients except olive oil in bowl.
2. Whisk to mix well.
3. Add olive oil; whisk well.
4. Note: It is important to mix olive oil in last as salt will not dissolve in oil.

Black Bean-Mango Salsa

This salsa is full of flavor and color.

Ingredients:

- ¼ c. finely chopped red onion
- 2 Tbs. chopped fresh cilantro
- 2 tsp. finely chopped canned chipotle chili in adobo sauce
- 1½ tsp. finely chopped jalapeño pepper
- ½ tsp. hot red pepper sauce
- ¼ tsp. salt
- 1 mango, peeled and chopped
- 1 can black beans (15-oz.), rinsed and drained

Directions:

1. Combine all ingredients in bowl.
2. Toss well.

Yields: 5 servings (½ cup each).

Creamy Italian Salad Dressing

This is a creamy version of Italian salad dressing that is very good.

Ingredients:

¾ c. dairy sour cream
2   Tbs. red or white wine vinegar
2   Tbs. dry white wine
2   cloves garlic
1   tsp. basil
1   tsp. oregano
2   tsp. chives
1   tsp. dried parsley
1   Tbs. Dijon mustard
1   Tbs. honey
2   Tbs. grated Parmesan cheese
2   Tbs. olive oil
½   tsp. black pepper

Directions:

1. In blender or food processor, process all ingredients except sour cream until completely mixed.
2. Add sour cream and process just until mixed.

Yields: 1¼ cups dressing.

Did You Know? . . . .

Did you know that 86 percent of Americans decorate their homes for Halloween?

Cowpea Chow Chow

When served with tortilla chips, this chow chow makes a tasty substitute for salsa.

Ingredients:
- 2 c. chopped seeded tomato
- 1 c. chopped onion
- 1 c. chopped green bell pepper
- 1 c. chopped red bell pepper
- ¼ c. chopped fresh cilantro
- 3 Tbs. fresh lime juice
- 2 Tbs. white vinegar
- 2 tsp. finely chopped seeded Serrano chili
- ½ tsp. salt
- ¼ tsp. pepper
- 1 can black-eyed peas (15 oz.), drained

Directions:
1. Combine all ingredients in large bowl; stir well.
2. Cover and chill at least 1 hour.

Yields: 14 servings (½ cup each).

Easy Homemade Salsa

This salsa is great with nachos or anything you like to eat with salsa. It is always great to have around at parties.

Ingredients:
- 2 cans diced tomatoes with juice (14 oz. each)
- ½ onion, chopped
- ¼ c. chopped green onions
- ¼ c. chopped fresh cilantro
- ½ tsp. dried oregano
- 1 Tbs. ground cumin

2   Tbs. chopped jalapeño peppers
    salt and pepper

Directions:
1. Add all ingredients to food processor or blender.
2. Process until desired texture is reached.

Yields: About 4 cups.

Warm-and-Spicy Salsa

This is a delicious spicy salsa that makes a great appetizer.

Ingredients:
1   c. white vinegar
1   lg. onion, diced
2   celery ribs, diced
3   cloves garlic, pressed
3   cans diced tomatoes and green chilies (10-oz. each), undrained
1   can crushed tomatoes (16-oz.)
1   tsp. salt
1   tsp. sugar
½   tsp. pepper

Directions:
1. Bring first 4 ingredients to a boil in saucepan over medium heat.
2. Add green chilies, tomatoes, and remaining ingredients.
3. Return to a boil, stirring occasionally.
4. Serve warm with tortilla chips.

Yields: 4½ cups.

Easy Italian-Style Spaghetti Sauce

Here is another version of a quick spaghetti sauce that is very good.

Ingredients:

- 3   Tbs. olive oil
- 2   med. onions, chopped
- 1   med. red bell pepper, chopped
- 1   clove garlic, minced
- 1   tsp. salt
- ¼   tsp. pepper
- 1   can tomato paste (6 oz.)
- 2   cans diced or crushed tomatoes (14.5 oz.)
- 1   tsp. dried leaf oregano
- ¾   c. grated Parmesan cheese

Directions:

1. Heat oil; add onions, pepper and garlic, sautéing until tender.
2. Add pepper, tomato paste, tomatoes, and oregano.
3. Simmer for 30 minutes, stirring occasionally.
4. Stir in cheese before serving or serve cheese separately.
5. Serve with hot, cooked and drained spaghetti or similar pasta.
6. Meat version: Sauté ½ pound lean ground beef with onions, peppers, and garlic until browned; proceed with recipe.

Yields: 6 to 8 servings.

Did You Know? . . . .

Did you know that an estimated $1.93 billion of candy is sold for Halloween, making it the sweetest holiday of the year?

Red Pepper Relish

Our family loves red peppers. Enjoy this tasty relish.

Ingredients:
- ½ c. purchased roasted red pepper, cut into strips
- 1   Tbs. finely chopped, pitted ripe olives
- 2   tsp. olive oil
- 2   tsp. snipped fresh thyme or ½ tsp. dried thyme, crushed
- ¼ tsp. pepper

Directions:
1. Combine red pepper strips, ripe olives, olive oil, thyme, and pepper in food processor bowl.
2. Cover and process with several on-off turns until coarsely chopped.
3. Cover and chill until ready to serve.

Pumpkin Pie Spice

This spice mixture is great to keep on hand, especially during the holiday season.

Ingredients:
- 2   Tbs. ground cinnamon
- 1   Tbs. ground ginger
- 1½ tsp. ground allspice
- 1½ tsp. ground cloves

Directions:
1. Mix all ingredients together thoroughly.
2. Store in airtight container.

Yields: ¼ cup.

Caramelized Black Bean "Butter"

Caramelized onions lend the black beans an intriguing sweetness and complexity which is highlighted by balsamic vinegar and cocoa. Spread on a sandwich of sliced ciabatta with grilled vegetables and arugula. It is also great with baked tortilla chips.

Ingredients:

1 Tbs. olive oil
4 c. chopped onion
2 cans black beans (15 oz. each), rinsed and drained
1 Tbs. balsamic vinegar
2 tsp. unsweetened cocoa
½ tsp. salt
½ tsp. paprika
1 Tbs. chopped fresh parsley

Directions:

1. Heat oil in large nonstick skillet over medium-high heat.
2. Add onion; sauté 10 minutes or until golden.
3. Place onion, beans, vinegar, cocoa, salt, and paprika in food processor; process until smooth.
4. Place bean mixture in bowl.
5. Sprinkle with parsley.

Yields: 3 cups.

After Work Spaghetti Sauce

This is a simple, easy-to-make sauce when you are busy and do not have much time to prepare a meal.

Ingredients:

2 Tbs. olive oil
1 lg. clove garlic
2 sm. cans tomato sauce

1   tsp. sweet basil, rounded
3   Tbs. Parmesan cheese, rounded
    salt and pepper to taste

Directions:

1. Sauté whole garlic clove, peeled, in hot oil until golden brown, watching carefully so that it does not burn.
2. Add tomato sauce; crush basil leaves before adding.
3. Add cheese, salt, and pepper.
4. Simmer partially covered until pasta is cooked.
5. Serve over your favorite pasta cooked al dente.
6. Serve with additional freshly grated Parmesan, a tossed salad, and dinner rolls.

Avocado Butter

This butter tastes great and is added here to decorate your Halloween fare.

Ingredients:

½ c. butter, softened
½ c. mashed ripe avocado
3   Tbs. fresh lime juice
2   Tbs. minced flat-leaf parsley
2   cloves garlic, minced
½ tsp. salt

Directions:

1. Combine butter and avocado in small bowl; mash with potato masher until smooth.
2. Add lime juice and remaining ingredients; stir well.
3. Cover and chill until firm.

Yields: 1 cup.

Barbeque Sauce

Try this simple barbeque sauce for your favorite meals.

Ingredients:

1	bottle ketchup (32 oz.)
1	c. dark molasses
1½	Tbs. red pepper sauce or to taste
1	c. finely chopped onions
1	med. red bell pepper, finely minced
½	c. lemon juice
1	tsp. garlic powder
2½	Tbs. dry mustard
3	Tbs. white vinegar
¾	c. brown sugar
½	c. water
¼	c. Worcestershire sauce

Directions:

1. Combine all ingredients except water in large, heavy saucepan.
2. Pour water into ketchup bottle and shake, then add to pan.
3. Bring to a boil, stirring constantly.
4. Reduce heat and simmer until onions and bell pepper are very tender, about 2 hours.
5. Stir occasionally.
6. Serve over your favorite meats.

***Did You Know?* . . . .**

Did you know that pumpkin is the best source of vitamin A of all canned vegetables and fruits?

Halloween Delights Cookbook

A Collection of Halloween Recipes
Cookbook Delights Series

Jams, Jellies, and Syrups

Table of Contents

Did You Know? . . . .

Did you know that the medieval chronicler Gervase of Tilbury associated the transformation of the werewolf with the appearance of the full moon, but this concept was rarely associated with the werewolf until the idea was picked up by fiction writers?

A Basic Guide for Canning Jams, Jellies, and Syrups

1. Wash jars in hot, soapy water inside and out with brush or soft cloth.
2. Run your finger around rim of each jar, discarding any with cracks or chips.
3. Rinse well in clean, clear, hot water, using tongs to avoid burns to hands or fingers.
4. Place upside down on clean cloth to drain well.
5. Place lids in boiling water for 2 minutes to sterilize and keep hot until placing on rim of jar.
6. Immediately prior to filling each jar, immerse in very hot water with tongs to heat jar (avoids breakage of jar with hot liquid).
7. Fill jar to within 1 inch of top of rim or to level recommended in recipe.
8. Wipe rim with clean damp cloth to remove any particles of food, and check again for any chips or cracks.
9. With tongs, place lid from hot bath directly onto rim of jar.
10. Using gloves, cloth, or holders, tighten lid firmly onto jar with ring or use single formed lid in place of ring to cover inner lid. Do not tighten down too hard as it may impede sealing.
11. Place on protected surface to cool, taking care to not disturb lid and ring. A slight indentation of lid will be apparent when sealed.
12. Leave overnight until thoroughly cooled.
13. When cooled, wipe jars with damp cloth and then label and date each.
14. Store upright on shelf in cool, dark place.

Did You Know? . . . .

Did you know that chocolate candy bars are the most popular candy for trick-or-treaters, with the Snickers bar being the favorite?

Halloween Freezer Jam

This is an easy-to-make Halloween jam, and because it is frozen, it is always on hand.

Ingredients:
- 2 c. strawberries, finely crushed
- 3 c. sugar
- 1 pkg. powdered fruit pectin
- 1 c. water

Directions:
1. Combine fruit and sugar; let stand 20 minutes, stirring occasionally.
2. Boil pectin and water rapidly for 1 minute, stirring constantly; remove from heat.
3. Add strawberries and stir about 2 minutes.
4. Spoon into freezer containers, wipe clean, and place lids on with date.
5. Place in freezer until ready to use.

Halloween Gooseberry and Strawberry Jam

This jam is a recipe that comes from a time when people grew gooseberries in abundance in the garden. If you have a gooseberry bush, give this jam a try!

Ingredients:
- 6 c. gooseberries
- 3 c. strawberries, hulled and mashed
- 1½ c. water
- 4 c. sugar

Directions:
1. Rinse, stem, and hull berries, then place in saucepan with sugar and water; bring to boiling.
2. Reduce heat and simmer until gooseberries and strawberries are soft, approximately 15 minutes.
3. Process following basic directions for canning jams and jellies found at beginning of this recipe section.

Halloween Mango and Strawberry Jam with Kiwifruit

This Halloween mango strawberry jam with kiwifruit is a great change of pace. The mangoes and kiwifruit add a tropical touch of flavor and make this an excellent jam for use as a glaze on pork or grilled chicken.

Ingredients:

2	c. mango, diced
1¾	c. strawberries, mashed
¾	c. kiwi, diced
¼	c. lemon juice
1	tsp. citric acid
7½	c. sugar
2	pouches fruit pectin

Directions:

1. Combine fruits, lemon juice, citric acid, and sugar in large, heavy kettle or saucepot; bring to boil.
2. Stir in fruit pectin and return to hard boil.
3. Boil 1 minute before placing in jars and processing.
4. Process following basic directions for canning jams and jellies found at beginning of this recipe section.

Halloween Guava and Strawberry Jam

This makes a delicious and different-tasting jam. Guavas are hard to find but are worth the effort.

Ingredients:

2	lb. ripe guavas, firm to the touch
1	lb. strawberries
6	c. water
5	c. sugar

Directions:

1. Rinse guavas and cut into quarters.
2. Rinse, hull, and quarter strawberries.
3. Boil strawberries and guavas, uncovered, in large pot over medium heat for 45 minutes.
4. Drain using colander; reserve liquid.
5. Use 5 cups reserved liquid and combine with boiled fruit and sugar, then return mixture to a boil.
6. Cook over medium-high heat, uncovered, for 35 minutes until thick or to 226 degrees F. on candy thermometer and fruit is disintegrated.
7. Process following basic directions for canning jams and jellies found at beginning of this recipe section.

Mint Jelly

Enjoy using mint jelly on bread, crackers, and meats.

Ingredients:

½   c. white vinegar
1   c. water
½   c. mint leaves
3½ c. sugar
½   c. powdered fruit pectin
       green food coloring

Directions:

1. Combine vinegar, water, mint leaves, and enough coloring to give tint desired.
2. Add sugar; stir and bring to a boil.
3. Add pectin at once, stirring constantly, and bring again to a full boil for 30 seconds.
4. Strain off mint leaves and pour jelly into glasses.
5. When cold, cover with paraffin.

Yields: Six 6-ounce glasses.

Black Raspberry Freezer Jam

Freezer jams are so easy to make. The dark color and the flavor of this black raspberry jam makes it an ideal complement to your Halloween fare.

Ingredients:

3	c. black raspberries, cleaned and picked over
5¼	c. sugar
2	Tbs. lemon juice
1	box powdered fruit pectin
¾	c. water

Directions:

1. Put raspberries in large bowl, and crush lightly with fork or potato masher.
2. Add sugar and lemon juice.
3. Set aside to allow sugar to dissolve with fruit for 10 minutes.
4. Place pectin and water in small saucepan and bring to a boil, stirring constantly.
5. Boil for 1 minute, stirring constantly. (Mixture will turn clear.)
6. Pour over fruit mixture and stir well for about 3 minutes.
7. Immediately spoon into clean, clear plastic containers, leaving about ½-inch headspace to allow for expansion during freezing.
8. Seal with lids and let stand at room temperature for 24 hours.
9. Freeze for up to 1 year.
10. May be refrigerated for up to 1 month.

Yields: 7 cups.

Did You Know? . . . .

Did you know that the spider symbolizes patience for its hunting with web traps, and mischief and malice for its poison and the slow death this causes?

Plum Nutty Jam

This combination of plums, orange, and walnuts makes a hearty jam that is great with meats. Try it as a topping for ice cream, too.

Ingredients:

- 2½ lb. fresh plums
- 1½ tsp. grated orange rind
- ½ c. orange juice
- 1 pkg. powdered fruit pectin
- 5½ c. sugar
- ½ c. walnuts, finely chopped

Directions:

1. Remove and discard pits from plums (do not peel).
2. Chop plums into ½-inch pieces.
3. Combine chopped plums, orange rind, and orange juice in large saucepan.
4. Stir in powdered fruit pectin.
5. Bring mixture to a rolling boil, stirring constantly.
6. Stir in sugar.
7. Return to a rolling boil, boil 1 minute, stirring constantly.
8. Remove from heat; skim off foam.
9. Stir 5 minutes then stir in walnuts.
10. Quickly spoon hot mixture into hot sterilized jars, leaving ¼-inch headspace.
11. Remove air bubbles; wipe jar rims.
12. Cover at once with metal lids and screw on bands.
13. Process in boiling-water bath for 15 minutes.

Yields: 9 half pints.

***Did You Know?* . . . .**

Did you know that the movie "Halloween," filmed in 1978, was made in only 21 days on a very limited budget.

Citrus Halloween Preserves

This Halloween preserve has just a hint of lemon, lime, and orange flavor added and is absolutely delicious. The strawberries make a festive Halloween color.

Ingredients:

5   c. strawberries, rinsed, hulled, chopped small
1   sm. lemon
1   sm. lime
1   sm. orange
5   c. sugar
1   pkg. liquid fruit pectin

Directions:

1. Place strawberries into large pot.
2. Remove skins in quarters from lemon, lime, and orange; lay skins flat.
3. Shave off and discard about half of inside white membranes, and then with sharp knife or scissors, slice remaining rind very fine.
4. Add to strawberries in pot.
5. Add sugar to berries and mix well; let stand 10 minutes.
6. Bring to full rolling boil; stirring constantly, boil hard for 5 minutes then remove from heat.
7. Immediately stir in liquid fruit pectin.
8. Stir and skim foam for 7 minutes to prevent floating fruit.
9. Process following basic directions for canning jams and jellies found at beginning of this recipe section.

Pumpkin Preserves

Pumpkin preserves are a great way to use up some of those pumpkins leftover from Halloween.

Ingredients:

4   lb. pumpkin, prepared
4   Tbs. sugar
3   lemons, thinly sliced

½ tsp. salt

1 Tbs. mixed spices (ginger, nutmeg, cinnamon, etc., to your taste)

Directions:

1. Wash pumpkin; remove peel and seeds and cut as desired.
2. Weigh; mix with sugar.
3. Let stand 12 to 18 hours in cool place.
4. Add thinly sliced lemons, salt, and mixed spices (tied in a bag), and boil until pumpkin is clear and syrup thick; remove spice bag.
5. Pour, boiling hot, into hot jars.
6. Process following basic directions for canning jams and jellies found at beginning of this recipe section.

Yields: 6 servings.

Blackberry Jam

Blackberry jam is always a favorite. Picking your own can add to the enjoyment of this tasty jam.

Ingredients:

3 c. blackberries

2 c. water

1 pkg. powdered fruit pectin

5 c. sugar

Directions:

1. Crush fruit thoroughly.
2. Add water and fruit pectin; stir until pectin is dissolved.
3. Heat to boiling; boil 5 to 10 minutes.
4. Add sugar; stir until dissolved.
5. Boil 3 to 5 minutes, stirring frequently or until thick.
6. Pour into jars; process following basic directions for canning jams and jellies found at beginning of this recipe section.

Yields: 6 servings.

Pumpkin, Ginger, and Apricot Preserves

This combination of dried apricots with fresh pumpkin, gingerroot, and cinnamon makes delicious and colorful preserves to use for Halloween as well as the holiday season.

Ingredients:

½   lb. dried apricots
1½ c. water
5   c. fresh, peeled, seeded pumpkin, cut into ½-inch dice
1   Tbs. fresh gingerroot, peeled and grated
1   cinnamon stick (3-in. length)
2½ c. sugar

Directions:

1. In bowl let apricots soak in 1½ cups water, covered, overnight.
2. Drain apricots, reserving water; cut into ¼-inch julienne strips.
3. In large saucepan combine reserved water, pumpkin, gingerroot, and cinnamon stick; bring to a boil over high heat.
4. Turn heat down to simmer and cook mixture, covered, stirring occasionally, for 30 minutes.
5. Discard cinnamon stick.
6. In food processor or blender, purée pumpkin mixture with any of its liquid; return to pan over moderate heat.
7. Add apricots and sugar.
8. Bring mixture to a boil, stirring constantly; reduce heat to simmer and cook, uncovered, for 30 minutes or until thickened.
9. Spoon preserves into hot, sterilized canning jars, filling to within ¼ inch of rims.
10. Wipe rims with dampened cloth or paper towel and seal jars with sterilized lids.
11. Place jars in canning kettle or deep steamer and add enough water to cover jars by 2 inches.
12. Bring water to a boil over high heat; boil for 10 minutes.
13. Transfer jars to dish towel to drain and cool.

Halloween Delights Cookbook

A Collection of Halloween Recipes
Cookbook Delights Series

Main Dishes

Table of Contents

Constricting Snake Bites

Have fun making this snake presentation for your Halloween-themed meal. Complete with olive eyes, this slithering fellow is so realistic, you expect him to hiss.

Ingredients:

- 3 loaves frozen white bread dough (16 oz. each), thawed
- 6 Tbs. brown mustard
- 16 oz. thinly sliced ham
- 12 oz. thinly sliced salami
- 6 oz. provolone cheese, shredded
- 6 oz. mozzarella cheese, shredded
- 3 lg. egg yolks
- 1 Tbs. water
- 2 whole cloves
- 3 Tbs. freshly grated Parmesan cheese (optional)
- 2 sm. pimiento-stuffed olives
  bottled roasted red sweet pepper strip (6 x 1-in.)
  green, red, and yellow liquid food coloring

Directions:

1. Line 3 cookie sheets with foil; grease foil and set aside.
2. Roll one loaf of dough on lightly floured surface to a 26 x 6-inch rectangle. (May need to allow dough to rest a few minutes occasionally while rolling out.)
3. Lightly brush 2 tablespoons mustard to within 1 inch of sides of dough.
4. Layer ⅓ of ham and salami over mustard.
5. Mix together cheeses.
6. Sprinkle ⅓ of cheese mixture over ham and salami.
7. Brush edges of dough with water.
8. Tightly roll up into spiral, starting with one of the long sides.
9. Pinch all edges to seal.
10. Shape dough on baking sheet in and "S" shape.

11. Combine 1 egg yolk, 1 teaspoon water, and several drops of desired food coloring.
12. Repeat, making green, red, and yellow egg wash.
13. Using a small paint brush, paint stripes crosswise over loaf, allowing wash to drizzle down sides.
14. Let loaf rise in warm place for about 20 minutes.
15. Sprinkle top of loaf with 1 tablespoon of Parmesan cheese if desired.
16. While one section of the "snake" rises, repeat with remaining bread dough and ingredients.
17. Taper one end of each of these 2 loaves to a rounded point making a head and tail.
18. Insert 2 whole cloves at one of these ends making nostrils of the "snake."
19. Place on remaining prepared cookie sheets.
20. Paint and let rise as above.
21. Preheat oven to 375 degrees F.
22. Bake snake sections for 25 to 30 minutes or until bottoms of loaves are golden.
23. Insert olives with toothpicks above cloves to form eyes.
24. Place red pepper strip in front for snake's mouth
25. Assemble snake portions on bamboo leaves if desired.
26. Slice and serve warm.

Yields: 24 slices.

Did You Know? . . . .

Did you know that although the Celts did not have demons and devils in their belief system, they did believe in gods, giants, monsters, witches, spirits, and elves? These were not believed to be evil but were considered dangerous.

Corpseloaf

This standard meatloaf is fun to decorate into a corpse.

Ingredients:

- 1½ lb. ground beef
- 1 egg, beaten
- 1 c. bread crumbs
- 1 tsp. ketchup
- 1 tsp. salt
- ¼ tsp. garlic powder
- ¼ tsp. pepper
- ¼ c. minced onion
- 2 black or green olives
  spaghetti sauce (recipes pages 206 or 208) or if in a hurry use a 26-oz. jar of spaghetti sauce
  corn kernels
  pimientos

Directions:

1. Preheat oven to 350 degrees F.
2. Combine ground beef, egg, bread crumbs, ketchup, salt, garlic powder, pepper, and minced onion.
3. Form into shape of a body and place in baking dish.
4. Place two olives on head for eyes.
5. Use corn for teeth and strip of pimento for mouth.
6. Pour spaghetti sauce around body.
7. Bake for 1 hour 15 minutes.
8. Right before serving, stick a dagger (butter knife) into the "heart" of the corpse as garnish.

***Did You Know?* . . . .**

Did you know that the fear of cats is called ailurophobia?

Count Dracula's Turkey Bites
with Peanut Sauce

This is a tasty marinade to serve with turkey. It is very good to serve alone with dipping sauce. It also makes great sandwiches.

Ingredients:

1½	lb. turkey breast, cut in strips
1	Tbs. packed brown sugar
2	cloves garlic, minced
4	Tbs. onion, minced
1	tsp. ground ginger
½	c. roasted peanuts, unsalted
1	Tbs. lemon juice
¼	c. soy sauce
1	tsp. coriander seed
½	tsp. cayenne pepper
½	c. chicken broth
¼	c. butter, melted

Directions:

1. Blend all ingredients except turkey, broth, and butter for 1 minute in blender.
2. Add chicken broth and butter, blend for another minute.
3. Marinate turkey strips in mixture for at least 6 hours.
4. Drain marinade into saucepan.
5. Bring marinade to boil, reduce heat, and cook for 5 minutes. (Use for dipping sauce.)
6. Grill or broil turkey strips for 7 to 8 minutes or until no longer pink.

Yields: 6 servings.

***Did You Know?* . . . .**

Did you know that the pumpkin comes from the same family as the cucumber?

Goblin Fingers and Toes

This makes a nice vegetarian pasta dish to add to your Halloween meal.

Ingredients:

- 14 manicotti shells
- 28 med. white mushrooms
- 2 Tbs. lemon juice
- 3 eggs
- 2 lb. ricotta cheese
- 2 c. Parmesan cheese, divided
- 2 c. mozzarella cheese, divided
- 2 tsp. garlic powder
- 2 tsp. onion powder
- ½ tsp. basil
- ½ tsp. oregano
- 3 c. favorite smooth tomato sauce
- salt and white pepper

Directions:

1. Preheat oven to 350 degrees F., and grease individual baking dishes or a large baking dish.
2. Cook manicotti shells according to package directions until al dente but not too soft.
3. Drain well and toss to remove most of water.
4. While manicotti is cooking, clean mushrooms well and toss with lemon juice to prevent browning.
5. Beat eggs, ricotta, half the Parmesan, half the mozzarella, and the spices in medium bowl until smooth.
6. Pour sauce into prepared baking dish(es).
7. Stuff manicotti with ricotta mixture using long-handled small spoon or pastry bag and tip. (Filling should be packed but not so tightly that it cracks or breaks shells.)
8. Add a mushroom to the end of each shell and place in baking dish.
9. Cover and bake for 20 minutes.
10. Remove cover and sprinkle remaining cheeses over bones.
11. Bake for an additional 15 to 20 minutes or until filling is hot and cheese is melted.
12. Serve hot.

Great Pumpkin Sandwiches

Visited by the Halloween Pumpkin? Your guests might think so when you serve this puffy layered tortilla sandwich. It is best served hot from the oven.

Ingredients:
- 3   c. shredded cheddar cheese (12 oz.)
- ¾   c. butter, softened
- 3   eggs
- ½   tsp. garlic salt
- ½   tsp. onion salt
- 9   flour tortillas (6 in.)
- 3   celery stalks with leaves (optional)
  paprika

Directions:
1. Preheat oven to 400 degrees F.
2. In food processor blend cheese and butter.
3. Add eggs, garlic salt, and onion salt; process for 1 minute or until creamy.
4. Spread ½ cupful on each tortilla.
5. Stack three tortillas, cheese side up, for each sandwich; sprinkle with paprika.
6. Place on ungreased baking sheet.
7. Bake for 10 to 15 minutes or until golden and bubbly.
8. If desired, add celery to resemble pumpkin stem.
9. Cut sandwiches into halves to serve.

Yields: 6 servings.

Did You Know? . . . .

Did you know that the original Halloween film directed by John Carpenter in 1978 cost just $320,000 to make, but it ended up making over $50 million worldwide?

Grilled Cheese Jack-O'-Lanterns

This recipe adds Halloween festivity to the traditional grilled cheese sandwich.

Ingredients:

    4   Tbs. butter, softened
    8   slices bread
    4   slices Monterey Jack cheese
    4   slices sharp cheddar cheese

Directions:

1. Preheat oven to 250 degrees F.
2. Spread butter on one side of each bread slice.
3. Place bread buttered side down on ungreased cookie sheet.
4. Using small, sharp hors d'oeuvre cutter or knife, cut out shapes from 4 bread slices to make jack-o'-lantern faces.
5. On remaining bread slices, layer 1 slice Monterey Jack and 1 slice cheddar cheese.
6. Bake 10 to 12 minutes or until cheese is melted.
7. Remove from oven; place jack-o'-lantern bread slice on sandwiches and serve.

Gnarled Witch's Fingers

This presentation can look quite disgusting. It also looks pretty sick if you want to boil the chicken instead of broil it. Have as much fun with this as you dare.

Ingredients:

    1   Tbs. vegetable oil
    4   boneless chicken breasts
    1   c. all-purpose flour
    1   egg, beaten
    1   c. bread crumbs
        pitted black olives, halved lengthwise
        shredded lettuce

Directions:
1. Grease cookie sheet with oil; set aside.
2. Carefully cut chicken breasts part way to create 5 fingers (uncut part will be the palm of the hand).
3. Dust in flour; dip in beaten egg then bread crumbs.
4. Broil 5 minutes on each side until golden brown and cooked through.
5. Trim fingertips with halved black olives and serve on lettuce.

Yields: 4 servings.

Bloody Turkey Medallions

This does not sound good, but it makes a great Halloween dish.

Ingredients:
- 2 lb. turkey tenderloin, cut into ¾-inch medallions
- 1 Tbs. butter
- 1 Tbs. oil
- 2 cloves garlic, minced
- 4 shallots, diced
- 1 c. cooking apples, peeled and diced
- ½ c. coarsely chopped cranberries
- ½ c. orange juice
- salt and pepper

Directions:
1. Salt and pepper turkey medallions.
2. Melt butter and oil in large skillet.
3. Brown turkey medallions quickly on each side.
4. Reduce heat and add garlic and shallots.
5. Cook until turkey is thoroughly cooked and no longer pink in center.
6. Place medallions on warm serving plate.
7. Add remaining ingredients to skillet and bring to boil.
8. Reduce heat and simmer until apples are soft.
9. Pour sauce over medallions and serve.

Jack-O'-Lantern Burgers

It is fun to "carve" cheesy faces for these nicely seasoned burgers.

Ingredients:

- 1 env. onion soup mix
- ⅓ c. ketchup
- 2 Tbs. brown sugar
- 2 tsp. prepared horseradish
- 2 tsp. chili powder
- 2½ lb. ground beef
- 10 slices process American cheese
- 10 hamburger buns, split

Directions:

1. In bowl combine soup mix, ketchup, brown sugar, horseradish, and chili powder.
2. Add beef and mix well.
3. Shape into 10 patties.
4. Grill, broil, or pan fry until meat is no longer pink.
5. Cut eyes, nose, and mouth out of each cheese slice to create a jack-o'-lantern.
6. Place cheese on burgers; cook until cheese is slightly melted, about 1 minute.
7. Serve on buns.

Yields: 10 servings.

***Did You Know?* . . . .**

Did you know that just ½ cup of pumpkin has more than three times the recommended daily requirement of vitamin A?

Meatloaf Mice

This is an easy-to-make meatloaf made into small meatloaves shaped into mice.

Ingredients:

½   c. ketchup
2   egg whites, beaten
6   oz. ground turkey
6   oz. ground beef
1   onion, chopped fine
⅔   c. oatmeal, uncooked
   salt and pepper to taste
   carrots
   spaghetti noodles, uncooked
   raisins
   spaghetti sauce (recipes pages 206 or 208)

Directions:

1. Preheat oven to 350 degrees F.
2. Cut 2 coins per mouse out of carrots for ears.
3. Make long thin strips out of remaining carrots for tails, one for each mouse.
4. Steam until crisp tender. (Do not overcook.)
5. Mix together ketchup, egg whites, turkey, beef, onion, and oatmeal for mouse bodies, and shape into 4 mouse-shaped loaves on baking sheet. (Shape to a point in front and rounded in back.)
6. Bake for 45 minutes or until desired doneness.
7. Cut slits for ears about ⅓ back from pointed end.
8. Place carrot coins in slits for ears.
9. Make tiny slit in rounded wide end, and place one of the carrot strips in slit for tail.
10. Use raisins for eyes.
11. Break uncooked spaghetti noodles into pieces and place around nose (pointed end) for whiskers.
12. Heat spaghetti sauce; place large spoonful of sauce on plate.
13. Place a meatloaf mouse on top of spaghetti sauce and serve.

Yields: 4 servings.

Hag Hash

Serve this Hag Hash with a cackle and a grin! It actually tastes good.

Ingredients:

1	pumpkin (4 lb.)
1	lg. onion
½	green pepper
½	zucchini
1	clove garlic
1	Tbs. vegetable oil
1	lb. ground beef
1	lb. pork sausage
1	can tomato juice (6 oz.)
1	tsp. salt
1	tsp. basil
1	tsp. thyme
	freshly ground pepper

Directions:

1. Cut off top of pumpkin, scrape out seeds and fibers, and rinse out with water.
2. Place pumpkin in cauldron (large pan), and cover with lightly salted water.
3. Simmer until almost tender, about 20 to 25 minutes.
4. While pumpkin is simmering, chop onion, green pepper, and zucchini into ½-inch pieces.
5. Mince garlic clove.
6. Preheat oven to 350 degrees F.
7. Carefully drain water from pumpkin. (Be very careful! Pumpkin will be hot, so remember to use oven mitts.)
8. After dumping out water, set pumpkin aside.
9. Add cooking oil and garlic to cauldron.
10. Cook for 1 minute.
11. Add onions to cauldron and cook for 1 minute.
12. Add ground beef and sausage, and brown meat.
13. Remove cauldron from heat.

14. Stir in green pepper, zucchini, tomato juice, salt, basil, thyme, and freshly ground pepper.
15. Spoon concoction into pumpkin; carefully replace lid.
16. Place pumpkin into baking dish; add about ½ inch of water to bottom of baking dish to keep pumpkin from burning.
17. Brush pumpkin with cooking oil.
18. Bake for 1 hour.
19. Using oven mitts, remove baking dish from oven.
20. Let stand for 5 minutes before serving.

Coffin Sandwiches

These are easy and fun to make for your Halloween tray or for a single serving for a quick Halloween surprise.

Ingredients:
  2   slices whole-wheat bread
  3   slices smoked ham
  1   slice cheese
  1   Tbs. mayonnaise
  1   lettuce leaf

Directions:
1. Layer one bread slice with sliced meat, sliced cheese, mayonnaise, and lettuce.
2. Spear each sandwich with plastic toothpick to hold it together if desired.
3. Cut sandwich into coffin shape using coffin template and sharp knife. (For an even stronger template, trace template onto piece of cardboard and cut out.)

Yields: 1 serving.

Did You Know? . . . .

Did you know that pumpkins have been growing for thousands of years?

Halloween Chicken Pizza Masks

These little pizzas are easy to make using English muffins. They make a popular, quick, and easy children's snack with or without the chicken.

Ingredients:

1	lb. ground chicken
⅓	c. chopped onion
1	tsp. salt
½	tsp. pepper
1	pkg. English muffins (6 count), split
2	Tbs. butter, divided
1½	c. pizza sauce, divided (recipe page 201)
1	tsp. oregano
1	lg. green pepper
4	oz. cheddar cheese, shredded
4	oz. mozzarella cheese, shredded
3	lg. pitted ripe olives, each sliced into 4 rings

Directions:

1. Preheat oven to 450 degrees F.
2. Heat frying pan to medium-high temperature.
3. Add ground chicken and onion.
4. Cook, stirring, until all red is gone, about 6 minutes; set aside.
5. Cover 10½ x 15½-inch baking sheet with aluminum foil.
6. Spread each muffin half with ½ teaspoon butter, and arrange in single layer on prepared pan.
7. Spread heaping tablespoon pizza sauce on each muffin half.
8. Cover generously with ground chicken and onion then sprinkle with oregano.
9. Cut 12 slivers of green pepper into "smiling" mouth shapes and set aside.
10. Chop remaining pepper and sprinkle on pizzas.
11. Mix together cheddar and mozzarella cheeses; sprinkle generously on mini-pizzas.
12. Bake for about 12 minutes; remove from oven.

13. Make mask face on each pizza by using 2 ripe olive rings for eyes and pepper slice for mouth. (Turn some slices up for smiles and some down for frowns.)

Yields: 12 mini pizzas.

Halloween Mummy Dogs

Try these easy-to-make hot dogs for a quick and fun meal.

Ingredients for:

1   c. mozzarella cheese, grated
¼   c. freshly grated Parmesan cheese
4   Tbs. pizza sauce (recipe page 201)
8   hot dogs
1   Tbs. Italian seasoning (recipe page 200)
    optional pizza toppings: onions, green peppers,
    olives, etc.
    pizza dough (recipe page 91, or use 2 tubes
    refrigerator pizza dough rolls when you are in a hurry)

Directions:

1. Prepare pizza dough or open packaged dough.
2. Preheat oven to 300 degrees F.; spray cookie sheet with nonstick cooking spray.
3. Divide dough into 8 sections and press dough thin into squares with fingers.
4. Add pizza sauce to each square.
5. Add hot dogs, pizza toppings, and pizza herbs to taste.
6. "Mummify" hot dogs by wrapping completely in dough and pinching ends.
7. Bake approximately 15 minutes or until crust begins to brown.
8. Serve warm with pizza sauce for dip.

Yields: 8 servings.

Haunted Taco Tarts

This has the ingredients of a taco made with the crust of a tart.

Ingredients for tart:

- 1 Tbs. vegetable oil
- ½ c. chopped onion
- ½ lb. ground turkey
- 1 clove garlic, minced
- ½ tsp. dried oregano leaves
- ½ tsp. chili powder
- ¼ tsp. salt
- 1 egg white
- ½ c. chopped tomato
- ½ c. taco-flavored shredded cheese
    double crust pastry (recipe page 246)
    egg yolk paint (recipe follows)

Ingredients for egg yolk paint:

- 4 egg yolks
- 4 tsp. water, divided
    red, yellow, blue, and green liquid food colorings

Directions for tart:

1. Preheat oven to 375 degrees F.
2. Heat oil in large skillet over medium heat.
3. Add onion and cook until tender.
4. Add turkey; cook until turkey is no longer pink, stirring occasionally.
5. Stir in garlic, oregano, chili powder, and salt; set aside.
6. Lightly grease baking sheets.
7. Prepare egg yolk paint; set aside.
8. Prepare double-crust pastry; divide in half.
9. On lightly floured surface, roll one portion of crust to 14-inch diameter.
10. Using 3-inch Halloween cookies cutters, cut out pairs of desired shapes.

11. Repeat with second portion of crust, rerolling dough if necessary.
12. Place ½ of shapes on prepared baking sheets.
13. Brush edges with egg white.
14. Spoon about 1 tablespoon taco mixture onto each shape.
15. Sprinkle with 1 teaspoon tomato and 1 teaspoon cheese.
16. Top with remaining matching shapes; press edges to seal.
17. Decorate with Egg Yolk Paint.
18. Bake 10 to 12 minutes or until golden brown.

Directions for egg yolk paint:

1. Place 1 egg yolk in each of 4 small bowls.
2. Add 1 teaspoon water and a few drops different food coloring to each; beat lightly.

Yields: 14 tarts.

Bat Sandwiches

Children and adults will have fun making these bat sandwiches for a Halloween tray.

Ingredients:
    3   c. shredded sharp cheddar cheese (12 oz.)
    1   container chive-and-onion flavored cream
        cheese (8 oz.), softened
    1   jar diced pimiento (4 oz.), drained
    1   c. chopped pecans, toasted
    24 whole-wheat or pumpernickel bread slices

Directions:
1. Stir together first 4 ingredients.
2. Using a 3- to 4-inch bat-shaped cutter, cut 2 bats from each bread slice.
3. Spread about 2 tablespoons filling over 24 bats.
4. Top with remaining 24 bats.

Yields: 24 sandwiches.

Spooky Eyeball Tacos

These tacos taste great and are prepared in an unusual presentation to go with the Halloween theme.

Ingredients for tacos:

- 1   lb. ground beef
- 1   recipe taco seasoning mix (recipe below)
- 12 taco shells
- ¾   c. Easy Homemade Salsa (recipe page 204)
- ¾   c. dairy sour cream
- 1   can sliced pitted ripe olives (2¼ oz.)

Ingredients for seasoning mix:

- 1   Tbs. all-purpose flour
- 1   Tbs. corn starch
- 1   Tbs. dried minced onion
- 1   tsp. beef bouillon granules or 1 beef bouillon cube, crushed
- 1   tsp. garlic salt
- 1   tsp. ground cumin
- 1   tsp. paprika
- 1   tsp. chili powder
- ½   tsp. onion salt
- ¼   tsp. cayenne pepper
- ¼   tsp. sugar

Directions for tacos:

1. Preheat oven to 350 degrees F.
2. Mix meat and seasoning mix. (Do not add water and cook as for regular tacos.)
3. Shape into 36 (1-inch) balls, and place on 15 x 10 x 1-inch baking pan.
4. Bake for 15 to 20 minutes or until cooked through.
5. Fill each taco shell with 1 meatball; drizzle with salsa.
6. Top with 2 meatballs dipped in sour cream.
7. Garnish with olives to make "eyeballs."

Directions for seasoning mix:

1. Combine all ingredients and store in air-tight container.
2. To make taco meat, brown 1 pound ground beef in skillet over medium-high heat; drain off fat.
3. Add seasoning mix and ¾ cup water.
4. Bring to a boil; reduce heat to medium-low.
5. Simmer, uncovered, for 10 minutes, stirring occasionally.

Yields: 6 servings tacos; seasoning mix equivalent to 1.25-oz. packet.

Ham with Wild Lice

Despite its ghoulish name, this dish will be a hit with your Halloween guests.

Ingredients:

2	c. orzo
⅓	c. light cream
3	Tbs. butter
¾	c. grated Parmesan cheese
1	Tbs. fresh parsley, chopped, or 1 tsp. dried
½	tsp. pepper
1	ham steak (about 1½ lb.)
	olive oil

Directions:

1. Preheat oven to 350 degrees F.
2. Prepare orzo according to package directions, making sure to not overcook the pasta.
3. Drain orzo through colander and pour into large bowl.
4. Add cream, butter, cheese, parsley, and pepper; toss well.
5. Grease casserole dish with olive oil.
6. Place ham steak in dish and cover with orzo (lice).
7. Bake 20 to 30 minutes.

Snakes in the Grass

Children will love these breadstick cheese sandwiches. They are fun to decorate.

Ingredients:

¾ c. dairy sour cream
¾ c. Easy Homemade Salsa (recipe page 204)
6 breadsticks (7½ in.), sliced in half lengthwise
10 slices deli American cheese (1 oz. each), each cut into 3
   strips
   chopped black olives
   cream cheese, softened
   sliced red bell pepper or pimiento
   sliced stuffed green olives
   shredded lettuce

Directions:

1. Combine sour cream and salsa in small bowl.
2. Spread cut sides of each breadstick with 1½ tablespoons sour cream mixture.
3. Place 4 strips cheese onto bottom half of each breadstick; cover with top half.
4. To decorate each snake sandwich, attach 2 pieces chopped black olive to one end of top of sandwich with dot of cream cheese for eyes.
5. Cut piece of red pepper into tongue shape; place between breadstick halves for tongue.
6. Attach slices of green olives to top of sandwich with dot of cream cheese for snake skin design.
7. Place shredded lettuce onto platter.
8. Place snake sandwiches onto lettuce.

Yields: 6 sandwiches.

Jack-O'-Lantern Cheeseburger Pie

This pie is easy to make ahead and cook for that Halloween-themed meal.

Ingredients:

- 1   lb. ground beef
- 1   med. onion, chopped
- 2   cloves garlic, pressed
- ¾   tsp. salt
- ½   tsp. pepper
- ¼   c. ketchup
- 1   tsp. Worcestershire sauce
- 1   recipe double-crust pastry (recipe page 246)
- 1   Tbs. prepared mustard
- 3   c. shredded Monterey Jack cheese, divided
- 2   Tbs. water
- 1   lg. egg
-     red and yellow liquid food coloring

Directions:

1. Preheat oven to 425 degrees F.
2. Cook first 5 ingredients in large skillet over medium-high heat, stirring until beef crumbles and is no longer pink; drain.
3. Stir in ketchup and Worcestershire sauce; cool.
4. Prepare pastry.
5. Roll out half of pie crust and place on lightly greased baking sheet; spread mustard evenly over crust.
6. Stir together meat mixture and 2 cups cheese; spoon onto center of crust, leaving 2-inch border.
7. Roll out remaining pie crust, and cut out jack-o'-lantern face, reserving pastry cutouts to use as stem.
8. Place crust over meat mixture; crimp edges of crust, and fold under; place stem on top of jack-o'-lantern face.
9. Whisk together 2 tablespoons water, egg, and 1 drop each of red and yellow food coloring; brush over crust.
10. Bake 20 minutes; remove from oven and brush again with egg mixture.
11. Fill eyes, nose, and mouth with remaining 1 cup cheese.
12. Bake 5 to 10 minutes or until golden brown.

Yields: 6 to 8 servings.

Monster Mouth

These stuffed pasta shells are actually very delicious and fun to decorate in the shape of a mouth.

Ingredients:

- 1 tsp. vegetable oil
- 1 med. onion, chopped
- 4 slices bacon, chopped
- 1 lb. ground beef
- 2 med. plum tomatoes, seeded and chopped
- ½ tsp. salt
- ¼ tsp. black pepper
- 8 oz. cheddar cheese, shredded
- ½ pkg. jumbo pasta shells (12 oz.), about 18 shells, cooked and drained
  baby carrots, olives, red bell pepper, small pickles, and cheese slices for decoration

Directions:

1. Preheat oven to 350 degrees F.
2. Lightly grease 13 x 9-inch baking dish.
3. Heat oil in large skillet over medium heat.
4. Add onion and bacon; cook until onion is tender.
5. Add beef; cook and stir about 5 minutes or until beef is no longer pink.
6. Stir in tomatoes, salt, and pepper.
7. Stir shredded cheese into beef mixture.
8. Spoon mixture into cooked shells; place in prepared baking dish.
9. Cut carrot into very thin strips.
10. Cut small slit into olives; poke one end of thin carrot strips into olives for eyes.
11. Cut red bell pepper into fang shapes.
12. Slice pickle lengthwise into tongue shape.
13. Cut cheese slice into zigzag pattern for teeth.
14. Bake shells 3 to 5 minutes or until shells are hot; remove from oven.
15. Decorate as desired with olive and carrot eyes, bell pepper fangs, pickle tongue, and cheese teeth; serve immediately.

Monster Claws

These chicken strips are full of flavor.

Ingredients:

- 2   Tbs. all-purpose flour
- 1   Tbs. plus 2 tsp. Cajun seasoning, divided
- 1   lb. boneless, skinless chicken breasts, cut lengthwise into ¾-inch strips
- 1½ c. cornflake crumbs
- 2   Tbs. chopped green onions
- 3   eggs, lightly beaten
- 1   red, yellow, or orange bell pepper, cut into triangles
    Barbeque Sauce (recipe page 210)

Directions:

1. Preheat oven to 350 degrees F.
2. Lightly grease baking sheets.
3. Place flour and 2 tsp. Cajun seasoning in large, resealable, plastic food storage bag.
4. Add chicken and seal; shake bag to coat.
5. Combine cornflake crumbs, green onion, and remaining 1 tablespoon Cajun seasoning in large shallow bowl; mix well.
6. Place eggs in shallow bowl.
7. Dip each chicken strip into eggs and then into crumb mixture.
8. Place coated chicken strips on prepared baking sheet.
9. Bake 8 to 10 minutes or until chicken is no longer pink in center.
10. When chicken is cool enough to handle, make ½-inch slit in thinner end.
11. Place bell pepper triangle into slit to form claw nail.
12. Serve claws with barbeque sauce for dipping.

Yields: About 30 strips.

Baked Worms

This is actually a tasty main dish casserole, once you get by the worm idea.

Ingredients:

3	lb. boneless, skinless chicken breasts
½	c. butter
1	lg. onion
4	ribs celery, chopped
2	red bell peppers, chopped
1	lb. sliced mushrooms
3	c. chicken broth
1	lg. can tomato juice
¾	c. stuffed green olives
3	Tbs. chili powder
2	tsp. salt
1	lb. dry spaghetti
1	lb. American or cheddar cheese, cut into cubes
½	c. dry sherry

Directions:

1. Poach chicken breasts.
2. Chop cooked chicken and set aside.
3. In large pan melt butter and sauté onion, celery, peppers, and mushrooms.
4. Add chicken, chicken broth, tomato juice, olives, chili powder, and salt; simmer for 30 minutes.
5. Preheat oven to 350 degrees F.
6. Break spaghetti up into worm-size pieces.
7. Cook spaghetti in boiling water until tender, about 6 minutes.
8. Drain spaghetti and fold into simmering sauce.
9. Stir in cheese and sherry.
10. Place in large greased casserole dish; bake 30 minutes.

Yields: 10 servings.

Halloween Delights Cookbook
A Collection of Halloween Recipes
Cookbook Delights Series

Pies

Table of Contents

Did You Know? . . . .

Did you know that the Count Dracula Society was formed in 1962?

A Basic Recipe for Pie Crust

This is a very good recipe for a delicious, flaky crust.

Ingredients for single crust:

    1½ c. sifted all-purpose flour
    ½   tsp. salt
    ½   c. shortening
    4-5 Tbs. ice water

Ingredients for double crust:

    2   c. sifted all-purpose flour
    1   tsp. salt
    ⅔   c. shortening
    5-7 Tbs. ice water

Directions for single crust:

1. In large bowl stir together flour and salt.
2. Cut in shortening with pastry blender or mix with fingertips until pieces are size of coarse crumbs.
3. Sprinkle 2 tablespoons ice water over flour mixture, tossing with fork.
4. Add just enough of remaining water, 1 tablespoon at a time, to moisten dough, tossing so dough holds together.
5. Roll pastry into 11-inch circle and wrap in plastic wrap; refrigerate for 1 hour.
6. Preheat oven to 425 degrees F.
7. Remove plastic wrap from pastry, and fit pastry into a 9-inch pie plate.
8. Fold edge under then crimp between thumb and forefinger to make fluted crust; prick crust all over with fork.
9. For filled pie with an instant or cooked filling (cream-filled, custard-filled, etc.), bake single crust 15 to 20 minutes until done.
10. If preparing single-crust pie with uncooked filling (such as pumpkin), do not prick crust; pour filling into unbaked pastry shell, and then bake as directed.

Directions for double crust:

1. Turn desired filling into pastry-lined pie plate; trim overhanging edge of pastry ½ inch from rim of plate.
2. Cut slits with knife in top crust for steam vents.
3. Place over filling; trim overhanging edge of pastry 1 inch from rim of plate.
4. Fold and roll top edge under lower edge, pressing on rim to seal; flute.
5. Cover fluted edge with 2- to 3-inch-wide strip of aluminum foil to prevent excessive browning; remove foil during last 15 minutes of baking.
6. Bake as directed in recipe.

Yields: 1 pie crust (9-inch single or double).

A Basic Cookie and Graham Cracker Crust

This is a great crust for use with cream pies or for an unbaked pie. Use your favorite flavor of cookie to complement your filling or use graham crackers.

Ingredients:

2 c. cookie or graham cracker crumbs, finely crushed
⅓ c. sugar
½ c. butter, melted

Directions:

1. Combine crumbs, sugar, and butter.
2. Press mixture firmly against bottom and up sides of 9-inch pie plate.
3. Baking is not necessary, but if preferred crust may be baked at 400 degrees F. for 10 minutes.

Yields: 1 pie crust (9-inch).

Black Cat Pie

This is a rich pie to top off your Halloween meal. Serve with sweetened whipped cream.

Ingredients:

- 1 deep dish pastry shell (9 in.), unbaked (recipe page 246)
- 2 sticks butter (1 c.)
- 2 eggs
- ½ c. all-purpose flour
- ½ c. sugar
- ½ c. brown sugar
- 6 oz. chocolate chips
- 1 c. nuts
- Sweetened Whipped Cream (recipe page 193)

Directions:

1. Melt butter and set aside.
2. Beat eggs until foamy.
3. Mix in flour and sugars.
4. Pour in butter and blend well.
5. Stir in chocolate chips and nuts.
6. Fill pie shell and bake at 325 degrees F. for 1 hour.

Candy Apple Pie

This candy apple pie makes a great Halloween treat.

Ingredients:

- 1¾ c. unsweetened apple juice
- 20 cinnamon red hot candies
- ¼ tsp. red food coloring
- ½ tsp. vanilla extract
- 5 Granny Smith apples, peeled, cored and thinly sliced
- 3 Tbs. cornstarch

1 single-crust pie shell (9 in.), baked (recipe page 246)
   Sweetened Whipped Cream (recipe page 193)
   cinnamon for garnish

Directions:
1. Combine 1½ cups apple juice, candies, food coloring, vanilla, and apples in saucepan.
2. Bring to a boil; simmer until apples are tender, stirring frequently.
3. Combine remaining ¼ cup apple juice and cornstarch.
4. Stir into apple mixture; cook until thickened.
5. Remove from heat and let cool.
6. Spread apple mixture into pie shell; chill several hours.
7. Before serving, top with whipped cream and sprinkle with cinnamon if desired.

Yields: 6 to 8 servings.

Meringue

Use this traditional recipe on any pie you want.

Ingredients:
3   egg whites
6   Tbs. sugar
¼   tsp. cream of tartar
½   tsp. vanilla extract

Directions:
1. Beat egg whites and cream of tartar until foamy.
2. Beat in sugar 1 tablespoon at a time; continue beating until stiff and glossy. (Do not underbeat.)
3. Beat in vanilla.
4. Spread on top of pie, sealing edges.
5. Bake at 350 degrees F. until brown.

Chocolate Chiffon Pie

Chocolate chiffon pie is an elegant dish to add to your Halloween meals.

Ingredients:

   1   pkg. unflavored gelatin
   ¼   c. cold water
   ½   c. boiling water
   6   Tbs. baking cocoa
   4   eggs, separated
   1   c. sugar, divided
   ¼   tsp. salt
   1   tsp. vanilla extract
   1   single-crust pie shell (9 in.), baked (recipe page 246)

Directions:

   1. Prepare pie shell.
   2. Pour cold water in bowl and sprinkle gelatin on top.
   3. Mix boiling water and cocoa until smooth.
   4. Add softened gelatin to hot cocoa mixture; stir until dissolved.
   5. Add egg yolks, slightly beaten, ½ cup sugar, salt, and vanilla; cool.
   6. While mixture is cooling, beat egg whites until soft peaks form.
   7. Gradually add remaining sugar and beat until stiff peaks form.
   8. When chocolate mixture begins to thicken, fold in beaten egg whites.
   9. Fill baked pie shell and chill.

Yields: 6 to 8 servings.

Did You Know? . . . .

Did you know that the fear of ghosts is phasmophobia?

Ghostly Chocolate Pie

An added "ghost" makes this basic chocolate pie work with the Halloween theme.

Ingredients:

1	single-crust pie shell (9 in.), baked (recipe page 246)
1½	c. sugar
⅓	c. cornstarch
½	tsp. salt
3	c. milk
2	sq. unsweetened chocolate (1 oz. each), cut up
4	egg yolks, slightly beaten
1	Tbs. plus 1 tsp. vanilla extract
2	chocolate chips for eyes
	Sweetened Whipped Cream (recipe page 193)

Directions:

1. Mix sugar, cornstarch, and salt in 1½-quart saucepan.
2. Stir in milk gradually then add chocolate pieces.
3. Cook over medium heat, stirring constantly, until mixture thickens and boils.
4. Boil and stir 1 minute.
5. Stir at least half of hot mixture gradually into egg yolks.
6. Blend into hot mixture in saucepan.
7. Boil and stir 1 minute.
8. Remove from heat; stir in vanilla.
9. Pour into pie shell; press plastic wrap onto filling.
10. Refrigerate at least 2 hours but no longer than 48 hours.
11. Remove plastic wrap.
12. Top with whipped cream in shape of a ghost; use 2 chocolate chips for eyes.

Yields: 6 to 8 servings.

Halloween Pumpkin Pie

This is a traditional recipe to decorate for Halloween.

Ingredients:

- 1 single-crust pie shell (9 in.), unbaked (recipe page 246)
- 2 eggs
- 1 can pumpkin (16 oz.) or 2 c. cooked pumpkin, mashed
- ¾ c. sugar
- ½ tsp. salt
- 1 tsp. ground cinnamon
- ½ tsp. ground ginger
- ¼ tsp. ground cloves
- 1⅔ c. evaporated milk

Directions:

1. Preheat oven to 425 degrees F.
2. Beat eggs slightly with hand beater.
3. Beat in remaining ingredients.
4. Place pastry-lined pie plate on oven rack; pour in filling.
5. Bake for 15 minutes; reduce oven temperature to 350 degrees F.
6. Bake until knife inserted in center comes out clean, about 45 minutes longer.
7. Decorating option: Make white icing and pipe a spider web over top of cooled pie; put on a plastic spider for effect.
8. Decorating option: Save pastry scraps when making pie shell; cut into shapes to make a jack-o'-lantern face, making sure they are slightly larger than what you want, because they will shrink when baked.
9. Bake shapes on cookie sheet then position them on cooked pie.

Yields: 6 to 8 servings.

Did You Know? . . . .

Did you know that in Mexico, starting the evening of October 31, they celebrate El Dia de los Muertos or The Day of the Dead?

Hobgoblins' Mud Pie

This pie is easy to make, tastes good, and presents the orange and black holiday theme.

Ingredients for crust:

    8   whole honey graham crackers, finely crushed (about 1¼ c. crumbs)
    ¼   c. sugar
    ⅓   c. butter

Ingredients for filling:

    1   jar chocolate fudge sauce (12 oz.)
    1½ pints orange sherbet
    ½   c. miniature chocolate chips

Directions for crust:

1. Preheat oven to 375 degrees F.
2. Mix all ingredients until well blended.
3. Press firmly onto bottom and up side of 9-inch pie plate.
4. Bake 8 to 10 minutes or until lightly browned.
5. Cool completely.

Directions for filling:

1. Using rubber spatula, spread chocolate fudge sauce evenly over cooled pie crust.
2. Place in freezer to harden.
3. Remove sherbet from freezer to soften.
4. In medium bowl combine sherbet and chocolate chips.
5. Spoon sherbet mixture into prepared crust.
6. Smooth top with spatula.
7. Return to freezer until ready to serve.

Yields: 6 to 8 servings.

Did You Know?...

Did you know that there are people who claim to be real vampires? They have their own clubs and societies.

Praline Pumpkin Pie

The praline layer adds a great touch to traditional pumpkin pie.

Ingredients for crust:

- 2   c. all-purpose flour
- 6   oz. cold butter, cut up
- ½   tsp. salt
- 5   Tbs. cold water

Ingredients for praline layer:

- 3   Tbs. soft butter
- 3⅔   c. packed brown sugar
- ⅓   c. pecan pieces

Ingredients for pumpkin filling:

- 1   c. evaporated milk
- ½   c. water
- 3   lg. eggs
- 1½   c. pumpkin purée
- ½   c. sugar
- ½   c. packed light brown sugar
- ¾   tsp. ground cinnamon
- ½   tsp. ground ginger
- ½   tsp. ground nutmeg
- ½   tsp. ground cloves
- ½   tsp. salt

Directions for crust:

1. In stand mixer with paddle attachment, combine flour, butter, and salt, mixing on slow speed until butter is size of small peas.
2. Add water all at once, and mix until dough comes together in a ball.
3. Wrap in plastic wrap and chill at least 4 hours. (Can be done one day in advance.)
4. Dust work surface with flour, and roll dough out to ⅛-inch thickness.

5. Carefully place dough into 10-inch pie plate.
6. Trim edges and crimp border, using thumb and forefinger.
7. Return crust to refrigerator until completely firm.
8. Prick all over with fork.

Directions for praline layer:

1. Preheat oven to 450 degrees F.
2. Cream butter and brown sugar in mixer with paddle.
3. Mix in nuts.
4. Spread onto bottom of chilled pie crust, and bake for 10 minutes.
5. Remove from oven and let cool completely.
6. Reduce oven heat to 350 degrees F.

Directions for filling:

1. In small saucepan bring milk and water just to a boil.
2. Remove from heat.
3. In large mixing bowl whisk together eggs, pumpkin, sugars, spices, and salt.
4. Gradually whisk in cooled milk and water.
5. Pour filling into prepared pie shell and bake until center is set, about 50 minutes. (Filling should not move when pie is jiggled.)
6. Let cool and refrigerate until ready to serve.
7. Top with whipped cream.

Yields: 8 to 10 servings.

*** Did You Know? . . . .***

Did you know that pumpkins originated in Central America, where they have been used as a food crop for centuries?

Midnight Madness Pie

This is another rich chocolate pie that is easy to make and tastes great.

Ingredients for chocolate crust:

    1½ c. chocolate wafer crumbs
    ¼ c. butter, melted

Ingredients for filling:

    8   oz. cream cheese, softened
    ½ c. mayonnaise
    ½ c. sugar
    2   eggs
    1   pkg. semisweet chocolate chips, melted
    1   tsp. vanilla extract

Directions for chocolate crust:

1. Heat oven to 350 degrees F.
2. Mix crumbs and butter.
3. Reserve 3 tablespoons mixture for topping if desired.
4. Press remaining mixture firmly against bottom and side of pie plate.
5. Chill until firm in refrigerator or bake for 10 minutes; cool.

Directions for filling:

1. Preheat oven to 350 degrees F.
2. In large bowl with mixer at medium speed, beat cream cheese and mayonnaise until smooth.
3. Gradually beat in sugar.
4. Beat in eggs 1 at a time.
5. Add chocolate and vanilla; beat until smooth.
6. Pour into prepared pie crust; place on cookie sheet.
7. Bake for 30 to 35 minutes or until set.
8. Chill 4 hours before serving.

Halloween Delights Cookbook

A Collection of Halloween Recipes
Cookbook Delights Series

Preserving

Table of Contents

Did You Know? . . . .

Did you know that in Greek mythology the story of Lycaon supplies one of the earliest examples of a werewolf legend? According to one form of it, Lycaon was transformed into a wolf as a result of eating human flesh.

A Basic Guide for Canning, Dehydrating, and Freezing

1. Place empty jars in hot, soapy water. Wash well inside and out with brush or soft cloth.
2. Run your finger around rim of each jar, discarding any that are chipped or cracked.
3. Rinse in clean, clear, very hot water, being careful to use tongs to avoid burning skin or fingers.
4. Place upside down on towel or fabric to drain well.
5. Place lids in boiling water bath for 2 minutes to sterilize and keep hot until ready to place on jar rims.
6. Immediately prior to filling jars with hot food, immerse in hot bath for 1 minute to heat jars. Heating jars avoids breakage.
7. If filling with room-temperature food, you need not immerse immediately prior to filling.
8. Fill jars with food to within ½ inch of neck of jars.
9. When ladling liquid over food, fill jars to 1 inch from top rim in each jar. This leaves air allowance for sealing purposes.
10. Wipe rims of jars with damp, clean cloth to remove any particles of food and again check for chips or cracks.
11. Using tongs, place lids from hot bath directly onto jars.
12. Place rings over lids, and using cloth, gloves, or holders, tighten down firmly while hanging onto jars.
13. Do not tighten down too hard as air may become trapped in jars and prevent them from sealing.
14. For fruits, tomatoes, and pickled vegetables, place each jar into water bath canning kettle so water covers jars by at least 1 inch.
15. For vegetables, process them in a pressure canner according to manufacturer's directions.
16. Follow time recommended for food being canned.
17. Do not mix jars of food in same canning kettle as times may vary for each kind of food.
18. At end of time recommended for canning, gently lift each jar out of bath with tongs, and place on protected surface.
19. Turn lids gently to be sure they are firmly tight.
20. Place filled, ringed jars on cloth to cool gradually.
21. Do not disturb rings, lids, or jars until sealed.

22. Lids will show slight indentation when sealed.
23. When cool, wipe jars with damp cloth then label and date each jar.
24. Leave overnight until thoroughly cooled.
25. Jars may then be stored upright on shelves.

Dehydrating

1. Always begin with fresh, good quality food that is clean and inspected for damage.
2. Pretreatment is not necessary, but food that is blanched will keep its color and flavor better. Use the same blanching times as you would for freezing. Fruit, especially, responds well to pretreatment.
3. Doing some research on pretreatments may help you decide what procedure you would like to use.
4. You can marinate, salt, sweeten, or spice foods before you dehydrate them.
5. Jerky is meat that has been marinated and/or flavored by rubbing spices into it; avoid oil or grease of any kind as it will turn rancid as the food dries.
6. Vegetables and fruit can be treated the same way.
7. Slice or dice food thin and uniform so that it will dehydrate evenly. Uneven thicknesses may cause food to spoil because it did not dry as thoroughly as other parts.
8. Space food on dehydrator tray so that air can move around each piece.
9. Try not to let any piece touch another.
10. Fill your trays with all the same type of food as different foods take different amounts of time to dry.
11. You can, of course, dry different types of food at the same time, but you will have to remember to watch and remove the food that dehydrates more quickly. You can mix different foods in the same dehydrator batch, but do not mix strong vegetables like onions and garlic as other foods will absorb their taste while they are dehydrating.
12. The smaller the pieces, the faster a food will dehydrate. Thin leaves of spinach, celery, etc., will dry fastest. Remove them from the stalks before drying them or they will be overdone, losing flavor

and quality. In very warm areas, they might even scorch. If they do, they will taste just like burned food when you rehydrate them.

13. Dense food like carrots will feel very hard when they are ready. Others will be crispy. Usually, a food that is high in fructose (sugar) will be leathery when it is finished dehydrating.

14. Remember that food smells when it is in the process of drying, so outdoors or in the garage is an excellent place to dry a big batch of those onions!

15. Always test each batch to make sure it is "done."

16. You can pasteurize finished food by putting it in a slow oven (150 degrees F.) for a few minutes.

17. Let the food cool before storing.

18. Store in airtight containers to guard against moisture. Jars saved from other food work well as long as they have lids that will keep moisture out.

19. Zip-closure food storage bags work well.

20. Jars of dehydrated carrots, celery, beets, etc., may look cheerful on your countertop, but the colors and flavors will fade. Dehydrated food keeps its color and flavor best if stored in a dark, cool place.

21. Dehydrating food takes time, so do not rush it. When you are all done, you will have a dried food stash to be proud of!

Freezing

1. Wash all containers and lids in hot, soapy water using soft cloth.
2. Rinse well in clear, clean, hot water.
3. Cool and drain well.
4. Place food into container to within 1 inch of rim. This allows for expansion of food during freezing.
5. Wipe rim of container with clean damp cloth, checking for chips or breaks.
6. Be certain cover fits the container snugly to avoid leaks. Burp air from container.
7. If food is hot when placing in container, cool prior to placing in freezer.
8. Label and date each container.
9. Store upright in freezer until frozen solid.

Canned Pumpkin Bread

This recipe is delicious. Canned pumpkin bread makes wonderful gifts for the holiday season.

Ingredients:

- ⅔   c. butter
- 2⅔ c. sugar
- 4   eggs
- 2   c. pumpkin purée
- ⅔   c. water
- 3⅓ c. all-purpose flour
- ½   tsp. baking powder
- 2   tsp. baking soda
- 1½ tsp. salt
- 1   tsp. ground cinnamon
- 1   tsp. ground cloves
- ⅔   c. chopped nuts

Directions:

1. Preheat oven to 325 degrees F.
2. Cream together butter and sugar.
3. Beat in eggs, pumpkin, and water.
4. Sift together dry ingredients; add to pumpkin mixture along with nuts.
5. Pour batter into clean, greased canning jars, filling half full.
6. Bake in jars, without lids, for about 25 minutes or until bread rises and pulls away from sides of jars.
7. When bread is done remove 1 jar at a time from oven, clean rim, and firmly screw on 2-piece canning lid.
8. Let jars cool on counter away from drafts.
9. After jars have sealed, store in cool, dry, dark place.

Yields: 8 pint jars.

Canned Pumpkin

Prepare this ahead of time and keep on hand the entire holiday season.

Directions:

1. Note: Pumpkin must be processed in a pressure canner.
2. Wash pumpkin, remove seeds, cut into large pieces, and peel; cut into 1-inch cubes.
3. Add to saucepan of boiling water; boil 2 minutes. (Do not mash or purée for canning.)
4. Pack hot cubes into hot jars, leaving 1-inch headspace.
5. Fill jars to 1 inch from top with boiling hot cooking liquid.
6. Remove air bubbles; wipe jar rims.
7. Adjust lids and process according to manufacturer's directions.

Pumpkin Pickles

This pickle spice is a nice deviation from the normal pickle flavor.

Ingredients:

1   pumpkin (4 lb.), peeled, seeded, cut into 1-in. cubes
4½ c. sugar
2   c. white vinegar
2   c. water
½   lemon, thinly sliced
1   cinnamon stick, broken
8   whole cloves
8   whole allspice

Directions:

1. Place pumpkin, sugar, vinegar, and water into large pot.
2. Tie lemon, cinnamon, cloves, and allspice in spice bag; drop into pot.

3. Heat until sugar dissolves; increase heat and bring to a boil.
4. Lower heat to a simmer, and cook for about 25 minutes or until pumpkin is tender.
5. Remove spice bag.
6. Pack hot cooked pumpkin into sterile jars and pour hot syrup over top.
7. Process following directions found at front of this section.

Yields: 4 pints.

Pumpkin Butter

My family loves this pumpkin butter. It goes great on muffins or any sweet bread.

Ingredients:

    10 c. raw pumpkin
    2   lemons
    1   tsp. ground ginger
    1   tsp. ground cinnamon
    ½   tsp. ground allspice
    ¾   tsp. salt
    2½ lb. brown sugar
    1   c. water

Directions:

1. Peel pumpkin and grind in food chopper.
2. Extract juice from lemons; add to pumpkin along with spices, salt, and sugar.
3. Let stand overnight.
4. Add water and boil gently until pumpkin is clear and mixture is thick.
5. Pour into sterilized jars and process following basic canning directions at front of this section.

Yields: 8 servings.

Gingery Pumpkin Pickles

These juicy, golden pickles are enlivened with lots of fresh, zesty ginger. They are great with grilled sausages, duck, lamb, or pork and are delicious with full-flavored or creamy cheese.

Ingredients:

- 2¼ lb. onions, finely chopped
- 5 oz. fresh gingerroot, peeled and finely chopped
- 12 oz. dried apricots, finely chopped
- 1½ lb. sugar
- 1½ pt. white wine vinegar
- 1 pumpkin (5½ lb.)

Directions:

1. Place onions, ginger, apricots, and sugar in large stainless steel saucepan or stockpot.
2. Stir in vinegar and bring to a boil, stirring frequently.
3. Reduce heat immediately so that mixture simmers gently.
4. Cover pan and let simmer for 1 hour, stirring once or twice.
5. Meanwhile, scoop seeds and fibers from pumpkin and cut off peel. (There should be about 4 pounds of flesh left.)
6. Cut flesh into ½- to ¾-inch cubes.
7. Add cubed pumpkin to simmering mixture; stir well.
8. Bring back to a boil, reduce heat, and simmer steadily, uncovered, for 45 minutes more.
9. Stir frequently during this second cooking stage to cook pumpkin evenly and prevent sticking.
10. Meanwhile, sterilize jars; drain and dry jars just before filling with pickles.
11. When pumpkin is tender and translucent, ladle into jars.
12. Top with discs of wax paper, and cover at once with airtight lids.
13. Store in cool, dark place when completely cooled.
14. These pickles taste good as soon as they are cooled, but they are best when matured for 3 to 4 weeks.

Freezing Pumpkin

This is great to have around during the entire holiday season.

Directions:

1. Wash pumpkin, remove seeds, cut into large pieces, and peel.
2. Cook until soft in small amount of boiling water, in steam, or in pressure cooker.
3. To bake, place cut side down on shallow baking dish, and bake at 350 degrees F. for 30 minutes or longer.
4. Test for doneness by piercing with fork.
5. When tender, remove from oven and allow to cool before handling.
6. To cool, place pan containing pumpkin in cold water and stir occasionally.
7. Package in zip-closure freezer bags or ridged container, leaving ½-inch headspace.
8. Seal and freeze.

Drying Pumpkin Seeds

Drying pumpkin seeds allows you to have this nutritious snack on hand year round.

Directions:

1. Carefully wash pumpkin seeds to remove clinging fibrous pumpkin tissue.
2. Dry in dehydrator at 115 to 120 degrees F. for 1 to 2 hours, or in oven set on warm for 3 to 4 hours.
3. Stir frequently to avoid scorching.
4. Store in airtight container in cool, dry place.

Pumpkin Marmalade

You will get rave reviews when you serve this delicious pumpkin marmalade. This recipe takes two days to make, so plan ahead.

Ingredients:

 20 c. small cubes pumpkin, peeled (1 large pumpkin)
 4 lb. sugar
 2 lemons, with zest
 2 oranges, with zest
 1 grapefruit, with zest

Directions:

1. Remove seeds from pumpkin.
2. Cut pumpkin into strips then cut meat away from peel.
3. Cut meat into small cubes.
4. Peel lemons, oranges, and grapefruit with zester or vegetable peeler; slice finely so you have thin strips of peel.
5. Remove seeds from citrus, then dice meat of citrus fruit.
6. Mix pumpkin cubes, citrus, and zest with sugar, and let stand at room temperature overnight in nonmetal bowl.
7. Transfer to large saucepan, and cook over low to medium heat for 1½ hours or until fruit becomes transparent.
8. Transfer hot marmalade to hot, sterilized jars, and cover immediately.
9. Store in cool, dark place.

Roasting Pumpkin Seeds

Make sure to keep roasted seeds in a cool, dark place so oil does not turn rancid.

Directions:

1. Preheat oven to 250 degrees F.
2. Toss dried pumpkin seeds with oil and/or salt.
3. Roast for 10 to 15 minutes; cool.
4. Store in airtight container in cool, dry place.

Halloween Delights Cookbook

A Collection of Halloween Recipes
Cookbook Delights Series

Salads

Table of Contents

Did You Know? . . .

Did you know that shape-shifters similar to werewolves are common in tales from all over the world, though most of them involve animal forms other than wolves?

Broccoli Boo Salad

This is a simple yet flavorful salad. You can always leave out the bacon for the vegetarians.

Ingredients:

1	c. mayonnaise
¼	c. sugar
2	Tbs. vinegar
8	c. broccoli florets
1	can mandarin oranges (11 oz.), drained
½	c. chopped red onion
6-8	bacon strips, cooked and crumbled
½	c. raisins

Directions:

1. In small bowl whisk mayonnaise, sugar, and vinegar.
2. Cover and refrigerate for at least 2 hours.
3. In large bowl combine broccoli, oranges, onion, bacon, and raisins; add dressing and toss to coat.
4. Cover and refrigerate for 1 hour.

Yields: 10 to 12 servings.

Buggy Pasta

This cold pasta salad may look slimy, but it is really delicious, and it can be made ahead, which is a nice plus.

Ingredients:

4	oz. fussili (twisted spaghetti)
4	oz. spaghetti
1	med. yellow squash and/or zucchini, halved lengthwise, sliced
1	c. small cherry tomatoes
1	c. fresh pea pods, tips and strings removed
1	c. pitted ripe olives
1	c. pimiento-stuffed olives
1	c. cubed cheddar cheese (about 4 oz.)

1   c. unblanched whole almonds, toasted
½   c. thinly sliced green onions
1   c. Italian salad dressing (recipe page 203)

Directions:
1. Cook pasta according to package directions, being careful not to overcook.
2. Drain pasta; rinse with cold water and drain again.
3. In large bowl combine pasta and remaining ingredients except dressing.
4. Add dressing to pasta mixture; toss gently to coat.
5. Cover and chill 2 to 24 hours.
6. To serve pasta Halloween-style, place in clean plastic cauldron embellished with well-secured plastic spiders.

Yields: 12 servings.

Varicose Veins (Salad)

This sign of getting older now takes ghoulish shape in this delicious salad.

Ingredients:
1   can French-style green beans (15½ oz.)
1   head iceberg lettuce
6   Tbs. sliced almonds
    red food coloring

Directions:
1. Heat beans in their liquid according to directions on can.
2. Wash and dry lettuce and arrange leaves on serving platter.
3. Pour beans and liquid into glass bowl.
4. Add red food coloring, drop by drop, until liquid turns color of blood.
5. Place bowl in refrigerator for 15 minutes.
6. Using slotted spoon, remove beans and place in "veinlike" pattern on top of leaves.
7. Sprinkle almonds over beans for added bony crunch and flavor.

Fungus Among Us Vegetable Salad

This salad definitely fits the theme and look of Halloween.

Ingredients:

9	oz. frozen creamed spinach
½	head iceberg lettuce
4	carrots
2	cucumbers
2	tomatoes
6-8	radishes
2	red onions

Directions:

1. Prepare creamed spinach in saucepan according to package directions; let cool in refrigerator for 30 minutes.
2. Wash lettuce, carrots, cucumbers, tomatoes, and radishes in cold water.
3. Pat lettuce dry with paper towels, tear into pieces, and place in salad bowl.
4. Peel carrots, cucumbers, and onions then slice all vegetables into small pieces.
5. Add to salad bowl.
6. Pour cooled creamed spinach (fungus) into salad bowl and toss.

Hairball Salad with Saliva Dressing

This looks disgusting but is a healthy salad for your Halloween party.

Ingredients:

1	lg. ripe avocado
2	c. alfalfa sprouts
6	carrots, grated
	Creamy Italian Salad Dressing (recipe page 203)

Directions:

1. Cut avocado in half and remove pit.
2. Scoop avocado out of shell and put in bowl.
3. Add sprouts to avocado meat and mash with fork. (It is okay to leave some lumps.)
4. Set mixture aside.
5. Divide grated carrots among four salad bowls.
6. Make walnut-size hairballs from avocado mixture, and arrange them on top grated carrots.
7. Pour Italian "saliva" dressing over hairballs and serve.

Yields: 4 servings.

Creepy Coleslaw

There is a refreshing blend of flavors in this coleslaw.

Ingredients:

½   sm. white cabbage
10 oz. carrots
1   can apricot halves (15 oz.), drained and halved
10 oz. red seedless grapes
3   oz. raisins
2   Tbs. roasted peanuts
1¾ c. mayonnaise

Directions:

1. Shred cabbage very finely and place in large bowl.
2. Peel and grate carrots and mix with cabbage.
3. Add apricot quarters, grapes, raisins, peanuts, and mayonnaise.
4. Toss well together.
5. Chill until ready to serve.

Yields: 2 servings.

Salmagundi Salad

This salad can be used as a main dish or a dish to serve at a party.

Ingredients for salad:

- 1 sm. bunch fresh spinach or other greens, washed and shredded
- 1 can anchovies, minced
- 4 c. cooked, diced chicken
- 1 c. diced smoked ham
- 4 stalks celery, chopped
- 7 hard-boiled eggs, whites and yolks chopped separately
- 3 lemons
- 1 c. chopped parsley
- 2 Tbs. fresh horseradish, grated

Ingredients for dressing:

- 2 Tbs. Dijon mustard
- ½ c. olive oil
- 3 Tbs. lemon juice
- 1 egg, beaten
  salt and pepper to taste

Directions for salad:

1. Place shredded spinach or greens in bottom of large glass bowl for a green "bed."
2. Add in layers the anchovies, chicken, ham, celery, egg whites and yolks, and pulp and chopped zest from 2 lemons.
3. Thinly slice remaining lemon.
4. Top bowl with parsley, put horseradish in a mound in center, and surround with overlapping lemon slices.

Directions for dressing:

1. Beat together dressing ingredients.
2. Pour into separate bowl and serve with salad.

Yields: 8 side-dish servings, 4 main-dish servings.

Werewolf in the Waldorf Salad

This frightening rendition of the Waldorf salad will complete your Halloween meal.

Ingredients:

- 2 lg. apples
- 1 Tbs. lemon juice
- ½ c. golden raisins
- ½ c. walnuts, chopped
- 1 c. diced celery
- ½ c. mayonnaise
- ½ Tbs. milk
- 1 tsp. sugar
- ½ head iceberg lettuce
- 1 lg. handful alfalfa sprouts
- 8 leaves endive (or other curly, leafy greens)
- 4 carrots, peeled and sliced lengthwise into 2-inch strips
- 4 radishes

Directions:

1. Peel, core, and dice apples.
2. Toss apples in large bowl with lemon juice.
3. Add raisins, nuts, and celery to apples; toss together.
4. In small bowl mix mayonnaise, milk, and sugar until well blended.
5. Add dressing to salad ingredients and toss.
6. Place 2 or 3 lettuce leaves on individual salad plates.
7. Spoon salad over lettuce in a "head" shape.
8. To create the werewolf in your Waldorf, decorate each salad with pointy endive ears, alfalfa sprouts hair and beard, pointy carrot fangs, and radish-half eyeballs.

Witches' Frog Eye Salad

This delightful salad will add color and variety to your Halloween buffet table.

Ingredients:

1   c. sugar
2   tsp. all-purpose flour
½   tsp. salt
1¾ c. pineapple juice
2   egg, beaten
1   Tbs. lemon juice
3   qt. water
2   tsp. salt
1   tsp. cooking oil
1   pkg. Acini de Pepe (pasta like orzo but round)
3   cans mandarin oranges (11 oz. each), drained
2   cans crushed pineapple (20 oz. each), drained
2   c. Sweetened Whipped Cream (recipe page 193)

Directions:

1. Combine sugar, flour, and ½ teaspoon salt.
2. Gradually stir in pineapple juice and eggs.
3. Cook over moderate heat, stirring until thickened.
4. Add lemon juice.
5. Cool mixture to room temperature.
6. Bring water, 2 teaspoons salt, and oil to a boil.
7. Add Acini de Pepe pasta.
8. Cook at a rolling boil until pasta is done.
9. Drain and rinse with water; drain again and cool to room temperature.
10. Combine egg mixture and pasta; mix lightly but thoroughly.
11. Refrigerate overnight in airtight container.
12. Add remaining ingredients; mix lightly but thoroughly and chill in airtight container.
13. Salad may be refrigerated as long as a week in airtight container.
14. For a dessert salad, add a package of colored marshmallows.

Yields: About 10 servings.

Black Mess Jello

This looks exactly as it sounds. Have fun making it.

Ingredients:

    6   oz. grape gelatin powder
    2   c. purple grape juice, chilled
    1   c. water
    1   sm. carrot
    4   lg. marshmallows
    16 oz. unsweetened pineapple tidbits
    16 oz. light peach slices
    2   c. green seedless grapes, washed
        ice cubes

Directions:

1. Place pineapple and peach slices in colander to drain (save juice for another use).
2. Dissolve gelatin in 1 cup boiling water.
3. When completely dissolved, add 2 cups chilled grape juice and 1 cup ice cubes, loosely packed. (This will be less than 1 cup of water due to spaces in-between cubes.)
4. Stir until ice cubes dissolve.
5. Shred carrot finely (do not grate it), and add to gelatin.
6. Snip marshmallows into small pieces and add.
7. Cut peach slices into small cubes.
8. If it is not Halloween and you do not need "eyeballs," cut each grape in half.
9. Add fruits to gelatin; chill.
10. Stir once or twice as it thickens to be sure fruit and carrot are evenly distributed.
11. If using a ring mold, place more grapes or other fruit in middle to serve.

Crudites with Vomit Vinaigrette

This vinaigrette tastes great in sandwiches. Try splattering some into pita pockets.

Ingredients:

- 2 c. cottage cheese
- 1 pkt. onion soup mix
- ¼ c. milk
- cherry tomatoes
- carrots, peeled
- zucchini
- celery stalks
- radishes
- mushroom caps
- yellow food coloring

Directions:

1. Rinse vegetables except mushroom caps in warm water.
2. Wipe mushroom caps gently with damp paper towel.
3. Slice carrots, zucchini, and celery into thin sticks.
4. Cherry tomatoes may be served whole, but remove stems.
5. Radishes and mushrooms may be halved or served whole.
6. If not serving right away, put vegetables in plastic bag and store in refrigerator to keep fresh and crisp.
7. In small bowl mix cottage cheese, onion soup mix, and milk.
8. Stir in food coloring until the desired yellowish color is achieved; do not overmix; lumpy is more realistic.
9. Arrange vegetables on platter surrounding Vomit Vinaigrette.

Yields: 6 servings.

Halloween Delights Cookbook

A Collection of Halloween Recipes
Cookbook Delights Series

Side Dishes

Table of Contents

Did You Know? . . .

Did you know that kornigou, antler-shaped cakes baked by Celts in western Brittany, commemorate the god of winter shedding his horns as he returns to his kingdom in the Otherworld?

Black Risotto

Our family enjoys risotto, and this black version is a great side dish for your Halloween theme.

Ingredients:

- 6   c. chicken broth
- 2   Tbs. olive oil
- 1   onion, chopped
- 2   cloves garlic, minced
- 2   c. Arborio rice
- ½   c. dry red wine
- 4   Tbs. black olive paste
- 2   Tbs. chopped fresh rosemary
- 2   Tbs. grated orange zest
- ¾   c. freshly grated Parmesan cheese, plus more to taste
  - salt and pepper to taste

Directions:

1. Place chicken broth in saucepan and bring to a boil.
2. Reduce heat to low, cover, and keep at low simmer.
3. Warm oil in large sauté pan over medium heat.
4. Add onion and garlic; sauté about 5 minutes or until translucent.
5. Add rice and cook until coated with oil, about 2 minutes.
6. Add red wine and cook until absorbed.
7. Add all but 1 cup of hot broth to rice mixture ½ cup at a time, making sure it is absorbed before adding another ½ cup.
8. Stir in black olive paste, and add remaining broth ¼ cup at a time.
9. Cook until rice is just tender and slightly creamy, about 25 minutes.
10. Stir in rosemary, orange zest, and ½ cup Parmesan cheese.
11. Add salt, pepper, and more Parmesan cheese to taste.

Creamed Eyeballs

This side dish adds to your Halloween holiday theme.

Ingredients:
- 4 lb. pearl onions
- 8 Tbs. butter
- 2 Tbs. all-purpose flour
- 2 c. light cream
- 3 tsp. freshly grated nutmeg
- salt and white pepper to taste

Directions:
1. Parboil onions with skins on for 1 minute.
2. Immediately rinse with cold water.
3. Slice off root end and squeeze onions out of skins.
4. Return onions to saucepan and simmer in enough water to cover for 10 minutes, until tender. (Be careful not to overcook; onions should be firm and retain their shape.)
5. Drain onions in colander while making sauce.
6. In same saucepan, melt butter; add flour and mix well.
7. Stirring constantly, pour cream in very slowly.
8. Cook sauce over medium heat, stirring constantly until sauce thickens.
9. Add spices and onions; cook just until onions are reheated.
10. Pour into serving dish and sprinkle with additional nutmeg if desired.

Did You Know? . . .

Did you know that there are not any words in the dictionary that rhyme with orange?

Devilish-Spicy Deviled Eggs

This recipe adds spice to traditional deviled eggs.

Ingredients:

6   lg. hard-boiled eggs, peeled
1   Tbs. horseradish
1½ Tbs. mustard
2   Tbs. honey-Dijon salad dressing
    cayenne pepper to taste

Directions:
1. Cut eggs in half lengthwise.
2. Remove yolks and put in small bowl.
3. Add remaining ingredients except for cayenne pepper; mix well.
4. Fill egg whites with filling, heaping up.
5. Sprinkle each egg with small amount of cayenne pepper.

Yields: 6 servings.

Spooky Eyeball Beans

Have fun serving these!

Ingredients:
1   jar oven-baked beans (18 oz.)
1   can kidney beans (16 oz.), drained, rinsed
1   jar small whole onions (10 oz.), drained
¾   c. honey barbeque sauce

Directions:
1. Mix all ingredients in saucepan.
2. Bring to boil over medium heat; reduce heat to medium-low, and simmer 20 minutes or until heated through, stirring occasionally.

Yields: 8 servings.

Gory Gorilla Tonsils

This is a great way to serve Brussels sprouts, while it adds to your holiday theme.

Ingredients:
- 2 doz. Brussels sprouts
- ¼ tsp. salt
- 4 oz. cheddar cheese, grated
- 2 Tbs. milk
- 12 iceberg lettuce leaves
- ¼ tsp. paprika

Directions:
1. Wash Brussels sprouts and remove any discolored leaves.
2. Trim off stem end, and cut an "X" into bottom of each sprout to make sure "tonsils" cook nice and tender.
3. Place sprouts in pot containing about 2 inches water, and sprinkle with salt.
4. Cover pot and cook over medium heat until boiling.
5. After 8 to 10 minutes, carefully stab a few sprouts with fork to see if they are tender.
6. When they can be easily pierced through their centers, remove pot from heat and carefully drain sprouts in colander.
7. Place grated cheese in small saucepan and add milk.
8. Simmer over low heat, stirring continuously with wooden spoon until cheese melts.
9. Remove saucepan from heat as soon as cheese melts.
10. Arrange bed of washed lettuce leaves on platter.
11. Place gorilla tonsils—in pairs, or course—on leaves.
12. Drizzle melted cheese (pus) over tonsils.
13. Sprinkle with paprika (blood specks) and serve.

Yields: 6 servings.

Moldy Cheese and Mashed Potatoes

This has great flavor and makes a delicious side dish for those who enjoy blue cheese.

Ingredients:

> 2   lb. red potatoes, cleaned and cut into wedges
> 4   Tbs. butter
> ½   c. crumbled Roquefort blue cheese
> 1   Tbs. minced fresh rosemary
> 2   Tbs. minced fresh parsley
>   salt and pepper

Directions:

1. Preheat oven to 375 degrees F.
2. Boil potatoes for 15 minutes in large pot of salted water.
3. Quickly drain potatoes, and mix with butter and Roquefort until cheese and butter melt.
4. Toss potatoes with rosemary.
5. Place potatoes on 2 large ungreased cookie sheets.
6. Bake 15 to 20 minutes or until crisp and tender in center.
7. Remove from oven and sprinkle with parsley, salt, and pepper.

Moldy Maggot Casserole

Despite its name, your family will love this cheese, spinach, and rice side dish.

Ingredients:

> 1   c. minced onion
> 2   Tbs. vegetable stock
> 1   lb. washed and chopped spinach
> 3   c. cooked rice
> 1   c. cottage cheese

¾ c. shredded cheddar cheese
2 eggs
3 Tbs. fresh parsley
1½ tsp. dill weed

Directions:

1. Preheat oven to 375 degrees F.
2. Spray 2-quart casserole with cooking spray.
3. In large skillet sauté onions and stock until soft.
4. Add spinach and cook over low heat until spinach is wilted and all liquid has evaporated, stirring constantly.
5. In large bowl combine remaining ingredients.
6. Fold in spinach mixture.
7. Spoon mixture into prepared casserole, and bake for 25 minutes.

Green Mashed Potatoes

This recipe uses natural green kale to color these mashed potatoes.

Ingredients:

¾ c. half-and-half
4 thinly sliced scallions
4 c. thinly sliced kale
6 lg. Yukon gold potatoes, cooked, peeled, and mashed
4 Tbs. butter
 salt and white pepper

Directions:

1. In large, heavy saucepan bring half-and-half to a boil.
2. Add scallions, kale, salt, and pepper and return to a boil.
3. Reduce heat and simmer until kale is very tender and bright green but not mushy.
4. While kale is cooking, whip potatoes with butter.
5. Fold kale mixture into potatoes; mix well to combine.
6. Serve hot.

Slash 'Em, Gash 'Em Spuds

Have fun decorating these spuds. They taste good, too.

Ingredients:

- 6   med. russet potatoes
- 2   tsp. salt
- ½   c. milk
- 4   Tbs. butter, softened
- 1   tsp. pepper
- 12 sm. mushrooms
- 2   red bell peppers, cored, seeded, and sliced
  assorted vegetables: broccoli, zucchini, carrots, etc.
  ketchup
  additional melted butter

Directions:

1. Peel potatoes with vegetable peeler.
2. Cut into quarters and place in large pot ¾ full of cold water.
3. Add 1 teaspoon salt to water; cover and boil for 15 to 20 minutes or until potatoes are soft.
4. Using slotted spoon, carefully remove potatoes from hot water and place in large mixing bowl.
5. Add milk, butter, pepper, and remaining teaspoon salt.
6. Beat with electric mixer for 3 to 4 minutes or until light and fluffy.
7. Spoon a mound of potatoes onto individual plates.
8. Allow to cool slightly then using clean hands, sculpt a human head on each plate.
9. Using vegetables of your choice, add eyes, a nose, and a mouth to each head.
10. Try mushrooms for eyes, red pepper slices for lips, broccoli for hair or mustaches, etc.
11. Using a blunt knife, slash a gash down the side of each head.
12. Pour ketchup (blood) into each gash and dribble on melted butter (pus) for a deliciously disgusting side dish.

Worms Au Gratin

Have a blast with the presentation of this dish. It is quite tasty.

Ingredients for worms:

- 4   qt. water
- 1   Tbs. salt
- 2   c. egg noodles
- 8   oz. spaghetti, broken into short pieces
- 2   Tbs. butter
- 1½ c. cheddar cheese, grated
- ½   tsp. olive oil

Ingredients for dirt:

- 2   whole-wheat bread slices, toasted
- 1   Tbs. butter, melted
- ¼   tsp. salt

Directions for worms:

1. Fill large pot with 4 quarts water and add salt.
2. Heat over medium to high heat until water comes to rapid boil.
3. Add noodles and spaghetti (worms), and allow water to return to boil.
4. Lower heat and cook worms on slow boil, uncovered, for about 8 to 10 minutes.
5. Drain; pour into large bowl.
6. Toss with butter and grated cheese.
7. Grease casserole dish with olive oil.
8. Pour cooked worms into dish and set aside.

Directions for dirt:

1. In small bowl crumble toasted bread into tiny crumbs.
2. Mix melted butter and salt with crumbs to create dirt.
3. Sprinkle dirt over worms and place under broiler for 5 minutes.

Yields: 5 servings.

Yams with Graveyard Dirt Topping

This mixture of flavors and textures makes a wonderful addition to your holiday plate.

Ingredients for yams:

- 22 oz. red-skinned sweet potatoes or yams (about 2 large), peeled and cut into 1-inch pieces
- 6 Tbs. unsalted butter, room temperature
- 1 lg. egg
- 3 Tbs. sugar
- ½ tsp. ground cinnamon
- ¼ tsp. ground nutmeg
- ⅛ tsp. ground allspice
- ⅛ tsp. ground cloves
- 1 pinch salt

Ingredients for graveyard dirt topping:

- 1½ c. cornflakes, crushed
- ½ c. packed brown sugar
- ½ c. pecans, chopped
- 6 Tbs. unsalted butter, melted

Directions for yams:

1. Open oven door and check inside for ghosts or goblins.
2. When your hands stop shaking . . . preheat oven to 400 degrees F. and continue with Halloween recipe, if you can!
3. Cook sweet potatoes in large pot of boiling water until tender, about 15 minutes.
4. Drain; transfer potatoes to large bowl and add butter.
5. Using electric mixer, beat until smooth.
6. Add egg, sugar, spices, and salt; beat to blend.
7. Transfer mixture to 8 x 8-inch baking dish.
8. Bake potatoes until beginning to brown around edges and slightly puffed, about 25 minutes; remove from oven.

Directions for graveyard dirt topping:

1. While sweet potatoes are baking, prepare dirt topping.
2. Mix together all dirt ingredients in medium bowl.
3. Spoon topping evenly over sweet potatoes.
4. Return to oven and bake until golden brown and crisp, about 10 minutes longer.

Yields: 6 to 8 servings.

Halloween Cat's Hairball Surprise

The cream sauce is a nice addition to this dish.

Ingredients:

- 1 lg. spaghetti squash
- 1 c. tomato sauce
- ½ c. heavy cream
- ¼ c. vodka
- 1 pt. ricotta cheese
- 2 c. shredded mozzarella cheese
- 1 c. grated Parmesan cheese
  salt and pepper to taste
  crushed red pepper flakes (optional)

Directions:

1. Preheat oven to 350 degrees F.
2. Cut squash in half, place halves in large baking dish with ½ cup water, cover with foil, and bake for 1 hour.
3. Let cool; scoop middle out of shell.
4. In small saucepan combine tomato sauce, cream, and vodka over moderate heat.
5. Bring to a boil; reduce heat and simmer for 15 minutes, stirring occasionally.
6. Combine squash, sauce, and cheeses in large casserole dish; mix well.
7. Salt and pepper to taste, and add some crushed red pepper flakes if you enjoy spicy food.
8. Bake for 30 minutes.
9. Serve hot.

Did You Know? . . . .

Did you know that the fear of cemeteries is called coimetrophobia?

Miniature Pumpkins Stuffed with Rice, Raisins, and Almonds

This is a fun side dish to make and decorate your meal theme.

Ingredients:

- 4   miniature pumpkins
- ¼ c. raisins, plumped
- ¼ c. butter
- ½ c. minced onion
- 1   c. cooked rice
- ½ c. slivered almonds or pine nuts
- ¼ tsp. ground cinnamon
- 1   egg, slightly beaten
  salt and pepper to taste

Directions:

1. Preheat oven to 350 degrees F.
2. Place whole pumpkins in baking pan and surround with 1 inch of water.
3. Bake 30 to 45 minutes until blade of knife penetrates pumpkins easily (or microwave for about 10 minutes).
4. Let cool then cut across top to make lid.
5. Scoop out flesh, discarding seeds and stringy fibers.
6. Coarsely chop flesh; set aside.
7. Cover raisins with water and bring to a boil.
8. Cover and let sit while proceeding with recipe.
9. Sauté onions in melted butter.
10. Combine with pumpkin, rice, almonds, raisins, cinnamon, and salt and pepper to taste.
11. Bind with beaten egg and fill pumpkin shells. (Filling will rise above top of shells.)
12. Top each with its hat.
13. Bake for 30 to 45 minutes.

Yields: 4 servings.

Halloween Delights Cookbook

A Collection of Halloween Recipes
Cookbook Delights Series

Soups

Table of Contents

Did You Know? . . . .

Did you know that the movie "Halloween" was filmed using fake autumn leaves because it was shot in the spring, and that although all the cars in the movie have California license plates, the film is set in Illinois?

All Hallows' Eve Soup

This delicious soup can be served as a main dish on a cool October evening.

Ingredients:

- 1 navel orange
- 1½ tsp. olive oil
- 3 med. onions, peeled, halved, and slivered lengthwise
- 4 med. carrots, peeled and grated
- ½ tsp. salt
- ¼ tsp. black pepper
- 2 tsp. dried marjoram
- 28 oz. plum tomatoes, crushed with juice
- 1 Tbs. tomato paste
- 1 tsp. brown sugar
- 6 c. chicken broth or vegetable broth
- 1 c. dried red lentils, rinsed
- ¼ c. parsley, coarsely chopped

Directions:

1. Cut rind off orange in one long strip.
2. Scrape off all excess pith from back and set aside.
3. Squeeze juice from orange and reserve.
4. Place olive oil in large, heavy pot over low heat.
5. Add onions and carrots and cook, stirring occasionally, until wilted, about 15 minutes.
6. Sprinkle with salt, pepper, and marjoram.
7. Add tomatoes, tomato paste, brown sugar, broth, reserved orange peel and juice, and lentils.
8. Bring mixture to a boil; reduce heat to medium and simmer, partially covered, for 30 minutes, stirring occasionally.
9. Remove orange peel and discard.
10. Adjust seasonings and stir in parsley.
11. Serve steaming hot with warm crusty bread.

Yields: 6 servings.

Acorn Squash and Apple Soup

This is a sweet version of squash soup.

Ingredients:

- 2   med. acorn squash (1 lb. each), halved and seeded
- 3   c. chicken stock (or unsalted canned chicken broth)
- 2   Granny Smith apples, cored, peeled, and chopped
- ½   c. onion, chopped
- 1   c. unsweetened apple juice
- 2   tsp. freshly grated gingerroot
- ½   tsp. salt
- 1   Tbs. fresh lemon juice
       freshly ground white pepper
       yogurt for garnish
       chives for garnish

Directions:

1. Place squash, cut side down, on rack set over gently simmering water in saucepan.
2. Cover and steam until tender, about 10 minutes.
3. Cool squash slightly.
4. Scoop pulp from shells.
5. Combine ¼ cup chicken stock, apples, and onion in heavy, medium saucepan.
6. Cover and cook over low heat 10 minutes.
7. Add squash pulp, remaining chicken stock, apple juice, ginger, and salt.
8. Cover and simmer until ingredients are very tender, about 20 minutes.
9. Purée soup in batches in processor or blender.
10. Strain through sieve into clean saucepan, pressing purée with back of spoon.
11. Reheat soup gently then add lemon juice.
12. Season with salt and generous amount of pepper.
13. Ladle into bowls.
14. Garnish with yogurt and chives.

Halloween Chili

This chili is best made during the last phase of the moon. If that is not possible, just do the best you can in a softly lighted kitchen after dark.

Ingredients:

1¼	lb. ground goblin gizzards (ground beef)
1	med. eye of Cyclops (onion)
1	can (15 oz.) soft-shelled beetles (kidney beans)
1	can (28 oz.) blood of bat (V-8 juice)
⅛	tsp. puréed wasp (prepared mustard)
¼	tsp. common dried weed (oregano)
1	dash red-tailed hawk toenails (crushed red pepper)
2	tsp. ground sumac blossom (chili powder)
1	tsp. hemlock (honey or sugar)
½	c. fresh grubs (sliced celery)
1	Tbs. eye of newt (pearled barley)
1	Tbs. dried maggots (uncooked rice)
	water from stagnant pond (tap water)

Directions:

1. Brown gizzards in iron cauldron over fire made from siding off a haunted house.
2. Add chopped eye of Cyclops and simmer until pieces of eye become translucent again.
3. Add soft-shelled beetles and blood of bat; bring to a slow bubbling boil.
4. At this time, add puréed wasp, common weed, toenails, sumac, hemlock, grubs, eye of newt, and maggots.
5. As it cooks, you may want to adjust consistency with pond water.
6. You can tell it is done when the eye of newt swells and the vertical tan-colored "cats eye" appears on one side.
7. Note: Substitutions are in parentheses. Leave a copy of the recipe out without the substitutions for your guests or kids to read.

Hobgoblin Stew

This is a delicious stew to add to the festive holiday party.

Ingredients:

2	Tbs. all-purpose flour
1½	tsp. salt
⅛	tsp. pepper
1	lb. stew beef
3	Tbs. vegetable oil
¼	c. onion, chopped
3	c. water
½	tsp. garlic powder
1	tsp. dried thyme
1	tsp. ground coriander
2	potatoes, peeled and cubed
6	carrots, peeled and sliced into rounds
1	c. frozen peas, thawed
½	c. evaporated milk
1	pumpkin, top cut off, seeds and strings removed

Directions:

1. On plate combine flour, salt, and pepper; set aside.
2. Cut meat into bite-size cubes, then roll in flour mixture to coat; reserve flour mixture.
3. Heat vegetable oil in saucepan over medium-low heat.
4. Add meat and brown, stirring occasionally with mixing spoon, then sprinkle in remaining flour mixture.
5. Add onion; cook until limp.
6. Add water, garlic powder, thyme, and coriander; bring to boil, cover, and cook over low heat for about 1 hour.
7. After the hour is up, add potatoes, carrots, and additional water as needed; cover and cook 10 minutes.
8. Add peas and continue to cook about 5 minutes or until vegetables are tender.
9. Stir in evaporated milk; heat through but do not boil.
10. To serve, pour into hollowed-out pumpkin shell which has been decorated to look like a spooky jack-o'-lantern by using black marker.

Moldy Cheese Soup

My daughter enjoys cheese soup, and this recipe is very tasty, despite its name.

Ingredients:

- 3 Tbs. butter
- 1 med. onion, chopped
- 1 lg. bunch broccoli
- 1 qt. chicken stock
- 1 c. dry white wine
- ¾ c. milk
- 2 c. heavy cream
- 2 oz. shredded mozzarella cheese
- 2 oz. freshly grated Parmesan cheese
- 2 oz. crumbled Gorgonzola cheese
- 2 oz. shredded fontina cheese
- ½ tsp. freshly grated nutmeg
  green food coloring (optional)
  salt and white pepper
  croutons

Directions:

1. Sauté onions in butter in medium-size stockpot until translucent.
2. Peel tough stem off broccoli stalk, and slice stalk into ¼-inch slices; break florets into small pieces.
3. Add broccoli pieces, chicken stock, wine, milk, and cream to pot.
4. Add green food coloring until soup reaches desired "moldiness."
5. Simmer until broccoli is bright green and tender.
6. Add cheeses to soup, and cook over low heat until cheeses all melt.
7. Season with nutmeg, salt, and pepper.
8. Serve soup with your favorite croutons.
9. Note: Do not heat soup too much or it will separate.

Maggot Stew

This is a perfect stew to complement your Halloween meal.

Ingredients:

2	T. vegetable oil
¼	c. all-purpose flour
½	tsp. salt
½	tsp. pepper
¼	tsp. garlic powder
1	lb. stew beef, cut in 1-inch chunks
2	cans plain stewed tomatoes (14.5 oz. each)
1	can beef broth (10.5 oz.)
1	tsp. dried thyme
1	bay leaf
3-4	med. carrots
1	c. fresh or frozen green beans
¾	c. orzo pasta

Directions:

1. Place oil in stewpot and turn heat to medium-low.
2. Measure flour, salt, pepper, and garlic powder into resealable plastic food bag.
3. Drop in stew beef, seal bag, and shake until well coated.
4. Pour contents of bag into stewpot; turn heat up to medium.
5. Turn meat every 3 to 4 minutes, letting meat brown well on all sides.
6. Cook until meat begins to look crusty.
7. Add tomatoes, broth, thyme, and bay leaf.
8. Bring to a boil, then reduce heat to low.
9. Peel carrots and cut into small coins with knife.
10. When stew has simmered 1 hour, add carrots and green beans; cover and simmer another 45 minutes.
11. Cook orzo in saucepan according to package directions.
12. When just tender, drain through a colander into sink, shaking out any excess water. (These are your maggots.)
13. Add orzo to stewpot, then turn off heat.
14. Serve hot.

Cream of Pumpkin Soup

This is a delicious pumpkin soup. Enjoy.

Ingredients for soup:

- 1   c. chopped onion
- 2   Tbs. butter, melted
- 2   cans chicken broth (14.5 oz. each)
- 1   can pumpkin purée (15-oz.)
- 1   tsp. salt
- ¼   tsp. ground cinnamon
- ⅛   tsp. ground ginger
- ⅛   tsp. ground black pepper
- 1   c. heavy whipping cream

Ingredients for cinnamon croutons:

- 3   Tbs. butter, softened
- 1   Tbs. brown sugar
- ¼   tsp. ground cinnamon
- 4   slices whole-wheat bread

Directions:

1. Sauté onion in butter in medium saucepan until tender.
2. Add 1 can chicken broth; stir well.
3. Bring to boil; cover, reduce heat, and simmer 15 minutes.
4. Transfer broth mixture into container of blender or food processor; process until smooth then return mixture to saucepan.
5. Add remaining can of broth, pumpkin, salt, cinnamon, ginger, and pepper; stir well.
6. Bring to a boil; cover, reduce heat, and simmer 10 minutes, stirring occasionally.
7. Stir in whipping cream and heat through. (Do not boil.)
8. Ladle into individual soup bowls.
9. Top each serving with cinnamon croutons.

Directions for cinnamon croutons:

1. Preheat oven to 400 degrees F.
2. Combine butter, brown sugar, and cinnamon.
3. Spread butter mixture evenly over one side of each bread slice.
4. Place bread buttered side up on baking sheet.
5. Bake 8 to 10 minutes or until bread is crisp and topping is bubbly.
6. Cut each slice of bread into 8 small triangles or squares.

Yields: 6 servings.

Frankenstein Stew

This stew is a family favorite that even Frankenstein would enjoy.

Ingredients:

> 1   onion, diced
> ¼ c. butter
> 1   can creamed-style corn
> 2   cans potatoes, drained and diced
> 1   can tuna fish, flaked
> 3   c. milk
> 1   tsp. seasoned salt
> ½ tsp. salt
> ¼ tsp. pepper

Directions:

1. Sauté onion in butter in large saucepan.
2. Add remaining ingredients.
3. Cover and simmer until well heated.
4. Serve with bread or rolls for dunking.
5. Reheats easily in microwave.

Spooky Pumpkin Soup in a Tureen

This is a simple pumpkin soup you will enjoy.

Ingredients:

1	pumpkin (8 to 10 lb.)
1	lg. potato, peeled and chopped
1	lg. sweet potato, peeled and chopped
2	med. white onions, chopped
6	c. water
1	tsp. salt
1	tsp. dried thyme
½	c. condensed milk (not sweetened)
	white pepper to taste

Directions:

1. With sharp, heavy knife cut off top ¼ of pumpkin, jack-o'-lantern style; scoop out seeds and strings.
2. Scoop out pumpkin flesh with heavy spoon, making sure to leave a 1-inch wall.
3. Refrigerate shell and its top.
4. In large pot combine 2 cups of pumpkin flesh with remaining ingredients except condensed milk.
5. Bring to a boil over medium heat, and cook until potatoes are tender, about 20 minutes.
6. Preheat oven to 200 degrees F.
7. Place pumpkin shell and top on baking tray and put in oven to warm up.
8. With slotted spoon, remove potatoes and onions from soup mixture and purée in food processor. (May be mashed by hand, making sure to smooth out all lumps.)
9. Return purée to soup and stir in condensed milk. (Add more condensed milk if you prefer it thicker.)
10. Heat over low heat until hot. (Do not boil.)
11. To serve, place warmed pumpkin shell on large serving tray.
12. Pour soup in carefully; cover with lid to keep warm.

Yields: 6 servings.

Halloween Delights Cookbook

A Collection of Halloween Recipes
Cookbook Delights Series

Wines and Spirits

Table of Contents

Did You Know? . . . .

Did you know that the fear of witches is called wiccaphobia, the fear of the dark is called nyctophobia, and the fear of spiders is called arachnophobia?

About Cooking with Alcohol

Some recipes in this cookbook contain, among other ingredients, liquors. It is for the purpose of obtaining desired flavor and achieving culinary appreciation and not to be abused in any way. In cooking and baking, alcohol evaporates and only the flavor may be enjoyed. When mixed in cold, however, such as in desserts, caution must be exercised. These recipes are intended for people who may consume small amounts of alcohol in a responsible and safe manner.

I live in Washington State and we are proud of our wine production. Washington State is rapidly gaining prestige as a premier wine producer. Do enjoy the art of wine tasting and enjoy the completeness and uniqueness of each wine. It is an art to enjoy and savor in moderation.

If consumption of even small amounts of alcoholic ingredients presents a problem, in whatever form, please substitute coffee flavor syrups, found in coffee sections of supermarkets. For example, instead of Southern Comfort liqueur, substitute with Irish Cream or Amaretto Syrup.

Karen Jean Matsko Hood

Black Magic

Once you taste this drink, you will feel the magic.

Ingredients:

> 1½ oz. vodka
> ¾ oz. espresso liqueur
> 3-5 dashes lemon juice
> cracked ice

Directions:

1. Mix ingredients with cracked ice in cocktail shaker.
2. Pour into chilled old-fashioned glass.

Witch's Tail

This drink is perfect for serving at a holiday celebration.

Ingredients:
- 1   oz. wild-berry schnapps
- ¼   oz. blue Curacao
- 3   oz. sweet and sour mix
- 3   oz. club soda
- ice cubes
- orange wheel for garnish

Directions:
1. Combine ingredients in ice cube-filled Collins glass; stir.
2. Garnish with orange wheel and witch's hat.

Witchypoo

This sweet drink tastes much better than it sounds.

Ingredients:
- ¾   oz. dark chocolate liqueur
- ¾   oz. white chocolate liqueur
- ¾   oz. green crème de menthe
- ¾   oz. vodka
- cocoa powder

Directions:
1. Dust martini glass with cocoa powder.
2. Combine ingredients in shaker.
3. Shake and strain.

Yields: 1 serving.

Vampire's Kiss

You will feel like you have been kissed by Dracula himself when you taste this drink.

Ingredients:

- 2 oz. vodka
- ½ oz. dry gin
- ½ oz. dry vermouth
- 1 Tbs. tequila
- 1 pinch salt
- 2 oz. tomato juice
  ice

Directions:

1. Shake with ice.
2. Strain over ice in old-fashioned glass.

Blood Bath

You will feel like a vampire as you sip this blood-like beverage.

Ingredients:

- 4 oz. blood orange juice
- 2 oz. rum
- ¼ oz. dark rum
- ¼ oz. grenadine
  blood orange segment for garnish

Directions:

1. Mix and strain into martini glass.
2. Garnish with blood orange segment.

Bloody Eyeball Martinis on the Rocks

This ghoulish beverage is perfect for a Halloween gathering.

Ingredients per eyeball:

    1   radish
    1   pimiento-stuffed green olive

Ingredients per drink:

    1   shot gin or vodka
    ¼   shot dry vermouth (more or less to taste)

Directions for eyeballs:

1. Prepare ice "eyeballs" at least a day before you plan to use them.
2. Peel radishes, leaving thin streaks of red skin on to represent blood vessels.
3. Using tip of vegetable peeler or small knife, carefully scoop out small hole in each radish, roughly the size of an olive.
4. Stuff a green olive, pimiento side out, in each hole.
5. Place 1 radish eyeball in each section of an empty ice cube tray.
6. Pare radishes down a bit to fit, if necessary.
7. Fill tray with water and freeze overnight.

Directions for drink:

1. Fill tall cocktail glass with 3 to 4 eyeball ice cubes.
2. Add ingredients in order given.
3. Shake or stir, as is your preference.

Did You Know? . . .

Did you know that the signs of a werewolf are a unibrow, hair palms, tattoos, and a long middle finger?

Swamp Water

To give this drink an eerie radiance, use a plastic glow-stick as a swizzle stick.

Ingredients:

    1 oz. vodka
       splash of blue Curacao
       orange juice
       ice

Directions:

1. Fill a very tall glass with ice.
2. Pour in alcohol.
3. Finish filling glass with orange juice.
4. Mix.

Witch's Brew

This spooky beverage will wow your Halloween guests.

Ingredients:

    2   oz. yellow chartreuse
    1½ oz. blue Curacao
    ½   oz. brandy, spiced
    ¼   tsp. ground cloves
    1   dash ground nutmeg
    1   dash ground allspice

Directions:

1. Shake all ingredients together.
2. Serve in chilled glass.

Black Cat

This is an easy-to-make drink with a name to match the season.

Ingredients:

   1¼ oz. black-cherry liqueur
   3   oz. cranberry juice
   3   oz. cola
        ice
        orange quarter for garnish
        maraschino cherry for garnish

Directions:
   1. Combine ingredients in ice cube-filled, black-stemmed goblet.
   2. Garnish with orange quarter and maraschino cherry.

Moonshine

The name of this drink conjures up an image of eerie nights.

Ingredients:

   ½ oz. vodka
   ½ oz. peach schnapps
        lemon-lime soda
        ice

Directions:
   1. Fill a very tall glass with ice.
   2. Pour in alcohol.
   3. Fill rest of the way with soda.
   4. Mix.

Festival Information

Following are just a few of the many Halloween celebrations throughout the country each year. You may use the following contact information or contact the local Chamber of Commerce or Visitor's Information Bureau of each town to find out what the exact dates for each festival are for that community.

Anoka Halloween
Late October of each year
Anoka, MN
763-427-1861 | http://www.anokahalloween.com

Bannack Ghost Walks
Late October of each year
Dillon, MT
406-834-3413 | Email: bannack@montana.com

Trick or Treat Street
Late October of each year
Denver, CO
303-433-744 Ext. 128 | Email: brookef@cmdenver.org
Website: http://www.cmdenver.org

Salem Haunted Happenings
October of each year
Salem, MA
978-744-3633 | Email: halloween@salem.org
Website: http://www.hauntedhappenings.org

Nightmare in Painesville
October of each year
Painesville, OH
440-255-4948 | Email: nightmarehelp@yahoo.com
Website: http://frightworldohio.com

Boo at the Zoo
Late October of each year
Little Rock, AR
501-666-2287 | Email: mshaw@littlerockzoo.com
Website: http://www.littlerockzoo.com

U.S. and Metric Measurement Charts

Here are some measurement equivalents to help you with exchanges. There was a time when many people thought the entire world would convert to the metric scale. While most of the world has, America still has not. Metric conversions in cooking are vitally important to preparing a tasty recipe. Here are simple conversion tables that should come in handy.

U.S. Measurement Equivalents

A few grains/pinch/dash, (dry) = Less than ⅛ teaspoon
A dash (liquid) = A few drops
3 teaspoons = 1 tablespoon
½ tablespoon = 1½ teaspoons
1 tablespoon = 3 teaspoons
2 tablespoons = 1 fluid ounce
4 tablespoons = ¼ cup
5⅓ tablespoons = ⅓ cup
8 tablespoons = ½ cup
8 tablespoons = 4 fluid ounces
10⅔ tablespoons = ⅔ cup
12 tablespoons = ¾ cup
16 tablespoons = 1 cup
16 tablespoons = 8 fluid ounces
⅛ cup = 2 tablespoons
¼ cup = 4 tablespoons
¼ cup = 2 fluid ounces
⅓ cup = 5 tablespoons plus 1 teaspoon
½ cup = 8 tablespoons
1 cup = 16 tablespoons
1 cup = 8 fluid ounces
1 cup = ½ pint
2 cups = 1 pint
2 pints = 1 quart
4 quarts (liquid) = 1 gallon
8 quarts (dry) = 1 peck
4 pecks (dry) = 1 bushel
1 kilogram = approximately 2 pounds
1 liter = approximately 4 cups or 1 quart

Approximate Metric Equivalents by Volume

U.S.   Metric
¼ cup = 60 milliliters
½ cup = 120 milliliters
1 cup = 230 milliliters
1¼ cups = 300 milliliters
1½ cups = 360 milliliters
2 cups = 460 milliliters
2½ cups = 600 milliliters
3 cups = 700 milliliters
4 cups (1 quart) = .95 liter
1.06 quarts = 1 liter
4 quarts (1 gallon) = 3.8 liters

Approximate Metric Equivalents by Weight

U.S.   Metric
¼ ounce = 7 grams
½ ounce = 14 grams
1 ounce = 28 grams
1¼ ounces = 35 grams
1½ ounces = 40 grams
2½ ounces = 70 grams
4 ounces = 112 grams
5 ounces = 140 grams
8 ounces = 228 grams
10 ounces = 280 grams
15 ounces = 425 grams
16 ounces (1 pound) = 454 grams

Glossary

Aerate: A synonym for sift; to pass ingredients through a fine-mesh device to break up large pieces and incorporate air into ingredients to make them lighter.

Al Dente: "To the tooth," in Italian. The pasta is cooked just enough to maintain a firm, chewy texture.

Amaretto: A liqueur with a distinct flavor of almonds, although it is often made with apricot pits kernels.

Bake: To cook in the oven. Food is slowly cooked with gentle heat, which causes the natural moisture in the food to evaporate slowly, concentrating the flavor.

Baste: To brush or spoon liquid fat or juices over meat during roasting to add flavor and prevent it from drying out.

Beat: To make a mixture smooth by briskly stirring or whipping with a spoon, fork, wire whisk, rotary beater, or electric mixer.

Bias-slice: To slice a food crosswise at a 45-degree angle.

Bind: To thicken a sauce or hot liquid by stirring in ingredients such as eggs, flour, butter, or cream until it holds together.

Blanch: To boil briefly to loosen the skin of a fruit or a vegetable. After 30 seconds in boiling water, the fruit or vegetable should be plunged into ice water to stop the cooking action, and then the skin easily peels off.

Blend: To thoroughly combine all ingredients until very smooth and uniform.

Boil: To bring to the boiling point.

Braise: To brown meat in oil or other fat and then cook slowly in liquid. The effect of braising is to tenderize the meat.

Bread: To coat food with crumbs (usually with soft or dry bread crumbs), sometimes seasoned.

Brew: To prepare (tea, coffee, etc.) by boiling, steeping, or the like.

Broil: To cook food directly under a heat source.

Brown: To quickly sauté, broil, or grill, either at the beginning or at the end of meal preparation, often to enhance flavor, texture, or eye appeal.

Bundt Pan: The generic name for any tube baking pan having fluted sides (though it was once a trademarked name).

Caramelize: To brown sugar over heat, with or without the addition of some water to aid the process. The temperature range in which sugar caramelizes is approximately 320 to 360 degrees F.

Chill: To place in refrigerator to reduce temperature.

Clarify: To remove impurities from butter or stock by heating the liquid then straining or skimming it.

Coat: To cover food evenly with flour, crumbs, or batter.

Cool: To allow to come to room temperature after cooking.

Core: To remove the inedible center of fruits such as pineapples.

Cream: To beat vegetable shortening, butter, or margarine, with or without sugar, until light and fluffy. This process traps in air bubbles, later used to create height in cookies and cakes.

Crimp: To create a decorative edge on a piecrust. On a double piecrust, this also seals the edges together.

Cruller: A twisted oblong pastry of doughnut dough, deep-fried and sugared or iced.

Crush: To condense a food to its smallest particles, usually using a mortar and pestle or a rolling pin.

Curd: A custard-like pie or tart filling flavored with juice and zest of citrus fruit, usually lemon, although lime and orange may be used, also.

Custard: A mixture of beaten egg, milk, and possibly other ingredients such as sweet or savory flavorings, which is cooked with gentle heat, often in a water bath or double boiler.

Cut In: To work butter into dry ingredients by chopping with knives or pastry blender.

Dash: A measure approximately equal to 1/16 teaspoon.

Deep-fry: To cook by submerging completely in hot oil.

Deglaze: To add liquid to a pan in which foods have been fried or roasted in order to dissolve the caramelized juices stuck to the bottom of the pan.

Direct Heat: A method of cooking that allows heat to meet food directly, such as grilling, broiling, or toasting.

Dollop: A spoonful of soft food, such as mashed potatoes or whipped cream. It may also mean a dash or "splash" of soda water, water, or other liquid if referring to liquid.

Dot: To sprinkle food with small bits of an ingredient such as butter to allow for even melting.

Dredge: To sprinkle lightly and evenly with sugar or flour.

Drippings: The liquids left in the bottom of a roasting or frying pan after meat is cooked. Dripping are generally used for gravies and sauces.

Drizzle: To pour a liquid such as a sweet glaze or melted butter in a slow, light trickle over food.

Dust: To sprinkle food lightly with spices, sugar, or flour for a light coating.

Dutch Process: A treatment used during the making of cocoa powder in which cocoa solids are treated with an alkaline solution to neutralize acidity. This process darkens the cocoa and develops a milder chocolate flavor.

Egg Wash: A mixture of beaten eggs (yolks, whites, or whole eggs) with either milk or water. Used to coat cookies and other baked goods to give them a shine when baked.

Fillet: To remove the bones from meat or fish for cooking.

Firm-Ball Stage: In candy making, the point at which boiling syrup dropped in cold water forms a ball that is compact yet gives lightly to the touch.

Five-Spice Powder: A seasoning mix that incorporates the five basic flavors of Chinese cooking—sweet, sour, bitter, savory, and salty.

Flan: An open pie filled with sweet or savory ingredients; also, a Spanish dessert of baked custard covered with caramel.

Flute: To create a decorative, scalloped, or undulating edge on a pie crust or other pastry.

Fold: To cut and mix lightly with a spoon to keep as much air in a mixture as possible.

Frittata: An unfolded omelet in which the eggs are mixed with vegetables, cheese, or other ingredients, cooked slowly over low heat, and then browned on top.

Ganache: A rich chocolate filling or coating made with chocolate, vegetable shortening, and possibly heavy cream. It is used to coat cakes or cookies and may be used as a filling for truffles.

Garnish: A decorative piece of an edible ingredient such as parsley, lemon wedges, croutons, or chocolate curls placed as a finishing touch to dishes or drinks.

Glaze: A liquid that gives an item a shiny surface. Examples are fruit jams that have been heated or chocolate thinned with melted vegetable shortening. Also, to cover a food with such a liquid.

Grate: To rub on a grater that separates the food into very fine particles.

Grease: To coat a pan, dish, or skillet with a thin layer of oil.

Grill: To cook over the heat source in the open air.

Hard-Ball Stage: In candy making, the point at which syrup has cooked long enough to form a solid ball in cold water.

Infusion: To extract flavors by soaking them in liquid heated in a covered utensil. The term also refers to the liquid resulting from this process.

Julienne: To cut into long, thin strips.

Knead: To work dough with the heels of your hands in a pressing and folding motion until it becomes smooth and elastic.

Marble: To gently swirl one food into another.

Marinate: To combine food with aromatic ingredients to add flavor.

Medallion: A small round or oval piece of meat.

Meringue: Egg whites beaten until they are stiff, then sweetened. It can be used as the topping for pies or baked as cookies.

Mince: To chop food into tiny, irregular pieces.

Mole Sauce: The generic term for several sauces used in Mexican cuisine, as well as for dishes based on these sauces. In English, it often refers to a specific sauce which is known in Spanish by the more specific name *mole poblano.*

Nonreactive Pan: Cookware that does not react chemically with foods. Glass, stainless steel, enamel, anodized aluminum, and permanent nonstick surfaces are basically nonreactive. Shiny aluminum is reactive.

Parchment: A heavy, heat-resistant paper used in cooking.

Peaks: The mounds made in a mixture. For example, egg whites that have been whipped to stiffness. Peaks are "stiff" if they stay upright or "soft" if they curl over.

Pesto: A sauce usually made of fresh basil, garlic, olive oil, pine nuts, and cheese. The ingredients are finely chopped and then mixed, uncooked, with pasta. Generally, the term refers to any uncooked sauce made of finely chopped herbs and nuts.

Pipe: To force a semi-soft food through a bag (either a pastry bag or a plastic bag with one corner cut off) to decorate food.

Poach: To simmer in liquid.

Poblano Chilies: Fresh dark green, chilies, often called pasillas.

Pressure Cooking: To cook using steam trapped under a locked lid to produce high temperatures and achieve fast cooking time.

Ramekin: A small baking dish used for individual servings of sweet and savory dishes.

Reduce: To concentrate by boiling away excess liquid. This is best done in an uncovered, heavy-bottom pan over medium to medium-high heat.

Rolling Boil: A boil that does not stop bubbling when stirred.

Sauté: To brown or cook in a small amount of hot oil or butter.

Scald: To heat a liquid, usually a dairy product, until it almost boils.

Sift: To remove large lumps from a dry ingredient such as flour or confectioners' sugar by passing it through a fine mesh. This process also incorporates air into the ingredients, making them lighter.

Simmer: To cook food in a liquid at a low enough temperature that small bubbles begin to break the surface.

Springform Pan: A pan that is round with high sides. The side rim expands when a clamp is opened, allowing it to separate from the base. This makes it easier to shape and then serve something like a cheesecake.

Steam: To cook over boiling water in a covered pan. This method helps foods keep their shape, texture, and nutritional value intact better than methods such as boiling.

Steep: To soak dry ingredients (tea leaves, ground coffee, herbs, spices, etc.) in liquid until the flavor is infused into the liquid.

Strain: To pass through a filtering agent such as a strainer; to draw off or remove by filtration.

Tomatillo: Green, tomato-like vegetables with paper-thin husks.

Truss: To use string, skewers, or pins to hold together a food to maintain its shape while it cooks (usually applied to meat or poultry).

Unsweetened Chocolate: The ground up center (nib) of the cocoa bean.

Vinaigrette: A general term referring to any sauce made with vinegar, oil, and seasonings.

Whisk: To mix or fluff by beating; also refers to the utensil used for this action.

White Chocolate: A blend of cocoa butter, milk, sugar, and flavor. Not really "chocolate" since no chocolate solids other than cocoa butter are present. Similar to milk chocolate in composition.

Zest: The thin, brightly colored outer part of the rind of citrus fruits. It contains volatile oils, used as a flavoring.

Recipe Index of Halloween Delights

Reader Feedback Form

Dear Reader,

We are very interested in what our readers think. Please fill in the form below and return it to:

Whispering Pine Press International, Inc.
c/o Halloween Delights Cookbook
P.O. Box 214, Spokane Valley, WA 99037-0214
Phone: (509) 928-8700 | Fax: (509) 922-9949
Email: sales@whisperingpinepress.com
Publisher Websites: www.WhisperingPinePress.com
www.WhisperingPinePressBookstore.com
Blog: www.WhisperingPinePressBlog.com

Name: _____

Address: _____

City, St., Zip: _____

Phone/Fax: (___) _____ | (___) _____

Email: _____

Comments/Suggestions: _____

_____

_____

_____

_____

A great deal of care and attention has been exercised in the creation of this book. Designing a great cookbook that is original, fun, and easy to use has been a job that required many hours of diligence, creativity, and research. Although we strive to make this book completely error free, errors and discrepancies may not be completely excluded. If you come across any errors or discrepancies, please make a note of them and send them to our publishing office. We are constantly updating our manuscripts, eliminating errors, and improving quality.

Please contact us at the address above.

About the Cookbook Delights Series

The *Cookbook Delights Series* includes many different topics and themes. If you have a passion for food and wish to know more information about different foods, then this series of cookbooks will be beneficial to you. Each book features a different type of food, such as avocados, strawberries, huckleberries, salmon, vegetarian, lentils, almonds, cherries, coconuts, lemons, and many, many more.

The *Cookbook Delights Series* not only includes cookbooks about individual foods but also includes several holiday-themed cookbooks. Whatever your favorite holiday may be, chances are we have a cookbook with recipes designed with that holiday in mind. Some examples include *Halloween Delights, Thanksgiving Delights, Christmas Delights, Valentine Delights, Mother's Day Delights, St. Patrick's Day Delights,* and *Easter Delights.*

Each cookbook is designed for easy use and is organized into alphabetical sections. Over 250 recipes are included along with other interesting facts, folklore, and history of the featured food or theme. Each book comes with a beautiful full-color cover, ordering information, and a list of other upcoming books in the series.

Note cards, bookmarks, and a daily journal have been printed and are available to go along with each cookbook. You may view the entire line of cookbooks, journals, cards, and gifts by visiting our websites at www. halloweendelights.com, or you can email us with questions and comments to: sales@whisperingpinepress.com.

Please ask your local bookstore to carry these sets of books.

To order, please contact:

Whispering Pine Press International, Inc.
c/o Halloween Delights Cookbook
P.O. Box 214, Spokane Valley, WA 99037-0214
Phone: (509) 928-8700 | Fax: (509) 922-9949
Email: sales@whisperingpinepress.com
Publisher Websites: www.WhisperingPinePress.com
www.WhisperingPinePressBookstore.com
Blog: www.WhisperingPinePressBlog.com
SAN 253-200X

We Invite You to Join the Whispering Pine Press International, Inc., Book Club!

Whispering Pine Press International, Inc.
c/o Halloween Delights Cookbook
P.O. Box 214, Spokane Valley, WA 99037-0214
Phone: (509) 928-8700 | Fax: (509) 922-9949
Email: sales@whisperingpinepress.com
Publisher Websites: www.WhisperingPinePress.com
www.WhisperingPinePressBookstore.com
Blog: www.WhisperingPinePressBlog.com

Buy 11 books and get the next one free, based on the average price of the first eleven purchased.

How the club works:

Simply use the order form below and order books from our catalog. You can buy just one at a time or all eleven at once. After the first eleven books are purchased, the next one is free. Please add shipping and handling as listed on this form. There are no purchase requirements at any time during your membership. Free book credit is based on the average price of the first eleven books purchased.

Join today! Pick your books and mail in the form today!

Yes! I want to join the Whispering Pine Press International, Inc., Book Club! Enroll me and send the books indicated below.

<u>Title</u>   <u>Price</u>

1. _____
2. _____
3. _____
4. _____
5. _____
6. _____
7. _____
8. _____
9. _____
10. _____
11. _____

Free Book Title: _____

Free Book Price: _____ Avg. Price: _____ Total Price: _____

Credit for the free book is based on the average price of the first 11 books purchased.

(Circle one)   Check | Visa | MasterCard | Discover | American Express

Credit Card #: _____Expiration Date: _____

Name: _____

Address: _____

City: _____ State: _____ Country: _____

Zip/Postal_____ Phone: (_____) _____

Email: _____

Signature _____

Whispering Pine Press International, Inc.
Fundraising Opportunities

Fundraising cookbooks are proven moneymakers and great keepsake providers for your group. Whispering Pine Press International, Inc., offers a very special personalized cookbook fundraising program that encourages success to organizations all across the USA.

Our prices are competitive and fair. Currently, we offer a special of 100 books with many free features and excellent customer service. Any purchase you make is guaranteed first-rate.

Flexibility is not a problem. If you have special needs, we guarantee our cooperation in meeting each of them. Our goal is to create a cookbook that goes beyond your expectations. We have the confidence and a record that promises continual success.

Another great fundraising program is the *Cookbook Delights Series* Program. With cookbook orders of 50 copies or more, your organization receives a huge discount, making for a prompt and lucrative solution.

We also specialize in assisting group fundraising – Christian, community, nonprofit, and academic among them. If you are struggling for a new idea, something that will enhance your success and broaden your appeal, Whispering Pine Press International, Inc., can help.

For more information, write, phone, or fax to:

Whispering Pine Press International, Inc.
P.O. Box 214
Spokane Valley, WA 99037-0214
Phone: (509) 928-8700 | Fax: (509) 922-9949
Email: sales@whisperingpinepress.com
Publisher Websites: www.WhisperingPinePress.com
www.WhisperingPinePressBookstore.com
Blog: www.WhisperingPinePressBlog.com
Book Website: www.HalloweenDelights.com
SAN 253-200X

Personalized and/or Translated Order Form for Any Book by Whispering Pine Press International, Inc.

Dear Readers:

If you or your organization wishes to have this book or any other of our books personalized, we will gladly accommodate your needs. For instance, if you would like to change the names of the characters in a book to the names of the children in your family or Sunday school class, we would be happy to work with you on such a project. We can add more information of your choosing and customize this book especially for your family, group, or organization.

We are also offering an option of translating your book into another language. Please fill out the form below telling us exactly how you would like us to personalize your book.

Please send your request to:

Whispering Pine Press International, Inc.
P.O. Box 214, Spokane Valley, WA 99037-0214
Phone: (509) 928-8700 | Fax: (509) 922-9949
Email: sales@whisperingpinepress.com
Publisher Websites: www.WhisperingPinePress.com
www.WhisperingPinePressBookstore.com
Blog: www.WhisperingPinePressBlog.com

Person/Organization placing request: _____

_____ Date: _____

Phone: (___) _____ Fax: (___) _____

Address: _____

City: _____ State: _____ Zip: _____

Language of the book: _____

Please explain your request in detail: _____

_____

_____

_____

_____

_____

Halloween Delights Cookbook

A Collection of Halloween Recipes

How to Order

Get your additional copies of this book by returning an order form and your check, money order, or credit card information to:

Whispering Pine Press International, Inc.
c/o Halloween Delights Cookbook
P.O. Box 214, Spokane Valley, WA 99037-0214
Phone: (509) 928-8700 | Fax: (509) 922-9949
Email: sales@whisperingpinepress.com
Publisher Websites: www.WhisperingPinePress.com
www.WhisperingPinePressBookstore.com
Blog: www.WhisperingPinePressBlog.com

Customer Name: _____

Address: _____

City, St., Zip: _____

Phone/Fax: _____   _____

Email: _____

- -

Please send me _____ copies of _____ _____
_____ at $_____ per copy and $4.95 for shipping and
handling per book, plus $2.95 each for additional books. Enclosed is my check,
money order, or charge my account for $_____.

☐ Check   ☐ Money Order   ☐ Credit Card

(*Circle One*)   MasterCard | Discover | Visa | American Express
☐☐☐☐   ☐☐☐☐   ☐☐☐☐   ☐☐☐☐

Expiration Date: _____

_____
Signature

_____
Print Name

Whispering Pine Press International, Inc.
Your Northwest Book Publishing Company
P.O. Box 214
Spokane Valley, WA 99037-0214 USA
Phone: (509) 928-8700 | Fax: (509) 922-9949
Email: sales@whisperingpinepress.com
Publisher Websites: www.WhisperingPinePress.com
www.WhisperingPinePressBookstore.com

Shop Online:
www.whisperingpinepressbookstore.com
Fax orders to: (509)922-9949

Gift-wrapping, Autographing, and Inscription
We are proud to offer personal autographing by the author. For a limited time this service is absolutely free!
Gift-wrapping is also available for $4.95 per item.

1. Sold To
Name: _____
Street/Route: _____
_____
City: _____
State: _____ Zip: _____
Country: _____
Gift message: _____
_____
Email address: _____
Daytime Phone: (___) ___-____
*Necessary for verifying orders
Home Phone: (___) ___-____
Fax: (___) ___-____

2. Ship To
☐ Is this a new or corrected address?
☐ Alternative Shipping Address
☐ Mailing Address

Name: _____
Address: _____
_____
City: _____
State: _____ Zip: _____
Country: _____
Email address: _____

3. Items Ordered

ISBN # /Item #	Size	Color	Qty.	Title or Description	Price	Total

4. Method Of Payment

☐ Visa ☐ MasterCard ☐ Discover ☐ American Express
☐ Check/Money Order   Please make it payable to Whispering Pine Press International, Inc. (No Cash or COD.)

Expiration Date
Account Number _____ / _____
                    Month Year

☐☐☐☐ ☐☐☐☐ ☐☐☐☐ ☐☐☐☐

Signature_____
                Cardholder's signature
Printed Name_____
                Please print name of cardholder
Address of Cardholder_____
_____

5. Shipping & Handling

Continental US
US Postal Ground: For books please add $4.95 for the first book and $2.95 each for additional books. All non-book items, add 15% of the Subtotal. Please allow 1-4 weeks for delivery.
US Postal Air: Please add $15.00 shipping and handling. Please allow 1-3 days for delivery.

Alaska, Hawaii, and the US Territories
By Ship: Please add 10% shipping and handling (minimum charge $15.00). Please allow 6-12 weeks for delivery.
By Air: Please add 12% shipping and handling (minimum charge $15.00). Please allow 2-6 weeks for delivery.

International
By Ship: Please add 10% shipping and handling (minimum charge $15.00). Please allow 6-12 weeks for delivery.
By Air: Please add 12% shipping and handling (minimum charge $15.00). Please allow 2-6 weeks for delivery.
FedEx Shipments: Add $5.00 to the above airmail charges for overnight delivery.

Subtotal	
Gift wrap $4.95 Each	
For delivery in WA add 8.7% sales tax.	
Shipping See chart at left	
6. Total	

About the Author and Cook

Karen Jean Matsko Hood has always enjoyed cooking, baking, and experimenting with recipes. At this time Hood is working to complete a series of cookbooks that blends her skills and experience in cooking and entertaining. Hood entertains large groups of people and especially enjoys designing creative menus with holiday, international, ethnic, and regional themes.

Hood is publishing a cookbook series entitled the *Cookbook Delights Series*, in which each cookbook emphasizes a different food ingredient or theme. The first cookbook in the series is *Apple Delights Cookbook.* Hood is working to complete another series of cookbooks titled *Hood and Matsko Family Cookbooks*, which includes many recipes handed down from her family heritage and others that have emerged from more current family traditions. She has been invited to speak on talk radio shows on various topics, and favorite recipes from her cookbooks have been prepared on local television programs.

Hood was born and raised in Great Falls, Montana. As an undergraduate, she attended the College of St. Benedict in St. Joseph, Minnesota, and St. John's University in Collegeville, Minnesota. She attended the University of Great Falls in Great Falls, Montana. Hood received a B.S. Degree in Natural Science from the College of St. Benedict and minored in both Psychology and Secondary Education. Upon her graduation, Hood and her husband taught science and math on the island of St. Croix in the U.S. Virgin Islands. Hood has completed postgraduate classes at the University of Iowa in Iowa City, Iowa. In May 2001, she completed her Master's Degree in Pastoral Ministry at Gonzaga University in Spokane, Washington. She has taken postgraduate classes at Lewis and Clark College on the North Idaho college campus in Coeur d'Alene, Idaho, Taylor University in Fort Wayne, Indiana, Spokane Falls Community College, Spokane Community College, Washington State University, University of Washington, and Eastern Washington University. Hood is working on research projects to complete her Ph.D. in Leadership Studies at Gonzaga University in Spokane, Washington.

Hood resides in Greenacres, Washington, along with her husband, seventeen children, and foster children. Her interests include writing, research, and teaching. She previously has volunteered as a court advocate in the Spokane juvenile court system for abused and neglected children. Hood is a literary advocate for youth and adults. Her hobbies include cooking, baking, collecting, photography, indoor and outdoor gardening, farming, and the cultivation of unusual flowering plants and orchids. She enjoys raising several specialty breeds of animals including

Babydoll Southdown, Friesen, and Icelandic sheep, Icelandic horses, bichons frisés, cockapoos, Icelandic sheepdogs, a Newfoundland, a Rottweiler, a variety of Nubian and fainting goats, and a few rescue cats. Hood also enjoys bird-watching and finds all aspects of nature precious.

She demonstrates a passionate appreciation of the environment and a respect for all life. She also invites you to visit her websites:

www.KarenJeanMatskoHood.com
www.KarenJeanMatskoHoodBookstore.com
www.KarenJeanMatskoHoodBlog.com
www.KarensKidsBooks.com
www.KarensTeenBooks.com

www.HoodFamilyBlog.com
www.HoodFamily.com

CPSIA information can be obtained at www.ICGtesting.com
Printed in the USA
LVOW12s1514171113

361652LV00003B/397/P